Educational Institutions in Horror Film

Educational Institutions in Horror Film
A History of Mad Professors, Student Bodies, and Final Exams

Andrew L. Grunzke

EDUCATIONAL INSTITUTIONS IN HORROR FILM
Copyright © Andrew L. Grunzke 2015.
Softcover reprint of the hardcover 1st edition 2015 978-1-137-46919-9
All rights reserved.

First published in 2015 by PALGRAVE MACMILLAN® in the United States—a division of St. Martin's Press LLC, 175 Fifth Avenue, New York, NY 10010.

Where this book is distributed in the UK, Europe and the rest of the world, this is by Palgrave Macmillan, a division of Macmillan Publishers Limited, registered in England, company number 785998, of Houndmills, Basingstoke, Hampshire RG21 6XS.

Palgrave Macmillan is the global academic imprint of the above companies and has companies and representatives throughout the world.

Palgrave® and Macmillan® are registered trademarks in the United States, the United Kingdom, Europe and other countries.

ISBN 978-1-349-50043-7   ISBN 978-1-137-46920-5 (eBook)
DOI 10.1057/9781137469205

Library of Congress Cataloging-in-Publication Data

Grunzke, Andrew L.
  Educational institutions in horror film : a history of mad professors, student bodies, and final exams / Andrew L. Grunzke.
     pages cm
  Includes bibliographical references and index.
  1. Horror
films—History and criticism. 2. Schools in motion pictures.
3. Education in motion pictures. I. Title.
  PN1995.9.H6G78 2015
  791.43'6164—dc23
                                                    2014040338

A catalogue record of the book is available from the British Library.

Design by Amnet.

First edition: April 2015

10 9 8 7 6 5 4 3 2 1

To my wife, Rebecca, who stayed up past midnight watching hundreds of scary movies with me

Contents

Acknowledgments		ix
1	Introduction	1
2	Is There a Doctor in the House? The Evolution of Van Helsing and Frankenstein as Intellectual Archetypes, 1931–1975	19
3	The Transformation of Dr. Jekyll: The Evolution of Film and Television Portrayals of Stevenson's Intellectual in the Age of Academe	67
4	Student Bodies: The School as Locus of Trauma in American Horror Films of the 1970s and 1980s	89
5	Final Exams and Greek Tragedies: Colleges and Universities in American Horror Films of the 1970s and 1980s	117
6	Survival Training: Summer Camp as Educational Institution in Slasher Films of the 1980s	135
7	Some Concluding Thoughts	167
Notes		177
Index		199

Acknowledgments

A project like this is not possible without owing numerous debts of gratitude to the people who have provided intellectual and emotional support over the course of years. My wife has been wonderful throughout this entire process, staying up late night after night watching (what were admittedly sometimes terrible) movies with me, serving as a sounding board for new ideas, and providing the encouragement to continue working.

I am also extremely thankful for my colleagues in the History of Education Society, especially the members of the "Florida Fringe." Your willingness to take an expansive definition of what it means to conduct history of education provided the intellectual space to hone the ideas contained in this book.

My friends and coworkers at Mercer University have created an atmosphere of congeniality and support that has given me the freedom to pursue the type of research agenda I believe represents important work. I am thankful for all of you.

Although it no longer exists, the discs-by-mail service of Blockbuster movies provided valuable access to films discussed in this book that would have been prohibitively expensive or otherwise unavailable to me. The discontinuation of this service certainly made this project more difficult. You are missed.

Finally, I owe a serious debt of gratitude to my dear friend Alex Trane. Your passion for horror movies was highly contagious. I have thought about you at every step in this project, and I likely would not have continued with it if not for the impact you had on my life. I only wish that you had survived long enough to have one of your movies included in this book.

Chapter 1

Introduction

The 1981 film *The Prowler* opens with newsreel footage from World War II of the British liner *Queen Mary* bringing victorious American troops home to begin their postwar lives. The scene shifts to a 1945 high school graduation dance. Two young lovers leave the dance to find an intimate moment. Their tryst is interrupted by a figure in combat boots who, upset about having received a "Dear John" letter from the young lady while at war and having a difficult time readjusting to his life in a time of peace, brutally murders the pair with a pitchfork.

The film moves the scene forward to the end of the school year in 1980. The graduation dance had not been held for the past 35 years, out of respect for those who had died on the night of the last dance. After the three-and-a-half decade hiatus, a group of high school seniors are planning to revive the dance. One by one, the horrors of the past graduation dance are revisited on the youth as a man in World War II gear—boots, helmet, and gas mask—stalks and kills them. One surviving female is finally able to overcome the attacker with a shotgun blast to the head, but she is left profoundly affected by the event and becomes seemingly unhinged by the viciousness of what she has seen.

Intense and savage, the film is, in many ways, a quintessential example of the slasher subgenre of horror films. Featuring a masked killer psychologically damaged by some nebulously described event in his past and employing sharp metal implements to hunt and slaughter a group of teenagers engaged in morally dubious behavior on the anniversary of a traumatic event, the film simultaneously inherited and helped establish the filmic language of the slasher movie.

Additionally, the film adopts a posturing toward violence that is typical of many films of its type. First, the tension of the film is predicated upon the idea that violence cannot exist in a psychological vacuum. The newsreel footage at the beginning of the film strongly implies that the violence that the American troops experienced on the battlefield would not be left there. They would struggle with shell shock and the return to their quotidian lives for years after their homecoming—a phenomenon that would have resonated with audiences a little more than half a decade from the end of US military involvement in Vietnam. *The Prowler* argues that it is not possible to leave violence behind; it will return to haunt and continuously victimize those unfortunate enough to experience it. As will be explored in greater detail throughout this book, horror film has a strong tendency to orient itself around the idea that the violence of the past does not stay in the past. In twentieth-century horror films, even the dead rarely stay in their graves.

Interestingly, though, the events of *The Prowler* take place against the backdrop of a high school graduation dance. Narratively speaking, there was little reason for this to be the case. The story of a jilted soldier returning home with post-traumatic stress disorder, becoming unhinged, and committing mass murder hardly requires the setting of a high school dance. In fact, such a filmmaking choice might seem at odds with the subject matter. *The Prowler* was hardly alone in the inclusion of important milestones in young adults' school life as integral parts of the story. Whether it was going to the prom (e.g., *Carrie*, *Prom Night*), high school graduation (e.g., *Graduation Day*), spring break (e.g., *Terror Train*), class reunions (e.g., *Slaughter High*), or numerous other important events on the school calendar, horror films in the latter half of the twentieth century frequently centered around various aspects of school life. As unlikely a choice as they may have seemed, educational institutions, whether they be high schools, colleges and universities, or summer camps, repeatedly served as the stage for the events of late twentieth-century horror films.

In the case of *The Prowler*, one can see how the stresses associated with high school graduation can create psychological tension. In that film, a girl, presumably not yet out of high school, does not wait for her boyfriend to return home from fighting overseas, and he ends her life. Nearly all the young characters in the film in either 1945 or 1980 were on the verge of major life changes; the future beyond that high school dance being unwritten. In the same way, many of the film's audience members—for the film is seemingly aimed predominantly at teenagers—would have been dealing with many of the same sets of stressors. The terror created by the presence of the adult killer, then, became a sort of visual metaphor for the angst associated with the transition into the adult world, a world of war and violence, rejection and uncertainty. At times in the film, this visual metaphor was not so subtle, as in a scene in which the film cuts from a young girl being impaled with a pitchfork to the graduation cake being sliced. The image of the end of this young woman's life was juxtaposed with a symbol of the end of her school life. In this way, the adolescents' struggle against the adult killer mirrored their struggle with the ending of their childhood.

The transition from high school to the period of adult life beyond the schoolhouse gates was not the only education-related anxiety horror filmmakers exploited to create feelings of dread in their audiences. Over the past 50 years, many school-focused fears served as fodder for the makers of scary movies, including bullying, sexual awakenings, social acceptance (including hazing and violent initiations into peer groups), parent/child relationships, the development of a moral self-identity, and academic performance. In concentrating on the fears of teenagers, educational institutions served as the focal point for huge numbers of horror films, making a veritable constellation comprising decades of adolescent anxieties.

Horror stories play an important social function. The storyteller exploits the anxieties of the audience to craft a story that employs those fears to create tension and dread. For historians, then, horror texts represent a unique opportunity. Scary stories give historians a chance to examine the preoccupations certain people possessed in any given era. At the same time, horror tales provide an opportunity for people to work through their anxieties. Horror stories often present societal fears in metaphorical terms. They depict abstract fears as monsters, and they give audiences a chance to work through those fears within the safety of the narrative. In the case of modern-era horror film, these fears were often either directly or indirectly linked to education. The sheer number of horror films set in educational institutions provides historians with an opportunity to examine trends and themes regarding the types of anxieties that resonated with young Americans over the second half of the twentieth century.

One possible explanation for the explosion in the number of movies using high schools as a setting is the unprecedented growth in high school enrollments in the first half of the nineteenth century. In the United States, one of the most drastic of changes to have occurred over the twentieth century is the near universalization of the educational experience. In 1890, less than 6 percent of 14- to 17-year-olds were enrolled in high school. By the 1970s, more than 90 percent of the same age group were high school students.[1] In the first few decades of the twentieth century, high school enrollments skyrocketed. Attendance at high school had become mandatory, and by mid-century it had become a common experience for nearly all the nation's youth. In less than a century, attending high school had gone from an experience shared by a small minority of American youth to one mutually held by virtually all American teenagers.

Prior to the 1970s, high schools had not figured prominently as settings for horror films. What few films featured high schools at all did so incidentally. In the 1958 creature feature *The Blob*, when the townspeople discover that the aggressive blob-like creature is adversely affected by cold temperatures, they break into the local high school because it is the building in town with the largest supply of fire extinguishers whose cool blasts keep the monster at bay. By 1977, in *The Spell*, one of a host of films that borrowed heavily from Brian De Palma's *Carrie* (1976), a slightly overweight girl is teased by the other kids at school and finds no comfort from her parents. When she discovers she has telekinetic powers, she takes revenge upon the classmates who tormented her because "People laugh at each other. People deserve to be punished." In *The Blob*, the high school represented a place of safety from an external threat. In the 1970s and beyond, the attitude of horror films toward educational institutions was markedly different. Filmmakers made common anxieties many people had about their own high school experiences the impetus for their films' horrific occurrences. They shifted the source of the horror from forces outside the school to those inside the school; threats that had once been external and alien were now internal and personal.

From the Gothic to the Slasher

Horror, with its tendency to try to create feelings of angst or disgust in its audience, often relegates itself to low-art status, especially the closer one gets to the closing of the twentieth century. However, in the case of Western European and American horror, there was a time in which major literary figures published significant horror works. Johann Wolfgang von Goethe's *Faust* (circa 1808), Mary Shelley's *Frankenstein* (1818), Washington Irving's "The Legend of Sleepy Hollow" (1820), and many of the macabre works of Edgar Allan Poe were well respected among nineteenth-century literary circles. The waning decades of the nineteenth century and the beginning of the era of mass media refashioned the horror genre. As scary and violent tales became staples of dime novels and, later, pulp fiction magazines, the artistic nature of the genre changed. While towering literary figures might, on occasion, have once written tales of terror, horror stories became the province of cheap, serialized literature.

Scholars of nineteenth-century American and British literature have produced quality research on many of the major works of horror literature, especially the works of Shelley, Poe,

Robert Lewis Stevenson, and Bram Stoker. However, as horror works became more serialized, more ephemeral, more cheaply produced, and more sensational, they placed themselves out of the canon. Scholars and critics, therefore, more frequently began to dismiss the genre as not worthy of serious study. Works of twentieth-century horror literature have received far less scholarly attention than their Gothic era counterparts. As the century progressed, this has become increasingly true; late twentieth-century works of horror, including horror films, chiefly because of their low-art status, have been left largely unexamined, especially by historians.

In the nineteenth century, people struggled to come to terms with a world that was being reshaped by industrialization and the growing influence of scientific rationalism. Tales featuring mad scientists (like Shelley's Dr. Frankenstein and Stevenson's Dr. Jekyll) monomaniacally ignoring traditional and religious standards of behavior to pursue their own research agendas only to fall upon tragic ends eased people's transition into the modern world. For audiences, these figures were threatening precisely because they were operating outside of the mitigating influence of academia. Without the college or university to rein in their ethically questionable research, horror films represented Frankenstein, Jekyll, and other mad scientists as a real danger to the world. This image, though, of the dangerous independent scholar presented a vivid argument in favor of the expansion of higher educational institutions at a time when such institutions were growing.

The first few decades of horror film production tended to be dominated by filmic translations of classic Gothic novels, in particular numerous film adaptations of Shelley's *Frankenstein*, Stevenson's *The Strange Case of Dr. Jekyll and Mr. Hyde*, and Stoker's *Dracula*. Due to the Romantic roots of Gothic horror, these filmic texts were inextricably linked to anti-Modernist suspicions about the ethics of scientific research. Education, when it appeared at all in horror films of the first half of the twentieth century, was overwhelmingly of the postsecondary variety. Like the horror literature that predated them, in older horror movies, professors whose research agendas were at odds with those of the respected educational community retreated from the colleges and universities, which sought to corral their interests into safer avenues more in line with traditional cultural and religious values, and continued their sacrilegious experiments in secluded, private laboratories. The anxieties about education embodied by these films were not grounded in the personal school experiences of the audience members. Instead, the attitudes of these films regarding education centered around the role of science and the scientist in broader society and the changing function of the university.

Indeed, with so few early twentieth-century Americans having any direct experience of university life, it would have made little sense for films to address the personal anxieties of college students. Instead, horror films in the first half of the twentieth century, as one might expect, concentrated on the changing role of the college in the larger society at a time when its influence was beginning to wax. At the turn of the twentieth century, with a matriculation rate of just over 2 percent, for most Americans enrollment at a college was nearly as remote as Stoker's Romanian countryside. But, like high school, even college attendance had become commonplace by the 1960s, with college enrollment rates approaching one-quarter of recent high school graduates in 1969.[2] The sense of mystery surrounding institutions of higher education had been stripped away, and, in response, scary stories employing this setting needed to change too. Abstract fears about the unintended effects of abstruse scientific research conducted by obsessively driven scientists and embodied by emblematic movie monsters could not resonate with young people who had developed more than a passing familiarity with the type of work that went on at universities—especially as the number of scientists actually performing work outside of the strictures of the scientific academy had dwindled. The type of fear tactics employed by horror storytellers, in film and elsewhere, had to move away from abstract and allegorical representations and toward tales of personal horror.

Indeed, this is a large part of the reason that prior to the 1960s, horror narratives generally—and horror films in particular—were less likely to be set in schools and other educational institutions than they would be thereafter. However, even early twentieth-century horror films were not completely devoid of references to the world of formal education. Many times it was the absence of the formal educational institutions that gave the films their horrific power. Society could benefit, the films seemed to argue, from the advancements represented by cutting-edge scientific research without having to worry about the potentially disastrous effects of allowing unbridled inquiry into any self-destructive or insidious topic of the scientist's choosing.

After the 1960s, the number of horror films finding their source material in nineteenth-century literature dropped precipitously. Indeed, the number of mad scientist films generally plummeted in the 1970s and beyond. Horror films from the latter half of the twentieth century dropped the Transylvanian countryside as a setting in favor of more everyday environs. By the time of the Vietnam War, the age of academe was well underway, and the violence of monster movies could not compete with the nightly news broadcasts.[3] The nightmares created by Frankenstein's laboratory were slowly replaced by those on Elm Street. As the often abstract and metaphorical terrors of faraway castles faded, personal, everyday horrors frequently set in suburbia took their place.

In the twentieth century, as new fears of nuclear annihilation rose, horror films like *Godzilla* and other atomic age creature features provided safe spaces in which audiences could see symbolic monsters overcome by bravery and ingenuity. Even today, the recent economic downturn has led many people to worry about what would happen in the event of global economic collapse. Outbreaks of SARS, swine and bird flus, and (presently) Ebola, periodically incite fears of global pandemics and death. Zombie narratives, which prominently feature the breakdown of societal structures as a result of plague, provide a metaphorical framework for people to work through those fears and are currently experiencing massive popularity. In each successive generation, audiences turn to horror narratives to help them psychologically cope with rapid social change and newly arising dangers.

Excepting the recent popularity of zombie narratives—which tend to trade heavily in global threats with the potential for massive societal collapse, the decline of the creature feature (which reached its zenith in the 1950s) brought with it a shift in the focus of the horror film. Once the threats depicted in horror movies were broad in scope, imperiling entire populations. These were displaced with horrors of a more personal variety. Where once King Kong and Godzilla stomped down city streets trampling thousands, Michael Myers, Jason Voorhees, and Freddy Krueger murdered their victims one by one. The more intimate focus of modern horror films, of course, affected the way that they approached the topic of education. Films of the 1960s and before tended to paint formal education with broad (and at times) implied strokes, focusing on the role of the intellectual in society and her or (in almost all cases) his relationship with the academic community and institutions of higher education. Films after the 1960s tended to approach the formal educational institution as the location wherein their characters grappled with the difficulties associated with growing up and the personal fears, anxieties, and violence associated with school life.

From Cultural Fears to Personal Terrors

This book aims to be a comprehensive examination of how horror films have historically addressed the issues of anxieties about education. In so doing, the book is divided into two major sections, largely representing these two eras of horror filmmaking. Early horror films tended to borrow heavily from Gothic source material. As a result, filmmakers returned repeatedly to the classic horror texts from the nineteenth and early twentieth century for their source material.

The figures of Dr. Frankenstein, Dr. Van Helsing, and Dr. Jekyll have made appearances in dozens, if not hundreds, of films over the course of the history of the cinema. As film after film provided depictions of intellectuals as deranged madmen, the stereotype of the mad scientist began to crystallize. Certainly, the frequency with which filmmakers translated *Frankenstein*, *Dracula*, and *The Strange Case of Dr. Jekyll and Mr. Hyde* onto celluloid played no small role in the creation of that stereotype. Because of the pervasiveness of the mad scientist icon, much work has been done on the figure of the stereotypical mad scientist in horror film (most notably, Andrew Tudor's *Monsters and Mad Scientists: A Cultural History of the Horror Movie* [1989] and David Skal's *Screams of Reason: Mad Science and Modern Culture* [1998]). This book does not seek to duplicate that work but rather to add to it. Some recent scholarship has begun to reevaluate whether this characterization of the scientist is a monolithic one. By adopting an approach of educational history and looking at the shifting public attitudes toward scientists, professors, and other academics, this books seeks to build upon the more nuanced view of the mad scientist by centering on the development of the image of horror film's three most prolific intellectuals (Shelley's Dr. Frankenstein, Stoker's Dr. Van Helsing, and Stevenson's Dr. Jekyll) over the course of the twentieth century. Instead of looking at these three characters as mad scientists, the first section of the book examines them as intellectuals. In particular, the first part of the book considers the relationships of these characters to the broader scientific community in their stories, and it seeks to delineate the ways in which the presentations of these characters represented the tensions associated with the culture's orientation toward public intellectuals in an era in which intellectuals were increasingly sequestering themselves in institutions of higher education. In other words, as public attitudes toward science, scientists, and higher education underwent major shifts in the first half of the twentieth century, horror films used and reused these narratives to explore the complex tensions associated with these shifts.

Because Frankenstein, Van Helsing, and Jekyll were doctors operating outside of the safety of the scientific academy, their violent acts were explicitly not acts of school violence. In fact, the lack of the mitigating influence of the school was a key factor in their ability to create the situations that made violence possible. In taking a closer examination of these figures, the first part of the book argues that in the first half of the twentieth century there was a commonly held sense that institutions of higher education could bring together powerful scientific minds for the protection of the general population—and that scientists operating outside of that system often represented a distinct threat.

The second part of the book, however, explores a very different kind of film. In the past 50 years, as horror filmmakers have begun to choose more everyday settings, the image of the school in film has shifted from a site of protection to a site of violence. The films no longer portrayed schools as places of safety. Instead, the films concentrated on creating the image of the school as the locus of the terror.

As a result, the second half of the book deals more explicitly with the ways that school violence was depicted on film. It explores how horror filmmakers interpreted the causes of school violence and its effects on young high school and college students. Many of these incidents were the result of social pressures, frequently resulting from failures of parents to understand the needs of their children and the cruelty of adolescents to one another. Sometimes the violent episodes were the product of academic anxieties. Other times they flowed from feelings of powerlessness over the life changes that occur in the high school and college years. Regardless, the second part of the book takes a historical approach to examining the themes around which horror films constructed their depictions of school violence.

The types of educational institutions chosen as settings for horror films in the latter half of the twentieth century were varied, and the films set in each of the respective educational venues tended to focus on the specific fears commonly experienced by young people attending each type of institution. Thus, the second part of the book is divided into three chapters, each one focusing on a distinct type of educational institution. Late twentieth-century high school horror films frequently dealt with issues of bullying and retribution and the transition from high school to adult life, while college and university horror films often dealt with issues of social class and fraternity and sorority hazing rituals. There were even a substantial number of horror movies set in summer camps that inherited many of the conventions of the traditional scary campfire tale. The second part of the book delineates the fears of school-aged youth and the way those fears were translated into on-screen film violence.

In shifting the threat from outside the school to inside it, filmmakers were changing the way that historians can approach these texts. External horrors give us a sense of how people were responding to the tension created by larger societal changes. They give historians a picture of the tactics people within a given culture were using to make sense of potentially traumatic shifts within that culture. Horror films constructed around internal, personal horror present historians with a much different opportunity. By looking at a variety of such texts, historians can get a stronger sense of the types of day-to-day anxieties that, if not directly experienced by members of the audience, resonated with them and were capable of inspiring strong emotion. Horror films of this kind provide unique primary sources useful for exploring the types of fears commonly experienced by students of a given era. By looking at horror films of both varieties, this book serves as a historical exploration of both the often anxious attitudes of the public about the expansion of public education, the disquietude regarding education and the transition to adulthood, and how these fears found symbolic representation in acts of violence both in and out of school.

A Few Words about Violence

The common thread running through all horror movies is violence. Horror films force their audiences to confront the effects of violence: physical, emotional, and sometimes spiritual. This is why, perhaps more than any other genre, horror films are so polarizing. People tend to be avid fans of horror films, or they refuse to watch them at all. The genre itself invites this sort of audience involvement (or lack thereof). The goal of the horror filmmaker is to create fear, terror, disgust, or revulsion. These films are often difficult to watch. They portray human beings as victims of violence. They dwell on that violence and its effects. Whether the agents perpetrating the violence are nonhuman or human, audiences are forced to confront those things that make them uncomfortable.

Asking audiences to focus on the effects of violence is one of the elements that distinguishes horror from other genres. One cannot categorize a film as a horror movie simply by cataloging the amount of violence depicted in the film. Action movies with huge death counts often contain substantially more violence than the average horror film. (Indeed, there are slapstick comedies, like the *Home Alone* series of films, that contain far greater violence than many horror films.) It is not the level of violence, in and of itself, that qualifies a movie to be considered a horror film. Rather, it is horror films' attitudes toward the violence they depict that defines the genre. Many horror films create a spectacle of their violence, as indeed do many action movies. The horror film, though, asks the audience to consider the causes and the effects of that violence; horror films are, in that regard, a unique film genre with respect to violence. They rip the decorum off killing, unlike, say, action films in which violence is almost always depicted as both justified and satisfying or comedies in which violence is usually portrayed as amusing. To use an action movie example, there is little narrative difference, for instance, between the Charles Bronson action vehicle *Death Wish* (1974) and Wes Craven's horror classic *The Last House on the Left* (1972). Both films are about a man seeking violent revenge after his family is victimized by savage criminals. The difference is that Craven's film shows a broken man with nothing left, even after his revenge. He has been twice degraded: once when his family is victimized, and again when he commits atrocities in their name.[4]

It is not the violence itself that makes a film horrifying; it is the way that the film approaches and treats the violence. Horror films force audiences to bear witness not just to the violence itself but also to the causes and impacts of the violence. It is rare in horror film for violence to exist for its own sake, tending, rather, to be part of a cycle. Acts of physical or emotional violence are committed. A survivor is left to grapple with the trauma of the experience. The survivor is either revisited by the memories of the experience and is repeatedly victimized by the violence of the past or is haunted by the trauma to such a degree that he or she becomes a perpetrator of even more violence.

In many film treatments, Frankenstein's monster is given the transplanted brain of a murderer, fresh from the gallows. After going through the traumatic experience of being brought back to life, being rejected by his creator, and realizing he is hideously disfigured, he revisits violence upon the innocent. Dracula attacks his victims, only to turn them into bloodthirsty killers like himself. The Prowler, for all the evils in which he engages, was never fully able to overcome the horrors of what he saw during World War II or the difficulty of transitioning back to civilian life. Jason Voorhees's mother puts on a hockey mask and commits a series of murders to prevent the summer camp at which her son drowned from reopening. Freddy Krueger haunts the dreams of the children whose parents used the school boiler to exact their angry mob justice against him. In horror film after horror film, the scenario revolved around the violence of the past returning to haunt people in the present. Moreover, as the twentieth century progressed, the school represented the site of both the violence and its retribution.

Many students, parents, teachers, administrators, and researchers are interested in the underlying causes of school violence. Over the course of the past century, the cinema has provided us with countless depictions of violence occurring in school and other educational institutions. Films have explored a variety of ways that students feel anxiety about the school system and their position in it. They have examined the ways in which schools have, on the one hand, promoted and, on the other, discouraged violence. They have developed a language for discussing the fluid relationships among school-aged youth and the dynamic between teenagers and their parents regarding the needs and fears of the young. Horror films provide visual documentation for shifting attitudes toward formal education over the past century, and they offer a unique window into the concerns of youth as they transitioned into adulthood.

Ultimately, this book seeks to chronicle the changes in attitudes regarding education by examining school anxieties through the lens of horror film. Horror stories serve an important cultural function. They provide a means for audiences to confront their fears in a safe, fictional narrative space. In so doing, they serve to ameliorate those fears—either by demonstrating to audience members that their personal fears are shared by others, by exhibiting strategies and providing opportunities for overcoming those fears, or by providing a cathartic experience wherein unexpressed fears are given expression. Neil Gaiman, in his dark fantasy novella for children *Coraline*, paraphrases G. K. Chesterton: "Fairy tales are more than true: not because they tell us that dragons exist, but because they tell us that dragons can be beaten." Horror stories focusing on those darker aspects of school life serve precisely this function. They provide narratives that describe the sources of dissatisfaction with adolescence and school life. They also provide dragons, metaphorical embodiments of these fears and anxieties. Moreover, by depicting young people overcoming these dragons, they often provide vivid examples of teenagers who are symbolically able to negotiate the complexities and challenges of adolescence and successfully transition into adulthood. Even in films in which the violence consumes the adolescent, horror films furnish stern warnings about the potential for the trauma of school life to awaken sleeping dragons.

The presence of dragons has done much to keep scholars away from horror films. Due to the type of graphic violence characteristic of the genre, their low-art status, and a predominantly adolescent audience, academics have often ignored horror films, especially slashers. While several excellent books have been written on slasher films, including Richard Nowell's *Blood Money: A History of the First Teen Slasher Film Cycle* (2011) and Adam Rockoff's *Going to Pieces: The Rise and Fall of the Slasher Film, 1978–1986* (2002), these works have focused heavily on the historical roots of and production considerations within the genre. This book turns its attention to content analysis within the context of historical trends in education to explore the ways in which school violence was depicted on film. In this way, this book adds a new layer of subtlety to the conceptualization of the image of the mad scientist that pervades the scholarship on silent, golden age, and postwar horror films, while also adding to the burgeoning scholarship on the more recent (and violent) history of the late twentieth-century slasher film.

In the twentieth century, compulsory elementary and secondary education universalized schooling as an experience for American youth. The academy also underwent a massive expansion, leading public intellectuals increasingly to find themselves employed at postsecondary institutions and serving ever-increasing numbers of college and university students. As the student population in both secondary and postsecondary institutions increased, the fears, anxieties, and stresses of academic life became part of the common experiences of American youth. The cinema likewise made vast commercial strides between the opening and closing of the twentieth century. In 1900, commercial film was in its infancy, but within a few decades, the cinema would come to be a dominant medium of American entertainment. It is little surprise that, with school experiences becoming such an important aspect of American childhood, that the burgeoning teenage film market would exploit commonly held sentiments about school life to serve as the underlying theme of many of its films.

Like film scholars, education researchers and scholars concerned with the image of school on film have been less than inclined to look at horror films, at least outside of the context of educational psychology. Even Robert Bulman's wonderful book about the school in films for teenagers, *Hollywood Goes to High School: Cinema, Schools, and American Culture* (2005), expressly excludes horror films from its analysis because the horror genre does not operate under the same filmic conventions as other teen films. This book helps to fill the hole in that scholarship by looking at the image of the school, students, educators, and administration in a sample of films largely unexplored in other education scholarship.

Bibliography

Bulman, Robert. *Hollywood Goes to High School: Cinema, Schools, and American Culture*. New York: Worth, 2005.
Gaiman, Neil. *Coraline*. New York: Harper Collins, 2002.

Mirel, Jeffrey. "The Traditional High School: Historical Debates over Its Nature and Function." *Education Next* 6 (2006): 14–21.

Nowell, Richard. *Blood Money: A History of the First Teen Slasher Film Cycle.* New York: Bloomsbury, 2011.

Rockoff, Adam. *Going to Pieces: The Rise and Fall of the Slasher Film, 1978–1986.* Jefferson, NC: McFarland, 2002.

Skal, David. *Screams of Reason: Mad Science and Modern Culture.* New York: Norton, 1998.

Tudor, Andrew. *Monsters and Mad Scientists: A Cultural History of the Horror Movie.* New York: Wiley, 1989.

US Census Bureau. "Education Summary—High School Graduates, and College Enrollment and Degrees: 1900 to 2001." Historical Statistics Table HS-21. http://www.census.gov/statab/hist/HS-21.pdf.

Filmography

Monument, Andrew, dir. *Nightmares in Red, White, and Blue: The Evolution of American Horror Film.* Lux Digital Pictures, 2009.

Phillips, Lee, dir. *The Spell.* Charles Fries Productions, 1977.

Zito, Joseph, dir. *The Prowler.* Graduation Films, 1981.

CHAPTER 2

IS THERE A DOCTOR IN THE HOUSE? THE EVOLUTION OF VAN HELSING AND FRANKENSTEIN AS INTELLECTUAL ARCHETYPES, 1931–1975

The mad scientist is one of the most pervasive images in both horror and science fiction film. The depiction of the socially isolated, wild-eyed, disheveled, and obsessive scientific researcher who engages in intellectual pursuits to the exclusion everything else (including moral and ethical considerations) has been so historically common in film as to become stereotypical. Researchers of mass media science fiction and horror have long pointed to the genres' preoccupation with the relationship between hyper-intellectualism and madness. Far too often scholars have written off this image as one of "knee-jerk anti-intellectualism," but closer examinations of the characterization have pointed to "a far more complicated symbol of civilization and its split-level discontents."[1] Especially in the era following Richard Hofstadter's landmark *Anti-Intellectualism in American Life*, a tendency has developed in scholarship to explain away the mad scientist icon as another example of the puritanical suspicion of intellect that has typified an important portion of the American character.

Since the advent of horror film, Shelley's groundbreaking novel *Frankenstein* and Stoker's Gothic masterpiece *Dracula* have appeared on film more than a combined four hundred times.[2] While this distinction makes the narratives important to film history, the prominence of professorial characters in both works, Abraham Van Helsing in *Dracula* and Victor Frankenstein in *Frankenstein*, make them particularly ripe for scholars concerned with the history of the image of the intellectual. Historians like Russell Jacoby have documented the decline of the public intellectual and the sequestering of academics in institutions of higher education throughout the first half of the twentieth century.[3] Others have outlined an antipathy toward intellectuals among the American public, distrustful and resentful of abstract thinkers, but dependent upon them for material and economic progress.[4] This chapter argues that this tension between suspicion of a decreasingly visible intellectual class and reliance upon them for scientific and material progress can be seen in the representations of horror's most famous scholars. In his secluded laboratory, Dr. Frankenstein ignores scientific ethics and unleashes a monster who murders innocents, while Dr. Van Helsing uses his profound learning and research abilities to protect the London populace from the menace of the bloodthirsty Transylvanian count. This examination also thereby seeks to add to the smattering of recent scholarship that has sought to provide this more nuanced picture of the mad scientist.

The era of the mad scientist film in horror is fairly well defined. There were certainly specific examples of silent film versions of both *Frankenstein* and *Dracula*. The first horror film ever made was Thomas Edison's 1910 *Frankenstein*. F. W. Murnau's thinly veiled retelling of the *Dracula* story, *Nosferatu* (1922), remains among the best-known examples of German Expressionist film. The vision of the mad scientist in horror film was largely solidified by the spate of film versions of both *Dracula* and *Frankenstein* that would become the hallmark of Universal Pictures. Variations to this mad scientist theme would provide the basis for the majority of 1950s creature features, in which newly discovered scientific knowledge would give rise to a threat to the ordered world that only the scientist would have the technical knowledge to contain. Prior to the 1960s, more than 50 percent of all horror and science fiction films were this type of narrative.

By the 1980s, fewer than 15 percent of horror films followed this basic pattern. By the late 1970s, it seems, the threat of science was no longer enough to carry a horror film. The decline of the mad scientist corresponded with the rise of the madman; 90 percent of all horror films involving psychotics were produced after 1960 (in the wake of Alfred Hitchcock's *Psycho*). The mad slasher had replaced the psychotic mad scientist. During this same period, there was also a corresponding and drastic shift in which the pursuer of the monster increasingly became the victim of the film. In 64 percent of films produced after 1960, the major pursuer was an "everyperson," not a scientific practitioner. Since 1960, the expert or scientist was a major figure in fewer than a quarter of all horror films. In the period from 1978 to 1983, science made an appreciable impact in only 14 percent of films, and a majority of those dealt with mutation.[5] After the British studio Hammer Films ceased their long-running *Frankenstein* and *Dracula* series in the mid-1970s, Drs. Frankenstein and Van Helsing all but disappeared from the horror film landscape. Thus, a logical delineation of the period for this examination of *Frankenstein* and *Dracula* films arises, beginning with the Universal films of 1931 and ending with the last of the Hammer films in the mid-1970s.

English Gothic Horror

Gothic horror is primarily an English invention.[6] The most prominent literary examples of the Gothic novel were published in England during the transition from the age of Enlightenment to the Romantic era. Many of them, including Shelley's *Frankenstein*, served to ease a certain cognitive dissonance. Romantics charged that because "[the Enlightenment] espoused nature instead of morality (or religion)" for answering ethical questions, it "expected adherents to act like civilized human beings—even though it could find no rational basis for doing so."[7] The difficulties associated with the transition to the Industrial Revolution cast suspicion upon the rationalist philosophies that had made it possible. By contrast, in seeking experiences of the sublime, Romantics emphasized emotions, especially horror and awe, over the powers of reason. As a result, the end of the Enlightenment marked the beginning of a new age of horror. In *Frankenstein*, science was presented as little more than successful magic, and the primary focus of the book was on the negative moral implications of scientific inquiry unrestrained by contemporaneous moral examinations.[8] The morality of horror narratives is a looking-glass morality. The existing social order is inverted with the addition of a "monster," and moral principles can be extrapolated by the struggle to return stability to the situation. Thus, Gothic horror was an attempt to use inverted logic to respond to moral questions that had been left unanswered in the rise of empiricism.

The Literary Context of *Frankenstein*

Both the *Frankenstein* myth and the modern literary vampire tale trace their roots to the same weekend in May 1816, spent in a villa on Lake Geneva, Switzerland. Lord Byron challenged the literary group he was entertaining, which comprised Mary Shelley, her future husband Percy Bysshe Shelley, and Byron's private physician, Dr. John Polidori, to a contest to see who could write the most terrifying story. Byron began, but never finished, a short story involving a gentleman who had returned from the dead.[9] After a falling out between Byron and Polidori, Polidori took the idea, remodeled the revenant gentleman after Byron, and published the tale under the title *The Vampyre*. This tale became the template for future vampire tales and a major influence on later horror writers, including Stoker. Shelley, of course, presented *Frankenstein* as her entry in the contest, and its subsequent publication quickly established her as an important figure in the Romantic movement.

The novel was itself a Romantic rebellion against scientific rationalism. Frankenstein's extreme dedication to scientific inquiry, without regard to the emotional needs of his loved ones or the moral implications of his actions, gives life to a murderous, uncontrollable being. While Frankenstein was able to create a man from reanimated parts stolen from corpses, he is poorly equipped to provide for the creature's emotional needs or help him to understand the meaning of his own existence. In one sense, this is a vivid demonstration of "the disparity between idealistic intentions and brutal consequences."[10] This example forms the center of Romanticism's Counter-Enlightenment focus. For all the dramatic impact rationalism was able to muster, it was unable to provide people with the framework for making sense of the changes it effected. Frankenstein, therefore, epitomizes the aspirations of the Enlightenment and explains why the Romantics believed it was doomed to failure.[11] If this idea forms the heart of the Frankenstein narrative, it also helps explain the story's role in shaping the twentieth-century image of the mad scientist in response to certain areas of scientific inquiry that outpaced the moral questions that surrounded them—namely, Nazi experiments in eugenics and the development of nuclear weapons.[12]

As a novel with a scientist as protagonist written by a major Romantic figure, *Frankenstein* seeks to address conflicting ideas between the scientific and ethical discourses. In order to build tension, horror tales frequently rely on certain dualistic tendencies. One of the techniques to achieve this effect is to divide "the narrative center, often the protagonist himself [as in *The Strange Case of Dr. Jekyll and Mr. Hyde*] into two sides, one subverting and one upholding the dominant social order."[13] In the case of *Frankenstein*, Shelley uses Dr. Frankenstein and his creature as doppelgängers of one another, with one serving to represent uncontrolled intellect and the other to embody the emotional ramifications of it. In Shelley's tale, the monster is part of the human scheme—while he seems supernatural in abilities, he is completely natural in his origins. Despite his propensity for murder, Shelley's creature engages in the sort of soul-searching that should have been performed by Frankenstein before his unholy experiment. In this respect, it is important that the monster is frequently called simply Frankenstein. This marks him as being one with his human creator. While this makes the creator seem more monstrous, it simultaneously serves to humanize the monster. Initially, Frankenstein's monster is not evil but lies outside of moral questions; he seeks love and companionship and education. Frustrated by people's inability to see beyond his monstrous visage, the creature is made evil by the inflexibility of the existing social structure. He is forced to become evil, in no small part, because of the rejection created by Frankenstein's inability to come to terms with the implications of his own discovery. In this way, *Frankenstein* creates "a sense of contradiction and dissatisfaction with social constructs—of identity, language, morality, law, knowledge, reason, time, and space."[14]

It is the complexity of the issues embodied by this early example of a mad scientist that caused writers, stage play producers, and filmmakers to return repeatedly to the narrative. *Frankenstein* first appeared on stage in 1823. Her journals tell us that Shelley attended that first performance.[15] The novel returned to the stage repeatedly over the next century. In 1910, another inventive scientist with a propensity for electrical experiments, Thomas Edison, created a silent film version of *Frankenstein*. This began a veritable flood of Mary Shelley–inspired films. All told there are more than two hundred versions of the Frankenstein story on film (some of which are, of course, very loose adaptations). The film versions of *Frankenstein*, most of which have come from less respected artistic traditions than their source material, have seen far less scholarly attention than the novel. While most of the film versions could fairly be called vulgarizations of Shelley's novel, as we will see, they also demonstrate how artists were able to adapt the image of the overly zealous scientist beyond nineteenth-century Romanticism.[16]

The Literary Context of *Dracula*

Stoker's works have received far less critical and scholarly attention than Shelley's writings. Shelley was the daughter of famed political philosopher William Godwin and early feminist thinker Mary Wollstonecraft. She was also wife to Percy Bysshe Shelley and compatriot of Lord Byron. She was, therefore, part of a respected literary and intellectual tradition. Such was not the case with Stoker. As an Irishman who began as a theater critic and was primarily known for horror novels and supernatural short stories, such as *The Lair of the White Worm* (1911) and *The Lady of the Shroud* (1909), Stoker garnered a reputation of being a purveyor of formulaic melodrama. It was not critical responses or canonization by scholars of literature, but, rather, the popularity of his work, especially *Dracula* (1897), that was responsible for Stoker's success. This popularity is also what attracted filmmakers to the novel as source material.

Dracula is, more or less, an invasion narrative.[17] In this subgenre, a plague descends, usually for unknown reasons, and the victims must seek the aid of an expert to help them contain it. In this case, Transylvanian Count Dracula relocates to London, and a mysterious affliction begins to affect the female gentility living in the area surrounding his new residence. Unable to fully explain the nature of the young ladies' illness, Dr. Seward seeks outside help, in the form of his colleague and mentor, Dr. Abraham Van Helsing of Amsterdam. "In the person of Van Helsing," *Dracula* "introduces the best known incarnation of the expert bourgeois individualist, whose role is to convince the world of the seriousness of the threat . . . and then act to destroy it."[18] Importantly, Van Helsing also represents a very different view of the intellectual. While Dr. Frankenstein's devotion to science was a liability that prevented him from seeing the negative consequences that would inevitably result from his work, Dr. Van Helsing actively seeks to use his knowledge to combat evil influences that he did not work to create. In juxtaposition with one another, these two figures (ironically both coming from the British literary tradition) embody the duality of the American attitude toward the intellectual: distrust and dependency.

Van Helsing is a far more complex archetype than Frankenstein. Like Dr. Frankenstein, Van Helsing is monomaniacal in his devotion to his studies. Also like Frankenstein, people consider Van Helsing mentally unstable and potentially dangerous. Unlike Frankenstein, who is obsessive in his dedication to science, Van Helsing is a Renaissance man. As a respected member of the medical community, he is a man of science, but his interest in occult matters makes him extremely knowledgeable in both religion and folklore. In this way, Van Helsing's identity is a conglomeration of three archetypes. He is a scientist, he is a devout Catholic (whose most effective weapons are the "crucifix, holy water, and the sanctified host"),[19] and he is a shaman (heavily steeped in peasant lore, including using garlic and wooden stakes to fend off vampires). While Frankenstein is wholly a scientist, Van Helsing uses religion, science, and superstition to achieve his desired ends.[20] His ability to seek answers outside of the scientific realm makes other intellectuals suspicious, but it also more closely links him with the people he is trying to protect. Frequently, this leaves Van Helsing alone in his resistance to Dracula. The intellectual community refuses to believe the threat is real, and the people's superstitious fear keeps them from joining him.[21]

In preying upon betrothed young females, Dracula represents a threat to marriage and family, cornerstones of civilization.[22] Moreover, Dracula is also a serious threat to the existing religious order. Dracula is an inversion of Christ; he sheds the blood of his followers for his own eternal life. In having achieved the secret of eternal life, Dracula is unable to age, perpetually locked in the present. Van Helsing creates a future in the face of Dracula's static present. By his vigorous resistance to the vampire, he "makes a new man [Stoker's words]" of Jonathan Harker, one of the book's protagonists who was brought by Dracula to Transylvania as an estate agent tasked with procuring a London residence for the count.[23] Dracula's threat is multifaceted, simultaneously natural and supernatural. He aims for the destruction of both the individual and the entire civilization. Such a problem requires an equally comprehensive solution. It calls for an approach that only a figure who is simultaneously scientist, philosopher, and metaphysician can bring.[24]

Frankenstein and Van Helsing in the Hands of Universal Films

In *Monster and Mad Scientists: The Cultural History of the Horror Movie*, Andrew Tudor divides the history of the horror film into five eras based on thematic, aesthetic, and structural similarities among the films: the classic period, 1931–1936; the war period, 1941–1946; 1950s boom, 1956–1960; 1970s boom, 1971–1974; and sustained growth, 1978–1983. Universal Pictures was the dominant producer of horror films throughout the classic and war periods. While the studio had made a name for itself producing gangster films, the signature film of Universal by the mid-1930s was the horror film. The studio was able to cultivate numerous popular film franchises, including *Dracula*, *Frankenstein*, *The Mummy*, *The Invisible Man*, and *The Wolf Man*.

For decades, the premiere American film studio was MGM, "a profitable, talent-laden studio geared to first run productions."[25] Universal was, in many ways, the antithesis of MGM. In order to be financially viable, Universal was forced to seek a European market and became increasingly dependent upon international distribution. In order to achieve these goals, the studio hired a number of German filmmakers who were well versed in European Gothic horror and the German Expressionist style of the teens and twenties. The style was typified by surreal landscapes, nightmare logic, and death. The fit was not entirely natural for a competitive American film studio seeking ways to reduce costs. The trajectory, then, from German to American horror was toward one of diminishingly complex lighting schemes and smaller numbers of dark, foggy sets.[26]

The production of German-styled horror films based on nineteenth-century British Gothic novels was not an intuitive business decision for an American company. Paramount had turned down *Dracula*, despite a successful Broadway stage production, because Paramount story editor E. J. Montagne had said of *Dracula* that it was "the type of story more palatable for Europe than the United States." This estimation was largely the product of the opinion that the "strictly morbid type of theme" would not appeal to American audiences. This opinion was more easily defensible in light of the strict American production code, which would have forbidden the depiction of blood sucking.[27] Nevertheless, Universal picked up the rights to *Dracula* and made the now classic Lugosi film, and Universal quickly became synonymous with horror.[28]

Dracula (1931)

The movie that began Universal's relationship to the horror film also made film icons of both Dracula (in no small part due to the magnetism of Bela Lugosi) and Van Helsing. When the audience is first introduced to Edward van Sloan's Van Helsing, he is a stereotypical scientist, mixing chemicals in a test tube and wearing thick coke-bottle lenses and a lab coat. On his first meeting with Dracula, the count's charming side is on full display: "Van Helsing, most distinguished scientist, whose name we know even in the wilds of Transylvania." He must be a very illustrious scientist, indeed, if his work is common knowledge in rural Romania. Certainly, he is a scientist of international repute. He was, after all, called in from Amsterdam to consult on cases of "mental illness" in London.

At the same time, the film undercuts the image of the celebrated doctor. Sloan's Van Helsing is a calm, reasoned man, but he has no compunction jumping to the "superstitious" conclusion for explaining the evidence before him, even when it puts him at odds with the rest of the scientific community. When he first hypothesizes that the outbreak of strange behavior may be attributed to vampires, the response of the other doctors is a disbelieving, "medical science does not admit of such a creature." Dracula's victims have a similar reaction to Van Helsing's offers of protection. Even Jonathan Harker's frustration with Van Helsing bubbles over, and he lashes out at the professor, blaming Van Helsing's strange theories for his newlywed wife Mina's unusual behavior, "Do you know what you're doing to her, professor? You are driving her crazy."

Van Helsing's response to the negativity surrounding him would be repeated throughout Universal's *Dracula* cycle. Van Helsing would remain resolute in the belief that the myth of yesterday becomes the "scientific reality of today." In the end, he realizes that in order to stand as humanity's last bastion against the evils that threaten it, his most effective strategy is to specialize in the "little known facts the world is perhaps better off not knowing." In concentrating on the esoteric for the protection of the public, Van Helsing's plight mirrors that of the twentieth-century American intellectual. The arcane nature of his intellectual pursuits make him the object of suspicion among the general population, even as these intellectual pursuits better position him as their protector.

Dracula's Daughter (1936)

The events of the second film in the Universal *Dracula* series all precipitate from the actions of Van Helsing. When the film opens, police discover a dead man with a broken neck at the bottom of a flight of stairs. They walk through a door and discover another man with a stake through his heart. Professor Van Helsing confesses to having staked the body in the room, and the police take him to Scotland Yard. Upon questioning, Van Helsing puts forth his theory on vampires, to which the police are less than receptive. They describe his story as either "mad or unbelievable." In light of his reputation in the intellectual community, the police decide to go with the latter interpretation. This still leaves our intellectual hero being held for murder. Van Helsing goes on trial for the murder of Count Dracula with an entirely ineffective defense: "In destroying Count Dracula, I have performed a service to humanity." Looking for someone to come to his defense, Van Helsing calls upon a former student, Jeffrey Garth, an American working as a psychiatrist.

Like the other medical scientists in the previous film, Garth calls Van Helsing's defense against his alleged crime "superstition." Van Helsing again claims that superstition is an important basis for scientific discovery. Hypnosis, he argues, has gone from superstition to science. Belief in the subconscious mind one hundred years prior would have been met with derision. Van Helsing strongly contends that his belief in vampires would be likewise vindicated. Garth, however, has a much clearer sense of the distinction between the culture of intellectuals and the mainstream. He pleads with his former mentor to find a better excuse: "Arguments of this sort are all right in academic circles. You're up against stern reality." Oblivious (or perhaps merely indifferent) to the idea that people will judge him negatively for his abstruseness, Van Helsing makes a Shakespearean play on words, telling Garth,

"There are more things on heaven and earth than are dreamt of in your psychiatry." Ultimately, Van Helsing is vindicated, as it becomes increasingly clear that Dracula's daughter is continuing her late father's evil machinations. Garth chases the countess to Transylvania to put an end to her reign of terror but still refuses to believe in Van Helsing's "spells" and "magic."

Son of Dracula (1943) and *House of Dracula* (1945)

While the first two entries in the Universal *Dracula* series were produced during Tudor's classic era of horror film, the final two entries in the series were typical of the war period. The trappings of German Expressionism had largely disappeared at this point. *Son of Dracula* moved the series from Europe to the United States, the Romanian Lugosi was replaced in the title role with American Lon Chaney, Jr., and neither it nor the following film featured Van Helsing. In the film, Dracula decided to come to the United States because it is "stronger and more virile" than the Transylvania he already drained.[29] Instead of Dr. Van Helsing, investigators call Professor Laszlo, an authority on the Hungarian occult, to help explain the strange occurrences. Laszlo adopts the same "I have uncovered data I cannot entirely explain" posturing as Van Helsing. He is likewise met with the same "It's strange to hear a man of science, such as yourself, express a belief in this superstition" reaction. Even Dracula uses, to his own advantage, the stereotype of the intellectual that Van Helsing helped forge. He poses as a scientist, figuring that obsessive scientific investigations are a good cover for not being seen during daylight hours.

The Universal *Dracula* series ends with *House of Dracula* (1945). Although the film returns the setting to Europe, Van Helsing is still not part of the action. Instead, various film monsters, including a vampire and the Wolf Man, seek the help of a scientist (named Dr. Edelmann) in hopes of finding a cure to their monstrosity. Scientific inquiry reveals that vampirism is caused by a blood parasite and lycanthropy by brain swelling. In his zeal to cure the vampire, Dr. Edelmann becomes infected with the parasite and goes mad, even attempting to revive Frankenstein's monster. His devotion to pure science links Edelmann to Frankenstein (more than Van Helsing), but Edelmann is a sort of Christ figure, taking on the sins of others even though they lead to his own death. This differentiates him from Frankenstein, who represents the danger presented by science when it becomes untethered from tradition. Rampant intellectualism, reason without morality to ground it, creates monsters.

Frankenstein (1932)

When James Whale was signed to direct Universal's *Frankenstein*, he was an established British stage director who was successfully transitioning into movies. Boris Karloff had a similar background. He was a British actor with stage experience who was languishing in a series of B-gangster pictures.[30] Together, the two of them were able to craft a new vision of Shelley's novel. The book's preoccupation with the narrowness of scientific understanding influenced a century of horror stories. If the "belief that science is dangerous is as central to the horror movie as is a belief in the malevolent inclinations of ghosts, ghouls, vampires, and zombies,"[31] this is due in no small part to the contribution of Whale's film.

The master of ceremonies begins the film with a description of its protagonist: "a man of science who sought to create a man after his own image, without reckoning upon God."[32] We are introduced to Colin Clive's Frankenstein, *in medias res*, as he waits outside the cemetery gate until the funeral party is done burying a new body. "He's just resting," Frankenstein says, "waiting for a new life to come." He cuts another corpse from the gallows on the way back to his home. From the beginning, the audience is given a strong sense that something is seriously wrong. Dr. Frankenstein has descended to some strange depths. It is obvious to both the audience and his own girlfriend, who receives such love letters as, "My work must come first, even before you," that the doctor's priorities are misaligned.

Van Helsing's relationship with the respected members of the scientific community was strained because of his willingness to seek metaphysical explanations for physical phenomena. Dr. Frankenstein is not part of the established medical community in his own village, but for entirely different reasons. Goldstadt Medical College lies near Frankenstein's laboratory. Frankenstein is not teaching at the college, nor is he a student there. He even sends his assistant there to steal organs (in this case, a brain) from the college's supplies. Eventually, we discover that Frankenstein has a brilliant, if erratic, mind. He left the university, but not because of his own failure. Rather, Frankenstein had advanced beyond the capabilities of the university—so much so that his old professor considered him dangerous. Frankenstein had discovered a ray beyond ultraviolet, one "that first brought life into the world." His recent experiments were not the kind that could be institutionally sanctioned.

As it turns out, the medical college had good reasons for disapproving of Frankenstein's areas of study. The product of his research was monstrous, and the monster was uncontrollable. In a fashion uncharacteristic of future *Frankenstein* films, the doctor has an epiphany and feels pangs of remorse. Gone mad with the results of his experiments, Frankenstein returns home to convalesce. When the monster's rampage comes close to home, Frankenstein even accepts responsibility for what he has created, saying, "I made it with these hands, and with these hands I'll destroy it." Frankenstein has undergone a complete transformation. Clive's Frankenstein is perhaps the only one in the entire film sample to do so.[33] Frankenstein even leads one of the search parties formed to find and destroy the monster. He actively pursues the monster's demise, and he becomes a sort of action hero.

Bride of Frankenstein (1935)

In *Bride of Frankenstein*, Frankenstein wonders, from time to time, about what he could have done if he had continued on the same intellectual course. Dr. Frankenstein is a recovered scientist, and because of the completeness of his transformation, the renewal of his obsession requires a catalyst. That catalyst takes the form of Dr. Pretorius, another scientist who seeks to build on

Frankenstein's work. Like Frankenstein, Pretorius "used to be a doctor of philosophy at the university," but he "got bored." Dr. Pretorius blackmails Frankenstein into being his new assistant. He wants to return Frankenstein to his rightful place, a world in which scientists prove the mysteries of life and death. He toasts the new endeavor: "To a new world of gods and monsters!" The philosophical orientation of these films toward science is one that elevates the scientist to the level of god by virtue of the nature of his research.

Pretorius is a figure worthy of his own study. He has had some success at creating life but has not been able to achieve the scale of Frankenstein. His life, he claims, was grown in cultures. Frankenstein is made uncomfortable by the nature of Pretorius's research. "But this isn't science," he claims. "It's more like black magic." Pretorius's true goal is to "create a man-made race on the face of this Earth." Of course, by 1935, Adolph Hitler had risen to power in Germany, and the horrific undertones of the Frankenstein story begin to tilt strikingly toward the creation of a master race.[34]

Getting Frankenstein to return to this ghastly research was difficult. Henry Frankenstein's complete reformation necessitated Pretorius's use of the monster as blackmail. The monster became a symbol of Frankenstein's past life, a life wholly devoted to scientific advancement. In the film's iconography, then, the creature represents the darker nature of the scientific inquiry. He is the product of the obsessive drive that drove Pretorius mad with the quest for power and keeps Frankenstein delving into the secrets of the world. In using Frankenstein's monster as a means to draw Frankenstein back into his research, the film establishes the monster as a symbol of the unholiness of unrestrained intellect.

The Son of Frankenstein (1939) and *The Ghost of Frankenstein* (1942)

Approaching the war period of horror films, the title role in *Son of Frankenstein* (1939) is an American. When the film opens, Baron Frankenstein has died, and the estate—including his castle, which is kept under lock and key—is bequeathed to his son,

Wolf Frankenstein (played by Basil Rathbone). Wolf's mother had escaped to England and then traveled to America. The younger Frankenstein followed in his father's footsteps, becoming a research scientist. He desires to get out of the *institutional* academic life in the United States ("no more college classrooms, no more faculty meetings") even if that means moving into a great tall tower "haunted because of the things [his] father did."

Wolf Frankenstein meets a cold reception in the town of his father's manor. The population is anti-intellectual, but they are not prejudicially so. They have had nasty experiences with the products of unrestrained intellect. Even though he understands the nature of the townspeople's objections to his presence, Wolf proceeds with a new research agenda, one suggested by his father's scientific notes inherited with the estate. When told that he is "rather like his father," Wolf does not run away from his family legacy, instead expressing admiration for his father's intellect: "If only I could have a fraction of his genius." Unfortunately for him, he too "burn[s] with the irresistible desire" for scientific knowledge that can only lead him to be "hated, blasphemed, and condemned."

Wolf is keenly aware of the stigma that surrounds the name of Frankenstein: "9 out of 10 people call that misshapen creature of my father's experiments 'Frankenstein.'" In his explorations of his new residence, Frankenstein runs across the comatose body of his father's creation. Frankenstein's motivations are not fully selfish, but he is stuck in a strange dilemma. In the name of humanity, he knows he should kill the monster. In the name of science, he believes he should reanimate it. It is family loyalty that convinces him to bring the creature back to life, if only to vindicate his father. The tipping point, however, was when Ygor, a broken-necked man who had been using the monster to murder the jurors who had sentenced him to an ultimately nonfatal trip to the gallows (played expertly by Bela Lugosi), asserted that both being products of the late Henry Frankenstein, Wolf Frankenstein and the monster were metaphorically linked as brothers.[35]

Ghost of Frankenstein (1942) features a second son of Henry Frankenstein, Ludwig Frankenstein, M.D., who specializes in "diseases of the mind." He has perfected a brain transplant surgery in which the brain could be removed from the skull, subjected to surgery, and then replaced.[36] Upon the death of his brother, he inherits both his father's diary and his brother's notes, which sets off a series of events that lead to Ludwig's downfall.

This Dr. Frankenstein is well respected within the established scientific community. When he walks into a room, everyone pays attention. The judge even delays a trial until he is available to appear as an expert witness. This Frankenstein is reluctant to become involved in his family's research. He is not the *obsessive* intellectual his father and brother were, but he is still the inheritor of the secret. In keeping with his reasoned approach to medical science, Ludwig decides to use the family secrets to disassemble the monster piece by piece. One night he sees the ghost of his father. His plans change, and he hatches a plot to transplant the brain of a deceased colleague into the monster.[37] At this point, the medical ethics Ludwig Frankenstein once possessed have all but disappeared. His plot hinges on performing a brain transplant on an unknowing, and almost certainly unwilling, participant. In the end, Ludwig is left with the realization that he created "one hundred times the monster [his] father did."

The Crossovers: *House of Frankenstein* (1944), *Frankenstein Meets the Wolf Man* (1946), and *Abbott and Costello Meet Frankenstein* (1948)

As the war period of American horror films was winding down, Universal released a series of messy crossovers, aimed at squeezing the last drops of life from the struggling genre. In both *House of Frankenstein* and *Frankenstein Meets the Wolf Man*, Chaney's Wolf Man comes to the belief that Dr. Frankenstein's scientific notes hold the key to curing his condition. In the latter film, he seeks the help of Dr. Frankenstein himself, but the former film does not feature Frankenstein at all. Instead, it introduces a new mad scientist who wishes to follow in the footsteps of Frankenstein's "genius," if he ever gets out of the lunatic asylum. Relying on many of the genre clichés that Universal helped establish (such as using a brain transplant to cure the Wolf Man), the films represent the end of a once vibrant horror film dynasty.

The era of Universal horror films officially ended, paradoxically, with both a bang and a whimper. As horror film profits began to decline, Universal recognized the increasing popularity of the buddy-buddy comedy. Bob Hope and Bing Crosby, Jerry Lewis and Dean Martin, and Bud Abbott and Lou Costello all rode to popularity in the late 1940s. In the marketing of films, Abbott and Costello represented a low-cost formula with widespread appeal. The duo made big money for Universal. It only stood to reason, then, that Universal would attempt a horror genre parody by Abbott and Costello (tentatively called *The Brain of Frankenstein*). The film sought to capitalize on the success of Abbott and Costello and reverse the fortunes of Lugosi and Chaney. American horror film was gasping for breath, and there were no serious hopes for it (especially if the macabre genre's final hopes were pinned on a comedy duo). Horror films "seemed rather antiquated after Hiroshima and the birth of the Atomic Age."[38] Even so, the Abbott and Costello film was a huge hit, and *Abbott and Costello Meet Frankenstein* was the number three film on the 1948 film exhibitor's poll.[39]

The opening credits of this film feature animated skeletons, a treatment that already marks it as a different sort of film and gives a strong indication of the level to which Universal was willing to exploit its legacy of horror films for financial gain. The film is peppered with slapstick comedy, such as piles of bags falling on a bellhop and the old secret rotating wall gag. The premise of the film is that Abbott and Costello, playing deliverymen, receive a phone call from Chaney's Wolf Man asking that they refuse receipt of some mysterious packages. They do not follow his advice. Rather, they accept a delivery for McDougal's House of Horrors, a delivery that, as it turned out, contained the corpses of Frankenstein's monster and Count Dracula.

The film presents some unforgiving depictions of scientists. First, upon awakening in the storehouse, Frankenstein's monster calls Dracula "master." In this way, Dracula has usurped the place of Dr. Frankenstein in this narrative, and the scientist has become literally conflated with the monster. Dracula ends up secretly using the equipment of the unwitting Professor Stevens. Dr. Stevens is so "completely engrossed in his own work" that he fails to realize the evil experiments involving Frankenstein's monster that are going on using his own equipment in his own laboratory. Dracula's goal with these experiments is to take away the "intellect" of Frankenstein's monster so that the monster will serve him as a "trained dog."[40]

This film is replete with strange role reversals (and is really no less convoluted than the other Universal crossover films). Here, even as Dracula serves as the Baron Frankenstein figure, the Wolf Man has taken the place of Van Helsing as the expert pursuer. The climax of the film hinges upon Dracula discovering Costello's idiocy. Dracula hunts Costello for his brain, thinking it would be the perfect organ to make Frankenstein's monster his slave. The Wolf Man and Abbott attempt to foil the plot. Silliness ensues, and the era of the Universal horror film comes to a close.

The Legacy of Universal's Frankenstein and Van Helsing

Spanning nearly two decades and a dozen films, Universal's *Dracula* and *Frankenstein* series established the stereotype of the horror film mad scientist that would reappear for decades to come. Hopefully, this examination of the *Dracula* films has provided a clear picture of Van Helsing as intellectual archetype. Van Helsing, as a symbol, embodies many contradictory cultural assumptions about the intellectual. As a leader in his field, his areas of inquiry are esoteric. He is misunderstood by scholars and laborers alike. He is obsessively dedicated to his work, and that devotion makes him potentially dangerous. However, he is able to seek answers from a variety of sources, including religion and superstition. While this places him at odds with his fellow intellectuals, it more closely aligns him with the people he is trying to protect. More importantly, it is his extraordinary ability to take a broad view of a problem that leaves him the only man capable of solving it.

Dr. Frankenstein represents a rather darker view of the intellectual. Like Van Helsing, he is obsessive and committed to his work. Unlike Van Helsing, however, Frankenstein is unable to see beyond the scientific questions he is investigating into a larger context of morality, religion, and tradition. His failure to examine the morality surrounding his research makes him a far more dangerous figure than Van Helsing. Throughout the Universal film series, the image of Frankenstein's monster is used as a hulking symbol of the doctor's fixation with scientific notions of life and death, absent a broader contextual understanding. While later film versions of Frankenstein take a bleaker view, Universal's Frankenstein is still capable of being reformed. Hammer Film's Frankenstein would be far less redeemable.

Van Helsing, Frankenstein, and Hammer Horror

The decade following the end of World War II experienced a dearth of horror films. Between 1951 and 1956, only 30 horror films were produced. During the 1950s boom period (1956–1960), 139 horror movies were released. In the United States, the bulk of these movies were creature features and alien invasion films. The British approach to horror was of a much different ilk; British films of the late 1950s presented monsters that were "more intelligent and urbane than the blind forces of chaos" typical of American horror.[41] This golden age of British horror began and ended with Hammer Film productions. Hammer Films produced the surprise science fiction hit *The Quatermass Xperiment* in 1956. The studio consolidated its success in 1957, using the profits from *Quatermass* to produce versions of both *Frankenstein* and *Dracula*. This represented the first time those two classics of British horror had ever been put to film by a British company. Meanwhile, there were no serious American attempts to revive the series from the 1950s through the 1970s.[42]

In the late 1950s, Great Britain was on the cusp of drastic social changes. Along with the 1957 Suez Canal crisis, the country was in the midst of a national identity shift. The Great Britain reflected in Hammer's first horror film was not

> the country of West End Espresso bars and Teddy Boys, the country soon to be hit by the rock and roll craze, the Angry Young Men, consumer property and the technological revolution. It was instead the country which had just shaken off rationing and building controls, a country of flimsy prefabricated housing and major cities still scarred by bomb sites, a country still in the grip of austere postwar greyness.[43]

In reaching back to horror narratives steeped in the British tradition, Hammer Films was reclaiming these narratives and bringing them back to their native soil, but in so doing they "revitalized, redefined, and revolutionized horror movies around the world."[44]

The Curse of Frankenstein (1957)

While Hammer Films might have been fighting to reclaim the classics of British horror for the motherland, their first *Frankenstein* film was far from a faithful adaptation. In fact, *The Curse of Frankenstein* is "about as far as you can get [from either Shelley's or Universal's *Frankenstein*] and still tell the same basic story."[45] Universal threatened a lawsuit if Hammer's first *Frankenstein* film bore any resemblance to theirs. For this reason, Hammer downplayed the importance of the monster and had the plot revolve around the mad doctor.[46] While Hammer's intent may have been to create a completely different-looking movie, the effect was to change the horrific center of the film. The scientist, not the creature, was the monster.

Despite, or maybe because of, the radical nature of the film's departure from both its source material and film tradition, *The Curse of Frankenstein* was resoundingly condemned by critics and massively popular with audiences. The film's use of primary colors (especially red) made the film more gruesome in tone than (basically any) prior film. Additionally, unlike the Universal films, this movie contained little moralizing. In total, the constellation of all these forces made the film the progenitor of the "gory" horror film that would experience a meteoric rise from the late 1960s through the 1980s.

In addition to the major changes in the horror genre the film presaged, it also represented a serious departure for the image of Dr. Frankenstein. *The Curse of Frankenstein* is the genesis of a new Frankenstein. In *The Curse of Frankenstein*, Frankenstein is "more ruthlessly obsessed"[47] than any of his filmic predecessors. While his willingness to bend morality is a slow progression, Hammer's Frankenstein is "a lethal combination of obsessive pride and cold, cruel idealism." He is a "monomaniac and a murderer."[48]

When the film opens, a priest has come to visit Frankenstein, who is locked up in a prison cell awaiting execution. The events leading to his imprisonment, comprising most of the rest of the film, are told in flashback. In this film, Frankenstein had been a baron from the age of five, which is also when he inherited the family fortune. As a child, he hired a tutor to teach him chemistry and physics. His obsession with the secrets of life and death began then (when he brought his dead puppy back to life). Upon discovering the success of his experiment, he exclaims, "We've discovered the secret of life itself." The tutor responds, "This can only end in evil."

Frankenstein's tutor could not have been more correct. By the end of the film, Frankenstein has committed multiple murders. He locks his servant (with whom he is having a secret affair) in the cell with his murderous creature, not to prevent her from telling his fiancée about the affair, but to keep her from exposing his secret experiments. He murders a famed intellectual to get an acceptable brain for his creature. Peter Cushing's brilliantly acted, icy, and ultrarational Frankenstein is the true monster of the film. Cushing's Frankenstein begs for mercy at the end of the first film as he is led to the guillotine. There would be no such lapse of character in the later films.

The Revenge of Frankenstein (1958)

The second film in Hammer's Frankenstein series begins where the first film ended. Grave robbers dig up the body of the baron, who had faked his own death. Quickly, the doctor moves to Carlsbruck and sets up his office there under the assumed name Dr. Stein. The ladies of the village flock to his office, and he performs free medical services for the poor. The good doctor is seemingly at his most humanitarian in this film. His own motivations are, however, less than honorable. He is, all the while, experimenting with body parts in his laboratory, body parts he has gleaned from medical procedures he performed at the clinic. So, for instance, when a pickpocket comes down with an infection, Dr. Frankenstein graciously amputates the arm and uses it for his experiments. These actions were, at worst, opportunistic. He seems genuine in his desire, for instance, to give a partially paralyzed man a new and healthy body, and this is as close as he ever comes to being depicted as a "victimized scientist."[49] His patients also seem to believe in Frankenstein's benevolence. When a member of the established medical community asks one of his patients, "So, you must have great faith in Dr. Stein?" The man responds with a heartfelt "Yes."

As is typical of reactions to Frankenstein by his fellow intellectuals, the medical community is extremely unhappy with Frankenstein and his decision to operate this clinic outside of their guild. Again, as with the Universal films, Hammer's Frankenstein always maintains a status outside of the accepted scientific community. This is the "revenge" that Frankenstein seeks to exact in this film. He does not want violent retribution. Rather, he seeks to be hailed as a great scientist and no longer to be reviled as the creator of a monster.

During the course of his experiments, Dr. Frankenstein discovers the secret to a successful brain transplant surgery. As with the last film, his creation goes wrong and becomes murderous, which exposes the baron's true identity. In the aftermath of this discovery, Frankenstein is nearly beaten to death, and his assistant uses his new technique to transplant the doctor's brain into another body. Prior to this film, Frankenstein's monster had always been his doppelgänger, a physical projection of the evils associated with the doctor's obsessive scientific mind. There is a drastic shift in this film; symbolically, the mad scientist has become his own monster.

Frankenstein Created Woman (1967)

This film[50] opens with a man being led to the guillotine. The man's young son, Hans, witnesses his father's beheading. As a grown man, Hans becomes a physician's assistant—to Dr. Frankenstein and his associate. The audience's introduction to Frankenstein in this film is as a frozen body. Frankenstein had his body frozen intentionally to demonstrate that the soul does not leave the body when it dies of freezing. "Dead for one hour," he muses, "but my soul did not leave my body. But why?" While all of the Universal *Frankenstein* films featured a doctor who was willing to exploit others in the interest of science, in none of those films does Frankenstein experiment on himself to discover the secrets of life and death.

As a result of this cryogenic experiment, Dr. Frankenstein is able to invent a device that can store human souls. In this way, the doctor intends to conquer death. When a person is dying (or recently deceased, since his freezing experiment demonstrated that the soul does not leave the body immediately upon dying), he can use the device to store the person's soul while he repairs his or her body. After he has provided all the necessary medical treatments, he can move the soul from the apparatus to the body, thereby cheating death.

Because of the strange and secret experiment he engages in, the townspeople think of Frankenstein as "the devil himself" and a performer of the "Black Mass." All the villagers are thoroughly convinced of Frankenstein's involvement with witchcraft. When Hans is arrested for a murder he did not commit (which was, instead, perpetrated by three libertine aristocrats), Frankenstein is brought into the courtroom as a character witness. When asked of his education, Frankenstein claims to be an expert in "medicine, law, and physics." The prosecutor snidely replies, "Of witchcraft?" Coldly and evenly, Frankenstein responds by saying, "To my knowledge, doctorates are not awarded for witchcraft, but, when they are, I shall no doubt qualify for one." This condescension continues throughout the film. When he eventually tells the authorities of his experiment and the soul of Hans occupying Christina's body, the police rhetorically ask the doctor,

"Do you take us for fools?" Frankenstein simply answers, "Yes." Frankenstein's work is not Black Magic. Like Clive's Frankenstein, Cushing's doctor is dedicated to the pursuit of science (and has little, if any, concern for the moral questions surrounding his work). Unlike Clive's Frankenstein, however, Cushing's depiction is openly classist his title and intelligence give Cushing's Frankenstein a less-than-subtle sense of superiority.

Like his father, Hans gets beheaded. Christina, the distraught and disfigured girl who loves him, jumps into the river. Dr. Frankenstein succeeds in capturing Hans's soul from his recently deceased corpse and puts the soul into the body of the woman Hans loved (but whom he was unable to save). Some vestiges of her soul seemingly remain in her body, and she develops massive identity problems. She exacts revenge on the group responsible for the murder for which Hans was convicted. Siren-like, she seduces them and kills them one by one. Frankenstein pursues her, under the auspices of trying to stop her murderous rampage. The film ends with Christina's suicide and Frankenstein's disappointment at his inability to preserve his creation. Ultimately, the film leaves the viewer with a strong sense of the disconnect between Frankenstein's sense of morality and common decency. In this film alone, Frankenstein has killed and revived himself, moved a human soul from one body to another (the person's lover, no less), and witnessed the resulting suicide. The film leaves it unclear as to whether the baron has even considered the larger questions surrounding his inquiries and instead portrays a man worried about the loss of the evidence of the success of his scientific experiment.

Frankenstein Must Be Destroyed (1969)

The theatrical trailer for *Frankenstein Must Be Destroyed* clearly demonstrates the new image of the scientist in horror film: "Scientist . . . Surgeon . . . Madman . . . Murderer . . . Search the length and breadth of Europe . . . Hunt him . . . Track him down . . . No matter what the risk . . . *Frankenstein Must Be Destroyed*." Notice that any reference to Frankenstein's monster or any of the doctor's creations is entirely missing. Christopher

Lee's monster might have been memorable in his own way, but the era of the lumbering, flat-headed, work-booted Karloff style monster had long since ended. It was not the products of science, but the scientist himself, who was the threat.

Scholars are nearly unanimous in their assessment that Cushing's baron in *Frankenstein Must Be Destroyed* is the most evil of all film depictions of the doctor. Tudor describes this film's Frankenstein as "embittered and ruthless; any sympathy that we may feel is directed at the film's pitiable monster," and Gary Smith asserts that the movie features the "most cold-blooded Frankenstein of the entire series."[51] *Frankenstein Must Be Destroyed* begins with the baron murdering someone for materials for his experiments. Given the starkness of the doctor's evil, Cushing is able to negotiate tricky acting waters with aplomb. He embodies a strange duality; his brutality punctuates an icy demeanor of courtesy and elegance. Near the opening of the film, a thief breaks into the laboratory and is attacked by a monster. The audience soon discovers the attacker was not a monster; instead it was Dr. Frankenstein in a mask. Frankenstein's appearance in a monster mask sets up a visual metaphor in which the doctor is equated with his monstrous creation. Like the ending of *The Revenge of Frankenstein*, the beginning of *Frankenstein Must Be Destroyed* leaves the audience with the impression that Frankenstein's creations are simply other victims; the scientist himself is the monster.

Negative comments about Dr. Frankenstein pepper the film. In one scene in which men, sitting in the lobby of an inn, are discussing a series of murders that have recently occurred, one man bemoans the downfall of Frankenstein's great scientific mind: "Madness is always sad, but for such a brilliant man to drive himself mad—what a terrible waste!" Another describes Frankenstein's colleague Dr Brandt, a man who had made a name for himself in brain transplantation, as "the devil's disciple." Unbeknownst to the men conversing in the lobby, Frankenstein overhears their comments. He does not respond kindly. He compares them to "cavemen" for dismissing the medical advances represented by the work of Drs. Frankenstein and Brandt. He claims that they should refrain from expressing opinions on subjects about which they are "ignorant." Further, he represents himself as a "Prometheus," bringing "progress" and civilization to the world. In this way, Cushing's Frankenstein harkens back to the Frankenstein of Shelley's novel, the full title of which was *Frankenstein: or, The Modern Prometheus*. Shelley's Frankenstein was a victim of his own hubris and, like the Prometheus of Greek myth, was severely punished for ignoring the will of the gods. Cushing's Frankenstein, however, seems to view his punishment as having to abide listening to the concerns of his colleagues about the viability of his research.

Beyond his interactions with his colleagues the Frankenstein of *Frankenstein Must Be Destroyed* is thoroughly despicable. He is highly misogynistic. He even goes so far as to rape the young woman he is blackmailing.[52] This depiction is over the top. The genre has moved away from the ambiguous depiction of the obsessive, but well-intentioned, scientist. The scientist is now largely evil. He is a man who does whatever he wants in the interest of his research (or in his own quest for power).[53] By the end, Frankenstein has transplanted the brain of Dr. Brandt into another body so that he can have access to the unpublished scientific discoveries housed therein. In one of the tiniest glimmers of the humanity of the obsessive scientist, Frankenstein seems to take pleasure in reuniting "Brandt" with his wife. He honestly seems to believe in the goodness of what he has done, irrespective of the means he used to orchestrate the reunion. In this respect, Cushing's Frankenstein should not be considered completely evil. Rather, he is solely concerned with the scientific impact of his research. While it may have been a taboo subject, Frankenstein's desire to aid humanity by keeping alive the brains of its greatest thinkers is not unreasonable. Rationalizing blackmail, rape, and murder to achieve these ends, however, exposes his inhumanity.

Frankenstein and the Monster from Hell (1973)

This final film in the Hammer *Frankenstein* cycle begins with a grave robbing, witnessed by a pair of policemen. The film cuts to a young, blond, attractive doctor, Simon Helder, who appears to be a younger version of Dr. Frankenstein, especially when we discover him looking over a copy of "The Collected Works of Baron Frankenstein." One of the police officers comes to the doctor's office and clumsily spills his jar of eyeballs (with attached optic nerves). Helder's frustration is apparent in his response: "If you could only understand the difficulty of finding specimens like these." The officer does not take too kindly to the insolence, arresting the young man "for sorcery." Equating science with sorcery was a staple of Hammer's everymen. This reaction certainly recalls the accusations that Dr. Frankenstein's research inspired in, for instance, *Frankenstein Created Woman*.

Despite the fact that the townspeople clearly misunderstand the nature of inquiry in theoretical science, Helder tries to use his status as a doctor to get him out of his legal troubles. When he is brought before the judge for the atrocities that take place in his lab, he responds with the weak excuse, "I am a doctor, you know." The judge's reply is clear (and mirrors the attitude of the horror genre to those who study science): "If we cannot trust even our men of science to behave in a manner proper to a decent and God-fearing citizen, then who are we to trust?" Helder is sentenced to a state asylum for the criminally insane for a period of five years.

After Simon is committed to the mental institution, the audience discovers that Dr. Frankenstein is also an inmate at the asylum. He gives orders followed by both his fellow patients and the doctors. Through a natural magnetism and intellectual weight, Frankenstein has assumed the responsibilities of the director of the asylum. Underlying this film seems to be an assumption of a natural aristocracy. In addition to his appropriated responsibility as director, Frankenstein also seems to care for his patients. He actively works to improve the lives of his charges, including teaching the medical trade to a mute female inmate. Frankenstein even makes the daily rounds and provides psychiatric treatment to all the inmates. It is through this ethic of caring that Dr. Frankenstein descends to the depths of human brutality. In the interests of furthering his philanthropic scientific research agenda, he is willing to commit atrocities. His single-minded focus seems largely due to his view that science is the foundation of all human progress.

With a new protégé in the ward, Frankenstein embarks on a new research project. The film seems to rely on the premise that there is an association between madness and hyper-intellectualism. One of the inmates is another intellectual, a professor of mathematics with musical acumen. The deeply disturbed professor hangs himself with his own violin strings. Frankenstein and his new apprentice attempt to save the man's brain by transplanting it into that of their new creature. The monster the two create is a grotesque "Neolithic" ape-man. Ironically, in his effort to advance human understanding, Frankenstein created a prehistoric monster. This monster is incredibly short-lived. Frankenstein is unable to control the inmates after they discover the monster, and they tear the creature from limb to limb.

Dracula (1958)

If Cushing's portrayal of Frankenstein was somewhat slightly revolutionary, his depiction of Abraham Van Helsing was iconoclastic. Sloan's Van Helsing was an elderly gentleman. He was intelligent and good-natured. One might even call him jovial. While he was not afraid of directly confronting evil, he always did so in highly structured social situations or within the context of his pleas for others to help implement his stratagems for defeating the evil menace. After more than a quarter century since Universal's first *Dracula* film, Van Helsing, vampire hunter, had become a fixed character archetype.

Against this backdrop, Cushing's portrayal was all the more groundbreaking. Cushing's Van Helsing was the most actively engaged in the intellectual community of all film representations of the Dutch professor. For instance, in one scene, Van Helsing listens to old lectures on vampires on his Victrola and takes notes. This film actually depicts Van Helsing doing secondary research, something entirely missing from any previous depiction of the professor. He also records his own voice on a disc, keeping an account of his observations on vampirism. Cushing's Van Helsing is an academic who is actively involved in the research community, including publishing his own research. This also distinguishes the Van Helsing of Hammer films from Frankenstein. Depictions of

Frankenstein almost always show him moving outside the intellectual community before he begins his obsessive experimentation. Every prior film version of Frankenstein shows a man who is not engaged with the larger scientific community, except insofar as he seeks to demonstrate its short-sightedness in rejecting his dangerous orientation to the discipline.

Cushing's Van Helsing is still the object of suspicion; in trying to aid a young woman who bears the mark of the vampire, he is met with the usual resistance: "Whoever you are and whatever your motives, please go!" This Van Helsing is both more forceful and more knowledgeable. Sloan's Van Helsing accepted the *possibility* of the supernatural. Cushing's Van Helsing is adamant that his way of thinking is *imperative*, saying, "If you don't do exactly as I say, she will die!" While the *Frankenstein* films implied that Frankenstein's scientific experiments were *like* magic, the *Dracula* films made no differentiation between the two. Van Helsing was not a natural scientist; he was a supernatural one.

The greatest difference between Sloan's and Cushing's Van Helsing is their level of agency. Sloan's Van Helsing is a medical consultant, brought in to give Dr. Seward a second opinion and advocate a course of treatment for a mysterious affliction. When his plans are heeded at all, others put them into motion. Cushing's Van Helsing is the active agent in the battle against evil. He recognizes the evil and actively investigates it. He is part Sherlock Holmes, scouring maps of the surrounding areas, locating graveyards, and hunting down Dracula's coffin.[54] He draws the conclusion that "the unholy cult must be wiped out." He arms himself for battle with crucifixes and wooden stakes. Cushing's Van Helsing is willing to get blood on his own hands, while burning the image of the Christ into the hands of Dracula's female victims. The climax of the film is an exciting chase through Dracula's castle, a physical contest between Dracula and Van Helsing. Outmatched by Dracula's strength, Van Helsing dashes across the dining room table, yanks open the curtains, and lets sunlight pour into the room. Van Helsing has become a variation on the swashbuckling action hero, "a quietly fanatical Christian warrior almost as frightening as [Christopher] Lee's Dracula."[55] Just as Cushing's Frankenstein blurred the line between well-meaning, misguided scientist and evil monomaniac, his Van Helsing oscillates between dispassionate, if not uncaring, professor and madman. Cushing's calm air of gentility contrasts uncomfortably with the bloody, violent acts he perpetrates. While Sloan's good-humored Van Helsing had some seemingly crazy ideas, Cushing's single-minded Van Helsing acted on them.

The Brides of Dracula (1960) and the Era Without Van Helsing

The Brides of Dracula (1960) is an interesting film in that Van Helsing, not Dracula, is the link to the first movie. Lee had decided not to do a sequel. He expressed a (likely reasonable) fear that his career would meet a similar fate to that of Lugosi, whose name was forever linked to Dracula. Viciously typecast, addicted to intravenous drugs, and unable to find work after the horror genre changed in the 1950s, Lugosi's later career was not one worthy of emulation. Lee approached the popular success of his *Dracula* film with a measure of trepidation. Cushing, who had an established and respected career in British film, had no such hesitancy in reprising his role as Van Helsing. Hammer's decision to make another *Dracula* film without Dracula lends credence to an important thesis. Cushing's Van Helsing was a charismatic enough character in his own right to carry a film. This is something that would have been unimaginable in the era of the Universal horror films. It is nearly impossible to envision Sloan's Van Helsing as the central character in any story. Van Helsing had moved beyond the image of the one-dimensional, socially awkward intellectual.

In this second film in Hammer's *Dracula* series, Van Helsing is still a physical presence on screen. Simultaneously, he is spiritually and intellectually self-assured, adding to the complexity of this new image of the intellectual in horror film. In one of Hammer's most visually unsettling scenes, Van Helsing succumbs to a vampire bite and burns out the poison with a branding iron. This "crystallizes all the Puritanical, God-fearing zeal which makes Cushing's Van Helsing every bit as uncomfortably charismatic as his undead opponent."[56] Hammer horror was not like American horror in the same period. At Hammer, adults were not producing movies aimed at teens that exploited their fears of the adult world. Hammer films were not teenage wish fulfillment. In this new vision of horror film, Van Helsing is both protector and threat.

Over the course of the next decade, Hammer released four more *Dracula* films, *Dracula: Prince of Darkness* (1965), *Dracula Has Risen from the Grave* (1968), *Taste the Blood of Dracula* (1969), and *The Scars of Dracula* (1970). None of these films featured Cushing or Van Helsing. Each of them featured a clergyman or intellectual vampire hunter. These films are worthy of an examination of their own but lie outside of the scope of this book.

Dracula A.D. 1972 (1972) and *The Satanic Rites of Dracula* (1973)

Van Helsing did not return to the Hammer *Dracula* series until 1972, a 12-year hiatus. Stylistically, the initial scene of the first of these films recalls the previous entries. It begins with a flashback in which Dracula and Van Helsing are battling atop a moving carriage. The carriage crashes. Van Helsing, seriously injured, crawls and grapples with Dracula, ultimately staking him with a piece of broken carriage wheel. While every representation of Van Helsing has him as spiritual and intellectual threat, Hammer's Van Helsing remains, as always, a physical threat to the undead.

After the opening flashback, *Dracula A.D. 1972* radically shifts in tone. It contains a jaunty, slightly funky soundtrack, highly reminiscent of a 1970s television police drama. This film's vampire hunter is Lawrence Van Helsing, the descendent of the great vampire hunter. He is an anthropologist and an author of a book on Count Dracula. His library contains books on Black Masses. When his daughter dismisses one of them as superstition, he retorts, "Our family has a tradition of research into the occult. For us, it has been a serious lifelong study." While the Universal films had long toyed with the idea of Dr. Frankenstein's sins being passed down to his sons,[57] this was the first film to suggest that Van Helsing's intellectual prowess and interest in the occult would revisit his offspring.

Dracula A.D. 1972 features not one, but two Van Helsings. Lawrence Van Helsing's daughter, Jessica, is something of a caricatured depiction of late 1960s, early 1970s youth culture. She attends "freak-out" rock-and-roll concerts and seeks out new experiences with her friends. Her youthful rebellious streak impels her to attend a Black Mass led by a young man by the name of Alucard (a thinly veiled inversion of the name Dracula).[58] Alucard tries to convince Jessica Van Helsing to allow him to baptize her with blood. She comes to her senses before participating. The Black Mass results in the resurrection of Dracula and the murder of one of her friends, and Scotland Yard is called in to investigate.

The plot of the rest of the film revolves around Dracula's plan to exact revenge on Abraham Van Helsing by changing his great-granddaughter into a vampire, as Scotland Yard tries to stop the serial killings Dracula leaves in his wake. The police are not left without aid in this effort. The audience is told in the film that Professor Lorimar Van Helsing, Lawrence's father, once helped Scotland Yard as a specialist in the occult. He was an expert in "psychophenomen[a] as related to history." In his son's estimation, "he was a scientist and his evidence was conclusive. There is evil in this world." Much of Van Helsing's information on vampirism does seem to be based on scientific evidence. He makes seemingly experience-based assessments of the relative effectiveness of certain tools, such as "silver bullets are impractical, and garlic is not one hundred percent effective." This incarnation of Van Helsing uses studies in cultural anthropology, Eastern European history and folklore, and written records of alleged vampire hunters to aid the police in tracking down their killer.

While this film's Van Helsing bears many of the characteristics of Cushing's previous depictions (e.g., his vast and varied intellectual curiosity), his function is quite different in this modern Dracula tale. Van Helsing in this film is an expert police consultant. In this capacity, he bears a strong resemblance to

Sherlock Holmes, another film role for which Cushing was famous. *Dracula A.D. 1972* also seems to be capitalizing on the rise of the police drama in the 1970s. Serving as a police consultant is an interesting way of pulling the intellectual into a modern monster tale, but it does not speak well of the intellectual. At this point, the demise of the public intellectual had been so completely effectuated that the only way to pull the intellectual out of the institution is to have him consult for the police. In the novel and the Universal films, Van Helsing had always been brought to the scene by another intellectual (usually Dr. Seward) to serve as a medical and metaphysical specialist. Ultimately, Lawrence Van Helsing destroys Dracula and saves his daughter's life by driving wooden crosses into the bottom of an open grave. He then throws holy water in Dracula's face so that he falls in and stakes himself with a cross. While the form of Van Helsing had changed, his plot function had not.

Another modern Dracula film followed on the heels of *Dracula A.D. 1972*. *The Satanic Rites of Dracula* (which was also released as *Count Dracula and His Vampire Brides* and *Dracula Is Dead and Well and Living in London*) begins with another Black Mass, during which a man being held against his will on an aristocratic estate escapes. The escapee does not survive, and Van Helsing (again as a police consultant) is brought in as "an academic type" who specializes in "anthropology and Eastern European history" with an emphasis on "satanic ritual, black arts, and . . . other things." His daughter, by the time of this film, has moved out of her rebellious phase and helps her father with his new job. The Van Helsing tradition of battling the evils of vampirism will continue for another generation.

In one of the least flattering depictions of a scientist of any film in this sample, a Nobel prize–winning friend of Van Helsing, it turns out, had become involved with a satanic cult. The cult was using his scientific acumen to develop a radioactively enhanced bubonic plague that it intended to use to aid Dracula in his quest to punish humanity for the repeated failure of his evil plots. The moral repugnance of his experimentation had driven the doctor mad. Van Helsing discovers his corpse hanging from the ceiling, either the victim of suicide or the dangerous cult with whom he associated.

When Dracula's plot becomes apparent to Van Helsing, he wonders about what would drive Dracula to destroy all of humanity, when this could only result in the destruction of his food supply, and, ultimately, his own demise. Van Helsing develops a theory about the "Death Drive" and Dracula's subconscious. In addition to anthropology, Eastern European history and folklore, and cultism, Van Helsing also appears to have some training as a psychologist. Van Helsing's psychological musings may have had an element of truth. In the finale of this film, Dracula destroys himself when Van Helsing leads him into a patch of the Hawthorn tree, the thorns of which, according to tradition, were used to make Christ's crucifixion crown.

The End of the Hammer Era

The Satanic Rites of Dracula was the last film in which Cushing and Lee appeared together as Van Helsing and Dracula. The modern Dracula films were certainly Hammer's attempt to breathe new life into its undead film series. The all-too-convenient police consultant excuse for explaining the existence of a modern-day vampire hunter added a new dimension to Van Helsing's character. Van Helsing had, since Stoker's novel, always been a multifaceted character—seeking knowledge from his books, spiritual strength from his Catholic faith, and wisdom from the cultural practices of the people. He was an invention unique to Great Britain's Gothic tradition. This was the tradition that had been reclaimed when Hammer brought *Dracula* and *Frankenstein* back to their native soil. The modern *Dracula* tales, while intriguing historical artifacts, moved Dracula and Van Helsing out of their Gothic past. This, in turn, undermined Hammer Film's identity. The films were not of appreciably lower production value than their predecessors, but they were radically different in tone and style.

By the mid-1970s, the *Frankenstein* film franchise had also lost it freshness and, hence, its ability to create terror. By the time Hammer's *Frankenstein* reached its seventh entry, the audience was left with a mad scientist "pursuing his, by now completely useless, experiments in a lunatic asylum" and drawing the conclusion that "a lunatic asylum is the best place for him."[59] The horror film landscape had changed drastically by 1974. Hammer's *The Curse of Frankenstein* had set a new standard in horror movie violence in 1957. Films like *Night of the Living Dead* (1968), *The Exorcist* (1973), and *The Texas Chainsaw Massacre* (1974) had inherited *The Curse of Frankenstein*'s legacy of gore and were driving the genre in an increasingly graphic direction. As a result, such mad scientist films as were left by the mid-1970s seemed quaint and "displayed neither the range nor the depth of narrative invention once familiar."[60] For instance, by the time of *Frankenstein and the Monster from Hell*, "the baron had become merely harsh and brutal . . . a stereotypical authoritarian, and such conviction as there is to this version depends on the graphic violence both of the monster's rampage and the lunatic asylum inmates who finally tear him apart."[61] By 1974, the *Frankenstein* films had moved well past questions of scientific ethics and were caught in the spiral of escalating violence they had been instrumental in creating. In less than two years, Hammer Films would produce their final film, *To the Devil a Daughter*, and the golden age of British horror film would end.

VAN HELSING AND FRANKENSTEIN IN THE UNITED STATES FROM THE 1950S BOOM TO THE 1970S

From the late 1950s to the mid-1970s, horror film's two great mad scientists were firmly in the control of the juggernaut that was Hammer Films. That is not to say that American film studios avoided two of the most prolific figures in the history of horror narratives. Certainly, the major film studios, including Universal, did not attempt any major cinematic events involving either Frankenstein or Van Helsing.[62] Instead, Frankenstein and Dracula became the staples of the smaller film studios. American *Dracula* and *Frankenstein* films in the postwar era came in three different varieties. The first and largest of the three groups included small, often regionally distributed drive-in fare. This group included such films as *Dracula vs. Frankenstein* (1971), *Frankenstein's Daughter* (1958), *Jesse James Meets Frankenstein's Daughter* (1966), and two more films that will be discussed later in this chapter, *Frankenstein Meets the Space Monster* (1965) and *I Was a Teenage Frankenstein* (1957). The second group of films consisted of movies of higher production value that responded to Hammer's inventiveness by attempting, with varying degrees of success, to stay as close as possible to the source texts. Among those films are Dan Curtis's *Dracula* (1974),[63] featuring Jack Palance as the infamous count, and *Frankenstein: The True Story* (1973).[64]

The third group of horror films was the product of a newly developing African American film industry. These titles, which included *Blacula* (1972), *Scream, Blacula, Scream* (1973), and *Blackenstein* (1973), form an interesting subgenre. The *Blacula* films do not contain an Africanized version of Van Helsing. Ironically, given the Hammer versions of *Dracula* that were being released contemporaneously, the man who pursued Blacula and sought to destroy him was a police investigator. While he may very loosely be considered a forensic scientist, Officer Gordon was not an obsessive bookworm. He was willing to accept supernatural interpretations for events he could not otherwise explain, and he did use his belief in folk wisdom (in this case, voodoo) to aid him in his quest to end Blacula's reign of terror.

The blaxploitation versions of *Dracula* and *Frankenstein* were the most explicitly political films of the more than 40-year span examined in this chapter. *Blacula* opens in Transylvania in 1780. Count Dracula is hosting an African dignitary, who tries to convince the count to aid his country in abolishing the slave trade. Dracula is less than receptive, instead offering to buy the prince's wife. Dracula intentionally created the black monster, cursing him for daring to defy him when he sought the man's wife: "You shall pay, black prince . . . You shall be Blacula." Blacula is an elegant, if pitiable character, seeking to break the violent curse that the white man has placed on him. At times, the vampire often serves as the antihero of the films, cleaning up the crime-ridden streets of Los Angeles and educating his African American brethren. In *Scream, Blacula, Scream*, for instance, he is approached by an African American prostitute and refuses her advances. Her pimps get involved, questioning Blacula's sexual orientation. They get a lecture from Blacula in return: "You make a slave of your sister, and you're still a slave—imitating your master." When they persist in their mockery, the vampire becomes violent and drains the men of their blood.[65]

Blackenstein has woeful production values—even for a film included in this sample. Its nonsensical plot is accentuated by continuity errors. Notwithstanding, the political undertones are even stronger in *Blackenstein* than in the *Blacula* dyad. In this film, a young black physician, Dr. Winifred Walker, arrives in Los Angeles to visit Dr. Stein, a famed white doctor who won a Nobel Peace Prize for "solving the DNA genetic code." Dr. Walker asks his help in treating her fiancé, Eddie, who lost his limbs to a landmine in Vietnam. After his experimental reconstructive surgery is complete, Dr. Stein, unaware that his patient is a lumbering Boris Karloff–style Frankenstein's monster, continues to provide the medical treatments that fuel his murderous rampage. Despite the picture's overall lack of production quality, it does make a powerful political statement. In *Blackenstein*, the monstrosity is a black man victimized first by the Vietnam War machine, then by his white captor.

Frankenstein Goes to the Drive-In

Many of the aforementioned drive-in theater *Dracula* and *Frankenstein* attractions are worthy of a more detailed discussion than is reasonable here. In this chapter, I argue that both American and British *Dracula* and *Frankenstein* films contain far more complex depictions of the intellectual than the one-dimensional mad scientist scholars and critics long assumed were the mainstay of twentieth-century science fiction and horror films. The depiction of Frankenstein in American horror films, in particular, exhibited the ambivalent cultural attitudes of suspicion and dependence associated with the scientist. With that in mind, I have selected the two extreme examples that best represent these competing values for the following discussion.

The first film, *Frankenstein Meets the Space Monster*, feels a great deal like a commercial for NASA. In this version of the *Frankenstein* tale, Dr. Steele plays the role of "Dr. Frankenstein." Dr. Steele is a NASA scientist who built a cyborg as a perfect astronaut for a "manned" Mars mission. The astronaut was built with synthetic skin and an electronic sensory control system. The rest of his body was composed of human parts. The doctor was able to control the cyborg using a radio signal. Dr. Steele used his scientific acumen to devise a plan that would allow for "extended space travel without the loss of a solitary life." It would also eliminate the possibility of human error. By the mid-1960s, Hammer had succeeded in making Cushing's icily rational aristocratic gentleman the new Dr. Frankenstein icon. This Dr. Frankenstein breaks the mold. Dr. Steele is an attractive young American male helping the United States win the Space Race with the help of a sexy young assistant.

Dr. Steele's best-laid plans go terribly awry. NASA launches the new robotic astronaut. The mechanical space traveler is severely burned when aliens shoot down his rocket. After he crashes to Earth, something goes wrong with the cyborg's circuitry. The robot's appearance is marred by the fire. Frankenstein's monster, as Dr. Steele's robot has now become, has corrupted programming that leads him to murder innocents.

Fearful the monster will alert Earth's scientists to the fact that they are hovering above the planet and are poised to attack, the aliens pursue the monster in hopes of destroying him. Likewise, Dr. Steele actively searches for his creation in an attempt to stop his rampage before anyone can discover the nature of his secret project. Much of the narrative arc in the first half of the film involves a race between the two sides, each hoping to find the cyborg first.

In the rest of the film, Dr. Steele attempts to thwart "Phase Two" of the aliens' plan. The aliens' home world was destroyed by nuclear war, and they are left in exile until the radiation levels drop to a safe range. They have come to Earth to acquire "breeding stock" to repopulate their planet. They are in "Phase

Two" of their plan: "the capture of the Earth women." Like much drive-in fare, the film also makes gratuitous use of the bikini, as the aliens round up Earth's women for "breeding stock."

Frankenstein Meets the Space Monster has a subtly esoteric title. The film itself makes no reference to Frankenstein or his monster. This movie is named after its subtext, highly unusual for a film in this era with such low artistic aspirations. Moreover, Dr. Steele is a complex character. On the one hand, he is the hero of the film. He is aiding the United States in its technological battles against the Soviets. He is developing technology to save the lives of American astronauts. Perhaps most importantly, he is engineering the means to bring about the end of "Phase Two," save the American family, and repel the alien invasion. On this level, this Dr. Frankenstein is a worthy protector. On the other hand, his research is so advanced that he is unable to control it. His creation is imperfect and murders innocent people. Although the overwhelming portion of the image of Dr. Steele is admirable, but there is still some reason to fear his research.

I Was a Teenage Frankenstein lies on the opposite end of the spectrum. This film features an almost entirely wicked Dr. Frankenstein. We are introduced to this incarnation of Professor Frankenstein during a faculty meeting. He has clear disagreements with his colleagues. Dr. Randolph, in particular, is extremely disrespectful, telling Frankenstein that a "high school sophomore" would not believe his ideas. As a result, Dr. Frankenstein loses faith in the educational institution as a locus for developing new ideas. For one thing, working outside the institution frees Frankenstein from the "publish or perish" mentality. He is able to tell his secretary/fiancée that he wishes her to hold all calls he may receive regarding "articles and periodicals and so forth." More importantly, he plans his newest experiment outside of the strictures of the institution. When you are going to engage in seriously unethical and hugely controversial research, under the watchful eyes of your fellow professors is not the best place to do it. His assistant, whom he has had to blackmail into helping him, attempts to clarify Frankenstein's intentions, "You mean [your new project will be done] under the sponsorship of some medical institution?" Frankenstein's completely even-tempered response is a simple, "No. On my own, in here, in my own laboratory." By this time in the history of American education, scientific research conducted outside of an educational or governmental institution had become nearly unfathomable.

Despite being played by an American actor who speaks without accent, this Dr. Frankenstein is not an American. He needs to finish his project "before [his] visa expires."[66] Frankenstein even seems proud of his adopted homeland: "When I think of all I've accomplished here, I will always remember America with deep gratitude." On the whole, Frankenstein films, both in America and in Great Britain, were hesitant to adopt the mad doctor as their own. His brand of scientific extremism was foreign, not homegrown. Prior to World War II and throughout the war period, it made a certain degree of nationalistic sense to maintain Dr. Frankenstein's German identity. In the postwar era, with the glut of German science-minded émigrés, it was easy to maintain the idea of the driven German scientist, rather than to try to recast Dr. Frankenstein as an American (or Englishman). With its idolization of the American space program, the exception of *Frankenstein Meets the Space Monster* makes sense within this context. The darts aimed at the threat of nuclear war and the dangers of radiation were easier to throw at foreign intellectuals, but Americans were willing to claim the laurels of success in the Space Race with nationalistic pride.

The hook for *I Was a Teenage Frankenstein* was that creating an adult human made him less educable. If science was to create a perfect race of human beings, scientists should begin by trying to create a more malleable teenager, because "only in youth is there any hope for mankind." Conveniently, a car full of teenagers crashes near Frankenstein's house. Frankenstein runs out to a veritable smorgasbord of raw material. Later in the film, Frankenstein also disinters a group of student athletes who died in a plane crash. Frankenstein's monster is made of all-American teenagers.

Like both Colin and Cushing, *I Was a Teenage Frankenstein*'s doctor ignores his fiancée in deference to the "pure, clear flame of science." Instead of engaging in a healthy romantic relationship, he perverts the natural order by patrolling Lover's Lane, "a private preserve for teenagers," for materials for his creature. His obsession with his project makes it impossible to even discuss wedding plans with his soon-to-be wife. The experiment is the most important thing in his life, and he keeps it a deep secret, even from her. Neither is Frankenstein above physically abusing her. When he loses his temper with her reasonable questions about wedding plans, he slaps her across the face. The best defense he can mount is the old mantra, "You understand a scientist's devotion to duty." He is unable to envision having both a romantic life and a professional one. "I must devote myself to science and research to the exclusion of all other interests." Once he is able to maintain a certain level of control over the creature—with the promise of an attractive new face—he even compels the "teenage Frankenstein" to murder his fiancée and end her snooping ways. He throws her body into the basement where he cartoonishly keeps the alligator to eat his scraps.

While taking the monster to Lover's Lane to pick out a new face, Dr. Frankenstein has the opportunity to give his grand soliloquy:

> After we have baffled the learned men of science I will tell the entire world the truth. How you were reborn. How I fashioned you from different parts, breathed life into you, pumped knowledge and wisdom into a brain that was hidden in a corpse. Then, I'll be honored by the entire world, having brought man one step further in the eternal battle against death.

What is intriguing about this quote is that, for all his blustery rhetoric about devotion to science as a discipline, he is not engaged in the pursuit of science for the benefit of the discipline. His desire to benefit mankind also seems, at best, secondary. Life expectancy may increase as a direct result of this research, but that is not the focus of Dr. Frankenstein's rant. He is concerned almost exclusively with his own renown as the person who made the discovery. Frankenstein's obsessive drive in this film was to prove himself better than his colleagues in the scientific community. This also puts him decidedly at odds with Cushing's Frankenstein for whom the experiment is more important, even, than his own health and safety.

Some Concluding Remarks

Looking at the development of the images of Van Helsing and Frankenstein provides a unique opportunity for scholars interested in the depiction of scientists in popular media. With several dozen examples extending across five decades, it is highly doubtful that there are any other intellectual figures on film with both the longevity and diversity of characterizations. In this chapter, I have attempted to use these discrete images of Van Helsing and Frankenstein to create constellations of these mad scientists across space and time. The results point to an archetype of the scientist in horror film that is far more nuanced than the stereotypical mad scientist.

Clive's Frankenstein was certainly obsessive and oblivious to the moral implications of the research to which he was unhealthily dedicated. Nevertheless, Clive's Frankenstein was also capable of reformation. He was able to step back into his family life and choose to leave his obsessions in the past, even if the draw to science was a monster always lurking in the background. Cushing's Frankenstein was so coldly rational and devoted to his intellectual pursuits that he no longer created monsters; he was one. His scientist was so singular-minded that he was able to overcome the grave itself. All the while, postwar American versions of Frankenstein were cultural artifacts that demonstrated far more ambivalent attitudes toward science.

The figure of Van Helsing—whose learning extended beyond natural science—was always a more complex (if not more convoluted) image of the intellectual. Sloan's Van Helsing was good-natured but eccentric. He was an elderly gentleman well versed in a variety of discourses. While Frankenstein fancied himself a god and toasted a new world of gods and monsters, Sloan's Van Helsing was a man of God. He did not, however, allow his devotion to either science or religion prevent him from considering folk wisdom. Cushing's Van Helsing could still be identified as a conglomeration of the same three archetypes: scientist, clergyman, and mystic. The demeanor of Cushing's Van Helsing was drastically different from Sloan's. The smiling joviality was replaced by cold extremism, the abstract planning with bloody violence.

Van Helsing, even in his most extreme versions, always served as a protector. Frankenstein, even in his mildest forms, forever posed a threat. Taken together, horror film's two most famous intellectuals provide a clear illustration of the antipathy toward the intellectual described in Hofstadter's *Anti-Intellectualism in American Life*. We rely on our scientists, hoping they turn out to be Van Helsings, eternally fearful that they may become Frankensteins.

Bibliography

Curti, Merle. "Intellectuals and Other People." *American Historical Review* 60 (1955): 259–282.

Foust, Ronald. "Rite of Passage: The Vampire Tale as Cosmogonic Myth." In *Aspects of Fantasy*, edited by William Coyle, 73–89. Westport, CT: Greenwood Press, 1986.

Fry, Carrol L., and John Robert Craig. "'Unfit for Earth, Undoomed for Heaven': The Genesis of Coppola's Byronic Dracula." *Literature/Film Quarterly* 30 (2002): 271–275.

Heffernan, James A. W. "Looking at the Monster: *Frankenstein* and Film." *Critical Inquiry* 24, no. 1 (Autumn 1997): 133–158.

Hofstadter, Richard. *Anti-Intellectualism and American Life*. New York: Knopf, 1963.

Howley, Craig, Aimee Howley, and Edwine D. Pendarvis. *Out of Our Minds: Anti-Intellectualism and Talent Development in American Schooling*. New York: Teachers College Press: 1995.

Jackson, Rosemary. "Narcissism and Beyond: A Psychoanalytic Reading of *Frankenstein* and Fantasies of the Double." In *Aspects of Fantasy*, edited by William Coyle, 43–53. Westport, CT: Greenwood Press, 1986.

Jacoby, Russell. *The Last Intellectuals: American Culture in the Age of Academe*. New York: Basic Books, 1987.

Jones, E. Michael. *Monsters from the Id: The Rise of Horror in Fiction and Film.* Dallas, TX: Spence, 2000.

Negra, Diane. "Covering the Feminine: Victor Frankenstein, Norman Bates, and Buffalo Bill." *Literature/Film Quarterly* 24, no. 2 (1996): 193–200.

Pirie, David. *A Heritage of Horror: The English Gothic Cinema, 1946–1972.* New York: Equinox Books, 1973.

Potts, John. "What I Owe to Hammer Horror." *Senses of Cinema*, no. 47 (2008). http://sensesofcinema.com/2008/feature-articles/hammer-horror/.

Rigby, Jonathan. *English Gothic: A Century of Horror Cinema.* London: Reynolds and Hearn, 2004.

Ryan, Alan, ed. *Vampires: Two Centuries of Great Vampire Stories.* Garden City, NY: Doubleday, 1987.

Schatz, Thomas. *The Genius of the System: Hollywood Filmmaking in the Studio Era.* New York: Henry Holt, 1988.

Schor, Esther. "Frankenstein and Film." In *The Cambridge Companion to Mary Shelley.* Cambridge: Cambridge University Press, 2003, 63–83.

Skal, David J. *Screams of Reason: Mad Science and Modern Culture.* New York: Norton, 1998.

Smith, Gary A. *Uneasy Dreams: The Golden Age of British Horror Films, 1956–1976.* Jefferson, NC: McFarland, 2000.

Terzian, Sevan, and Andrew Grunzke. "Scrambled Eggheads: Ambivalent Representations of Scientists in Six Hollywood Film Comedies from 1961 to 1965." *Public Understanding of Science* 16 (October 2007): 407–419.

Tudor, Andrew. *Monsters and Mad Scientists: A Cultural History of the Horror Movie.* Oxford, England: Basil Blackwell, 1989.

Wiebel, Frederick. *Edison's Frankenstein.* New York: BearManor Media, 2010.

Young, Elizabeth. *Black Frankenstein: The Making of an American Metaphor.* New York: New York University Press, 2008.

Filmography

Universal Films

Browning, Ted, dir. *Dracula*, 1931.
Whale, James, dir. *Frankenstein*, 1932.
———. *Bride of Frankenstein*, 1935.

Hillier, Lambert, dir. *Dracula's Daughter*, 1936.
Lee, Rowland V., dir. *Son of Frankenstein*, 1939.
Kenton, Erle, dir. *Ghost of Frankenstein*, 1942.
Siodmak, Robert, dir. *Son of Dracula*, 1943.
Kenton, Erle, dir. *House of Frankenstein*, 1944.
———. *House of Dracula*, 1945.
Neill, Roy William, dir. *Frankenstein Meets the Wolf Man*, 1946.
Barton, Charles, dir. *Abbott and Costello Meet Frankenstein*, 1948.

Hammer Films

Fisher, Terence, dir. *The Curse of Frankenstein*, 1957.
———. *The Horror of Dracula*, 1957.
———. *The Revenge of Frankenstein*, 1958.
———. *The Brides of Dracula*, 1960.
———. *Dracula: Prince of Darkness*, 1965.
———. *Frankenstein Created Woman*, 1966.
Francis, Freddie, dir. *Dracula Has Risen from the Grave*, 1968.
Fisher, Terence, dir. *Frankenstein Must Be Destroyed*, 1969.
Sasdy, Peter, dir. *Taste the Blood of Dracula*, 1969.
Baker, Roy Ward, dir. *Scars of Dracula*, 1970.
Sanster, Jimmy, dir. *The Horror of Frankenstein*, 1970.
Gibson, Alan, dir. *Dracula A.D. 1972*, 1972.
Fisher, Terence, dir. *Frankenstein and the Monster from Hell*, 1973.
Gibson, Alan, dir. *The Satanic Rites of Dracula*, 1973. (Also known as *Count Dracula and His Vampire Brides* and *Dracula Is Dead and Well and Living in London*.)

Others

Adamson, Al, dir. *Dracula vs. Frankenstein*. Independent International Pictures, 1971.
Beaudine, William, dir. *Jesse James Meets Frankenstein's Daughter*. Circle Productions, 1966.
Crain, William, dir. *Blacula*. American International, 1973.
Cunha, Richard E., dir. *Frankenstein's Daughter*. Layton Film Productions, 1958.
Curtis, Dan, dir. *Dracula*. Latglen Limited, 1974.
Floyd, Calvin, dir. *Terror of Frankenstein*. Independent International Films, 1977.

Gaffney, Robert, dir. *Frankenstein Meets the Space Monster*. Vernon Films, 1965.
Kelljan, Bob, dir. *Scream, Blacula, Scream*. American International, 1973.
Levey, William A., dir. *Blackenstein*. Frisco Productions, 1973
Morrissey, Paul, dir. *Blood for Dracula*, 1974.
———. *Flesh for Frankenstein*, 1973.
Smight, Jack, dir. *Frankenstein: The True Story*. Universal Television Pictures, 1973.
Strato, Herbert L., dir. *I Was a Teenage Frankenstein*. Anglo-Amalgamated Film Distribution, 1957.

Appendix

Frankensteins (By Name):[67]

Frankenstein	*Frankenstein* (1910)
Baron Victor Frankenstein	*Curse of Frankenstein* (1957)
	Revenge of Frankenstein (1958)
	Evil of Frankenstein (1964)
	Frankenstein Created Woman (1967)
	Frankenstein Must Be Destroyed (1969)
	The Horror of Frankenstein (1970)
	Frankenstein and the Monster from Hell (1974)
Baron Victor Von Frankenstein	*Frankenstein* (1970)
Baron Von Frankenstein	*Mad Monster Party* (1967)
Charles Frankenstein	*The Bride* (1985)
Dr. Frederick Frankenstein	*Young Frankenstein* (1974)
Henry Frankenstein	*Frankenstein* (1931)
	Bride of Frankenstein (1935)
Dr. Ludwig Frankenstein	*Ghost of Frankenstein* (1942)
Victor Frankenstein	*Frankenstein: The True Story* (1974)
	Frankenstein (1992)
	Mary Shelley's Frankenstein (1993)
Wolf von Frankenstein	*Son of Frankenstein* (1939)

CHAPTER 3

THE TRANSFORMATION OF
DR. JEKYLL: THE EVOLUTION OF
FILM AND TELEVISION PORTRAYALS
OF STEVENSON'S INTELLECTUAL IN
THE AGE OF ACADEME

There are at least 88 film and television adaptations—very loosely speaking—of Stevenson's novella *The Strange Case of Dr. Jekyll and Mr. Hyde*. Most of the scholarship has focused on a handful of these adaptations (especially the 1931 version). This chapter is, in part, an attempt to remedy that situation—by drawing from a larger pool. To keep it manageable, however, I have limited the pool to North American and British adaptations of the novella and have not included those texts that only borrow in part from Stevenson's work (like *Monster on the Campus*, *The Nutty Professor*, *Altered States*, or *The Incredible Hulk*).

A full treatment of the films in their entirety would also be a difficult endeavor. Instead, this chapter focuses on the character of Dr. Jekyll as an intellectual and a man of science. *The Strange Case of Dr. Jekyll and Mr. Hyde* was written at a time when scientific discourse was undergoing rapid changes; Stevenson was writing on the cusp of a time of "ever-increasing specialization, which sharply limits the extent to which non-specialists are able to take part in such debates."[1] Jekyll's experiment placed him outside of the respected scientific discourse and ethical scientific practices that were quickly becoming codified by a newly developing academy of science. As more intellectuals found themselves moving out of the public eye by retreating to colleges and universities in the twentieth century, the figure of Dr. Jekyll, an independent scholar with his own ethically questionable research agenda, became increasingly the object of suspicion or even, it seems, horror. With this in mind, this chapter outlines the ways in which the figure of Dr. Jekyll transformed over the first 70 years of television and film adaptations.

The Silent Jekylls

The first filmic appearance of "Dr. Jekyll and Mr. Hyde" came in 1912 and featured James Cruze as Jekyll. This film was a short, bare-bones production, essentially containing only the required elements to make it a retelling of the Jekyll tale. It did, however, introduce the film world to the idea of Dr. Jekyll as a romantic figure (which was not a focus of Stevenson's work). In the movie, Jekyll "becomes the accepted suitor" of a lovely young woman, becomes Hyde against his will, attacks his fiancée, kills her father, and runs from the law. Jekyll's fabricated romance with a young woman would be repeated in many of the later Jekyll films, including the 1920 version with John Barrymore in the title role. There is more of the tragic in the 1912 film than in others. In this film, Jekyll is a good man begging, struggling to keep the evil in himself at bay. As shall be discussed, in other Jekyll and Hyde films, the scientific obsession, exotic sense of morality, psychological experimentation, propensity for unethical human and animal subject research, and ego make Jekyll less likable.

In the 1920 version of the film, Jekyll still remains the tragic hero. The central theme of Stevenson's source material, the downfall of a good man through the stripping away of the veneer of civilization, remains strong in this film. The intertitles of the film describe Dr. Jekyll's character as an "idealist and philanthropist—by profession a doctor of medicine."

Jekyll does his clinical rounds. He is a decidedly good man: "The human repair shop, maintained by Dr. Jekyll at his own expense, for the treatment of the poor." In this film, Jekyll seems far less obsessed with even his own research than in later film versions. For instance, when he is late for dinner (and he is still late for dinner), he is late because of the amount of free clinical work that he does, not as a result of losing track of time in the lab. His colleagues comment on his devotion to his profession as a physician by saying things like, "In devoting yourself to others, aren't you neglecting the development of your own life?"

Hyde, however, seems far removed from the moral character of the good doctor. Dr. Jekyll renounces "the dark influence of Hyde," but the evils "burst forth." Jekyll remains remorseful for Hyde's actions, but Hyde "made [him] long for a knowledge of evil." It feels as though Barrymore's Jekyll could commit no evils acts, so he created Hyde to do the evil for him. The murder of his lady friend's father fits into this context quite well. The father was tempting Jekyll into evil, refusing to allow his marriage to his daughter because of his long, unexplained absences. Hyde is represented as the "creeping horror that was his other self" that came from the "black abyss." This visual metaphor is striking when the double-exposed film is used to create the effect that Hyde is a spider creeping over Jekyll while he sleeps. It is easy, when watching this film, to forget that Jekyll and Hyde are the same person, two different aspects of the same personality. While future films would depict Jekyll and Hyde as having an almost close or at least symbiotic relationship, in doing so they tend to undermine the duality established in Stevenson's source material. This film presents a distinct bifurcation of Jekyll and Hyde.

The Golden Age of Dr. Jekyll

Perhaps the *Dr. Jekyll* film that has received the most scholarly attention is Rouben Mamoulian's 1931 version (with Frederic March in the title role). The film opens with the sound of an organ playing. The camera presents a first-person perspective, as if the viewer is the one walking through the mansion. Stevenson's *The Strange Case of Dr. Jekyll and Mr. Hyde*, with its underlying theme of the body playing host to more than one psyche, invites the reader to consider the idea of another soul looking through one's eyes. Mamoulian's film opening allows the audience to see the world through Jekyll's eyes, and the viewer, by virtue of occupying Jekyll's body, becomes metonymically linked to Mr. Hyde. This idea is reinforced in the same opening shot by an unsettling special effect: the camera pans to a mirror in which the viewer sees the image of Jekyll.[2]

In this film, we have (with the possible exception of Jack Palance's turn as Jekyll in 1968) the closest thing to a depiction of Dr. Jekyll as a university professor. Eventually, the camera comes out of the first-person perspective. When Dr. Jekyll walks into the classroom and is set to deliver a lecture on violence, the camera returns to the third-person perspective. Jekyll's rather unusual lecture on violence focuses on "the soul of man," and he gives a scientific (or at least pseudoscientific) explanation of violent behavior that posits that violent tendencies are not rooted in the body of the person who commits the acts. Jekyll proposes to liberate the soul from evil by separating the two Freudian selves. The other members of the scientific community want nothing to do with this line of research, calling Jekyll's ideas "ridiculous" and claiming that he "talk[s] like a lunatic."

Still, Jekyll's station makes him an esteemed member of the community. Like Dr. Frankenstein in *The Curse of Frankenstein*, Dr. Jekyll is heavily involved in charity work. He cancels a meeting with the duchess in order to devote his time to charity cases at the free clinic. He also skips a meeting with a well-respected general in order to perform surgery. Time and time again, Jekyll in this film is portrayed as a worthy protector, someone uniquely dedicated to his profession and to helping people overcome their physical health limitations. People would make comments about the good doctor, like "he ought to come down to Earth" from his charity cases and think about his own needs. We know from other film doctors (like Dr. Frankenstein) that overattentiveness to one's scientific studies (even if they are under the auspices of helping one's fellow man) is a marker of something potentially dangerous lurking in the heart of the scientist.

Jekyll's downfall is made all the more tragic because he is a romantic and an idealist. He is young and intelligent and has a promising future (which distinguishes him from Stevenson's elderly gentleman). Perhaps as a result of youthful indiscretion, Jekyll seeks to aim the light of modern science onto questions of morality. After all, he claims, "It is unscientific not to admit the possibility of anything." Jekyll's colleagues see morality as an extension of living in a civilized society. They are merely uncomfortable with the idea of doing a scientific experiment involving the human soul. One would expect that this would stem from a desire to ground science in observable, natural (as opposed to supernatural) phenomena. Rather, however, the scientific community's reticence to accept the work of Dr. Jekyll apparently extends from a belief that his work is heretical—not heresy relating to the tenets of science, but heresy with respect to religion. Much of these beliefs seem to come from Victorian sexual attitudes, though, and distaste for the ideas of Freud and his preoccupation with sex. They prefer to believe that civilization will keep sexual feelings repressed than to advocate for a drug that will remove those desires from the human soul.

US involvement in World War II also seems to have had an effect on the Jekyll and Hyde tale. The 1941 version featuring Spencer Tracy as Jekyll is more full of masculine bravado (as compared with the 1931 version, anyway), and the depiction of Hyde almost seems more akin to one of Tracy's gangster characters than a cinematic monster, spouting off sentiments to naysayers questioning his research like, "Sometimes we have to gamble—or haven't you the courage?" This Jekyll is also a little older. He is no adolescent, and he is far surer of himself than previous incarnations. Even the difference in appearance between Dr. Jekyll and Mr. Hyde is less pronounced in this film than in its predecessors.

Identified as a psychologist (as opposed to the usual chemist), Jekyll's project is about more than merely helping individual patients with their psychological issues. Instead, the goal is to resolve the internal battles inside each person for the overall improvement of society. Nazi eugenics programs seem to have influenced the debate over human experimentation as depicted in the film. Jekyll is aware of the questionable ethics of his investigations, openly making rather ethically harrowing declarations like "When I get the proof, ethics or no ethics . . .," but he believes the result of his research justifies whatever means he deems necessary. In this way, the experience of Dr. Jekyll in this film undermines the film's effectiveness. In previous film incarnations, it is Jekyll's youthful enthusiasm (and rebellion against the scientific academy) that lead to his subversive research. In this film, the scientific community does not object to Jekyll's personal qualities. The result is to emphasize the identity of Jekyll as a scientist. In terms of actual time on film, the 1941 version spends a greater proportion of screentime showing Jekyll's work in the lab but proportionally less showing other scientists and members of the medical community talking about the theory behind his work.

This Jekyll's experiment is also more clearly blasphemous than that of his predecessors. Tracy's Jekyll attempts to solve the Original Sin problem by circumventing God. The filmmakers never made it fully clear in the 1931 version why Jekyll's experiment is unholy. The scientific community clearly labeled the research as heretical, but the theological nature of the heresy was never fully explored in the earlier film. In the 1941 film, a priest labels the doctor's research unholy. Jekyll explicitly makes the argument that the problems of civilized society are a direct product of the battle between good and evil waged inside the soul of the individual. This battle, it seems, may justify some unethical scientific practices, at least in the mind of Dr. Jekyll.

The two major American film versions of *Dr. Jekyll and Mr. Hyde* were different in tone and focus. Between 1931 and 1941, Dr. Jekyll had gone from being a chemist to a psychologist. He went from being young, reckless, and idealistic to being masculine, mature, and self-assured. Moreover, the psychological distance between Jekyll and Hyde had also decreased, with the physical markers of Jekyll's transformation being less great in the latter film.

The British Jekyll Revival

As Great Britain's Hammer film studios began successfully reappropriating the *Dracula* and *Frankenstein* narratives from American film studios in the late 1950s, it only made sense that Great Britain's third great Gothic horror narrative would receive the same treatment. British film studios produced three Jekyll and Hyde films during the great British horror film revival (two by Hammer Films and one by Amicus). The first of these, *The Two Faces of Dr. Jekyll*, anticipates the drug and sexual revolutions of the 1960s. The filmmakers give a strange time and place marker for this film's setting. Set in London in 1874 (oddly before the publication of Stevenson's original story), the story begins *in medias res*. The doctor is already married at the start of the film. It is also clear that he has been injecting himself with his experimental serum for some time. He gets a look of ecstasy on his face as he "shoots up." Part of the effect of beginning the story in the middle is to close the distance between Jekyll and Hyde (even further than the 1941 version already had). At times in this film, Hyde appears more "civilized" than Dr. Jekyll, even, at one point in the film, dancing with Jekyll's wife. In this film, Mr. Hyde lacks even a beard—one of the "ape-like" markers of Hyde that had been present in every film version since the publication of the original volume.

In this film, even Dr. Jekyll is made to appear less moral. In addition to smoking opium, Jekyll injects his serum intravenously and becomes embroiled in several sexual (and quasi-sexual) relationships. Dr. Jekyll in 1941 may have donated his valuable time to charity hospitals, but, at one point in *The Two Faces of Dr. Jekyll*, Jekyll (not Hyde) shoves a mute girl to the ground. Even the title, *The Two Faces of Dr. Jekyll*, makes no mention of Hyde. Instead, the title asks the audience to focus on the idea that Jekyll and Hyde are not two separate people. Rather, Hyde is merely a part of Jekyll's personality—albeit one that remains hidden, if Jekyll chooses to maintain his sobriety. This theme is further maintained by Mrs. Jekyll's own marital infidelities in the film. While Hyde eventually kills Jekyll's wife's lover by locking him in a room with a snake, the entire scenario imbues the Victorian setting with a "free love" sensibility. In the end, the overall effect of depicting the traditionally "moral" characters as deeply flawed, as simultaneously (rather than separately) depicting the film's characters as both Jekyll and Hyde, is to change the theme of the story. Rather than a tale of a civilized man whose scientific obsession leads to tragic downfall, *The Two Faces of Dr. Jekyll* is the story of a flawed man whose unethical experiments into the human psyche represent a desperate attempt to keep his uncivilized traits at bay.

It follows then that Jekyll would attempt to justify his experiment in this film as an attempt to create "man as he could be." He wishes to create an individual free of all of society's restrictions, a man (in highly Nietzschean terms) "beyond good and evil." The change in theme of the narrative also makes the animosity between Jekyll and Hyde feel more personal. In this film, Hyde kills people close to Jekyll as a sort of blackmail so that Jekyll will continue to frequently take his serum. Ultimately, Jekyll refuses to be blackmailed any longer and intentionally sacrifices himself by reverting to Hyde—knowing that this is the only way Hyde will go to the gallows for his murders. This film ushers in a new phase in filmic representations of *The Strange Case of Dr. Jekyll and Mr. Hyde* by stripping away elements of the faux-Victorian setting and opening up new film versions to create new manifestations not only of Hyde but also of Jekyll himself.

In *Dr. Jekyll and Sister Hyde* ([1971] with Ralph Bates as the good doctor), Jekyll is neither a chemist nor a psychologist; rather, he is a virologist searching for an antivirus, a universal panacea. He seeks to cheat death so that he can continue his own scientific research to benefit mankind. In order to create this serum, Jekyll has turned his scholarly attention to the science of longevity, attempting to create an "elixir of life." The key ingredient involved in the creation of this elixir is female "life hormones." Chemistry as an academic discipline was changing in the late nineteenth century. The discoveries were coming very rapidly, including Mendeleev's development of the periodic table of elements (1869) and the Curies' discovery of radium (1898). There was also a strong move toward "academic formalization." Jekyll in all of his incarnations (and particularly in *Dr. Jekyll and Sister Hyde*) is a sort of alchemist. His research lies in the intersection between chemistry and religion. In *Sister Hyde*, Jekyll becomes Hyde as a result of his experiments attempting to unnaturally extend his own life—not at all unlike the alchemical search for the philosopher's stone. The overall effect of associating Jekyll's work with alchemy is to make it feel out of step with legitimate, academic late nineteenth-century chemical research. Additionally, by portraying Jekyll as a sort of alchemist, Jekyll's work is endowed with a sense of magic—depicting it not only as taking place outside of respectable scientific endeavor but also as being religiously blasphemous.

Normally, the Jekyll and Hyde films portray Jekyll as either implicitly good or the beneficiary of the positive effects of civilization. In general, Jekyll brings about his own downfall by bending scientific ethics. This brings about a good/evil dichotomy in which Dr. Jekyll is good (but flawed) and Mr. Hyde is evil. This dichotomy is far less true for *Dr. Jekyll and Sister Hyde*. For one thing, most Jekyll films start before Jekyll has the idea for the experiment. Like the previous Hammer interpretation of Jekyll's story, this one, too, begins *in medias res*. When the film opens, Jekyll is already fully engaged in his research. If anything, this Jekyll is even more obsessive than his filmic predecessors. He sleeps for three whole days after working for ten days straight. Bates's Jekyll seems more aware of his own immoral practices, at first buying the corpses of young women on the black market (even though the film strongly implies that he is aware that the sellers are likely murdering the women for him to purchase) and eventually becoming a serial killer himself (to procure organs for his research). This represents the first time in filmic interpretations of Stevenson's work that Jekyll himself (not in the form of Hyde) commits murder.

As one could have easily guessed from the title, this film has strong homosexual and transgender undertones, and the end result of Jekyll's experiment is the development of a serum that causes Jekyll to become a female himself—whom he passes off to his neighbors as his sister. When Jekyll becomes a woman, his "sister" Hyde uses sex as a weapon, dressing in red and seducing her victims before murdering them. From here, the film sinks into a battle between the sexes within one person: the male and female personality, the yin and the yang, the anima and the animus. In this way the film becomes a metaphor for a man unable to come to terms with his own sexual desires. Jekyll's attraction to a female becomes a source of tension. His *sexual* feelings cause an identity crisis, which gives rise to a murderous woman. In this way, the film almost seems to be channeling Alfred Hitchcock's *Psycho*—another film in which a man who is unable to come to terms with his sexual desire for a woman becomes a cross-dressing murderer. Jekyll plans to perform "one final experiment" but draws an important conclusion: "I write this lesson as a scientist and as a solitary lesson to those who would tamper with nature." When he dies, he is androgynous, neither man nor woman, but simultaneously both. This is how the tension is resolved at the end of the film; he can no longer be either man or woman, so he must remain an androgyne. Some scholars have pointed out that in all Jekyll and Hyde narratives, Jekyll is, in a certain sense, pregnant with Hyde. Hyde exists within the body of Jekyll, and Jekyll is never sure where he will be when Hyde emerges.[3] *Dr. Jekyll and Sister Hyde* takes an underlying gender tension in the Jekyll story and makes it explicit. Jekyll had become a more masculine figure in the 1940s; by the 1970s the character had been reinvented. During the sexual revolution and the fight for women's rights, while not in perhaps the most progressive of ways, Dr. Jekyll's character was recast in a way that allowed the traditional narrative to explore the new sexual politics of the era.

Due to the relatively close temporal proximity of Stevenson's story (1886) and the Whitechapel murders (1888), film versions of Dr. Jekyll tend to conflate the fictional murders committed by Hyde and those real-world murders committed by Jack the Ripper. *Dr. Jekyll and Sister Hyde* is no exception. In one of the opening sequences of the film, the murder of a prostitute is juxtaposed with the butchering of a rabbit; she is another victim of the "Whitechapel Murderer." Jack the Ripper was a killer presumably able to masquerade in genteel society as a moral gentleman. Jack the Ripper, like Dr. Jekyll, was a person capable of existing as a monster, on the one hand, and yet blending into a life of Victorian self-restraint, on the other. Jekyll and Jack the Ripper both represent "a sense of the precariousness of a culture caught between outward respectability and secret violence."[4] In the case of Dr. Jekyll, though, that sense of outward respectability is undermined by the site of his research, which takes place outside of the supervision of the scientific academy and in direct opposition to their tempered objections to Jekyll's line of inquiry.

Christopher Lee's *I, Monster* (1973), is not, strictly speaking, a true Jekyll and Hyde film, at least in name. In this movie, we have Dr. Charles Marlowe and Mr. Edward Blake. Nevertheless, the film declares that it is "based on a story by Robert Louis Stevenson." The film, oddly, invites the viewer to see it as a retelling of the Jekyll and Hyde tale but changes the names of the title character. The new names do, however, seem pregnant with meaning. Marlowe calls to mind the name Christopher Marlowe (of *Dr. Faustus* fame). This already marks the main character as someone who is obsessive to the point of (at least metaphorically) selling his soul to Satan. The name Blake calls to mind the Romantic writer William Blake, and it links this tale with the Gothic works of the Romantics. Despite being inspired by a work of Stevenson's, this film is, in many ways, a conflation of *The Strange Case of Dr. Jekyll and Mr. Hyde* and Oscar Wilde's *The Picture of Dorian Gray*. As Marlowe's alter-ego's criminal acts worsen, Marlowe himself becomes uglier and uglier, until eventually he is murdered by a friend who cannot recognize him. Previous film incarnations have treated Dr. Jekyll as a flexible enough character that they could change his area of scientific expertise to suit the concerns of the era in which the film was made. Some had even changed the gender of the doctor. Still, aside from those issues, the Dr. Jekyll narratives clung fairly close to their source material. This was especially true in comparison to either the *Frankenstein* or *Dracula* narratives, for which filmmakers were always willing to deviate from the author's original storyline or create sequels the author had never penned. Until the late Hammer horror period, Dr. Jekyll stories remained at least relatively true interpretations of Stevenson's work.

While *Dr. Jekyll and Sister Hyde* portrays Dr. Jekyll as a virologist, *I, Monster* portrays its Jekyll figure as a clinical psychologist. Despite the fact that Stevenson's novella predated the advent of Freudian psychology, many of the film versions reinvent Dr. Jekyll as a Freudian psychologist. Marlowe's colleagues are not particularly receptive to the ideas of Freudian psychology, and they like those of Marlowe even less: "It's bad enough you practice in these ideas of Dr. Freud in Vienna, but your own ideas are even more dangerous." Dr. Marlowe is aware of the ideas "discovered by Dr. Freud" and justifies his own experiment because those ideas "haven't been fully worked out." The drug, Marlowe argues, breaks down the barrier between the conscious and subconscious mind, grounding it fairly solidly in a Freudian conception of human psychology.

How Dr. Marlowe chooses to work out these ideas lacks the ethical standards of his colleagues. Dr. Marlowe conducts a single-blind study. He creates a chemical in his lab and injects it into his patients using a hypodermic syringe without their full understanding of the nature of his experimental medicine. In the year following the 1972 revelation of the Tuskegee syphilis experiments—in which scientists conducted research to determine the long-term effects of untreated syphilis on African-Americans who were unknowingly infected with sexually transmitted diseases and who, to maintain the validity of the study, were not informed of their illness or available treatments—Marlowe's unethical research design has a far different meaning in 1973 than it did in previous incarnations of the Jekyll story. In *I, Monster*, the Dr. Jekyll narrative proves malleable to the concerns about the ethics of experimental medicine in a new era.

The Animated Jekylls

Children's animation, it seems, has long held a fascination with the Jekyll and Hyde tale. Warner Bros. made no fewer than three Jekyll and Hyde cartoons in the 1950s. The first of these, "Dr. Jerkyl's Hyde," featured Sylvester the Cat hiding in Dr. Jerkyl's lab to get away from two cockney dogs looking for a fight, where he chances upon Jerkyl's serum and turns the tables on his bullies; it does not, however, feature an actual Dr. Jerkyl. The second, "Hyde and Hare," is a Bugs Bunny cartoon in which Bugs decides to go live with the generous Dr. Jekyll (or "Doc," as Bugs prefers to call him). Eventually, Bugs Bunny discovers that the mousy Jekyll is not what he appears to be as he is chased around the house by a grotesque monster. The final Warner cartoon, "Hyde and Go Tweet," features a very similar milquetoast Jekyll who maintains a lab in a downtown office to which Tweety escapes from an unsuspecting Sylvester. MGM's "Tom and Jerry" was actually the first of the animated shorts to feature the Jekyll/Hyde motif. In their 1947 cartoon, "Dr. Jekyll and Mr. Mouse," Tom stands in for the infamous doctor and tries to create a poison to kill Jerry using household chemicals. The formula fails to kill Jerry and instead unleashes his inner strength.

In the stop-motion animated children's film *Mad Monster Party*, Dr. Frankenstein has a plan to create a matter-destroying serum. In order to do so, he draws a large number of film monsters to a secret island to participate in his plot. Dr. Jekyll makes an appearance in this film. Here, though, he plays second fiddle to Dr. Frankenstein, getting very little screen time. The character is used mostly for laughs, like getting seasick on the boat ride over to the island and generously drinking some of his special "elixir." Dr. Jekyll becomes Mr. Hyde in this film to avoid peer pressure for the most part. Tired of being the only normal man on the island, Dr. Jekyll drinks his elixir so he can become Mr. Hyde and his colleagues will no longer be suspicious of the only non-monster in the congress of film monsters.

Of the three figures discussed in this part of the book, Drs. Jekyll, Frankenstein, and Van Helsing, only Dr. Jekyll seems to be fodder for cartoon humor. This fact appears to stem, in large part, from Dr. Jekyll's frequent characterization as a mousy intellectual and the premise of his elixir as being able to instantaneously change both his personality and his physical appearance. Several of the filmic adaptations of Jekyll portray a doctor who intentionally drinks his potion to give him the moral freedom to do things he would not otherwise do. In animated shorts, Dr. Jekyll's potion becomes a humorous way of creating situational irony; small figures (like Tweety Bird) are able to rapidly turn the tables on their would-be oppressors. The overall effect of this use of the Jekyll narrative, though, is to make the figure of Dr. Jekyll seem harmless without his elixir. Live-action film versions of Stevenson's tale are less uniform in adopting this attitude toward Jekyll. At times, like Dr. Frankenstein, Jekyll's preoccupation with his research and his inability to consider the ethical consequences of his scientific inquiry are the source of his evil. Frankenstein's own personality flaws create his monster, and sometimes it is Jekyll's flaws that create Hyde. The cartoon versions of the story do not adopt this attitude. For them, Jekyll (or Sylvester, Tweety, or Jerry) is the victim *until* he drinks his potion.

North American Television Adaptations

Michael Rennie played Jekyll in a Gore Vidal–penned 1955 television adaptation of Stevenson's story. In certain respects, it was one of the more faithful adaptations, but in other ways it stands in stark contrast to the film and television versions that predated it and those that would follow. When the film opens, Jekyll has been locked in his laboratory for more than two weeks, having his meals brought to him and left outside his door. This is the first of the filmic representations of Jekyll to begin *in medias res*. Jekyll is shot dead within the first five minutes of the film. The rest of the film is told in flashback, while Jekyll's friend Utterson reads the doctor's found journal.

Despite much of the story's resolution coming so early in this film, the nature of Jekyll's experiment is only gradually revealed. Utterson slowly discovers what was going on. Jekyll was proposing to find the human soul. He delighted in the horror and destruction, focusing on the dualities of nature: good and evil, monster and angel. This film is not as Freudian in its emphasis as some of the films both before and after. Instead, it seems to borrow from puritanical theology. Jekyll's descriptions of his experiments lead his fellow scientists to complain to him, "I came for tea, not a Black Mass." His colleagues protest his suggestions, saying things like, "Suppose you uncage the monster." His response to this concern is that "it's a risk one would have to take in the interest of science." In the end, the 1955 version of Jekyll and Hyde featured a view of science and religion as being heavily entwined and drastically downplayed the psychological elements of the story (that had increasingly become the emphasis of film interpretations). "By day I was the good, kind doctor. By night, I was a strange, violent creature," Jekyll reminisces. He was "the wickedest man in London."

The ill-fated romance pioneered by the 1912 version is also absent from the film, but this Jekyll also has far more agency than any other Jekyll. This trait undermined what had become the traditional view of Jekyll as victim of his own personality flaws. He can change into Hyde "at will." Jekyll enjoys being Hyde. He gets a thrill from the sense of danger. The flip side of this coin is that Hyde is also Jekyll's ally. Hyde works to promote Jekyll's name as a scientist. Jekyll is hardly even ashamed of Hyde, saying strange things like, "You, who have always derided my theories, behold!" Jekyll is portrayed not as a victim, but as an evil man. He is accused of "witchcraft" and of having "fallen into the pit." He defends his "research into the criminal mind," but few of his colleagues buy the argument, especially when he brings up such metaphysical motivations as wanting to "find the soul, as an experiment." The appearance of Hyde is implied to be some sort of side effect to the drug, an accident and an impurity. Jekyll's sin in this film is not against medical ethics, it is a sin against God.

In one of the odder casting decisions among Jekylls, Jack Palance played the role in the Canadian television version of 1968. Like Mamoulian's 1931 version, we are presented with a Dr. Jekyll who is a member of a scientific community. The film opens with Jekyll, an aged gentleman with salt-and-pepper hair, lecturing to a meeting of doctors (clearly demarked as members of the scientific academy). His status as insider is quickly undermined, though, as the other doctors are clearly unreceptive to his lecture on how the psyche of man is broken into two parts: one animal and one higher being. Again, this television version seems to try to cleave more closely to Stevenson's story.

The selection of an older gentleman and the elimination of the love interest do much to hold the narrative more closely to the source material. One of the ways in which the story deviates, though, is that Hyde is finally dispatched in the lecture hall in which the film opened—perhaps the most extreme metaphor for the scientific community's rejection of Jekyll's ideas and methods.

Palance's Jekyll is engaged in the "private development of a new drug." As an unaffiliated researcher, he would not have to seek approval from an institutional review board (IRB) to conduct his research (and could, in fact, use himself as a research participant). Over the course of the twentieth century, this scenario became decreasingly likely. For one thing, the proliferation of IRBs in the 1960s and 1970s made unsupervised and unethical research significantly less common. By the 1960s, scientific researchers were working in a climate in which ethics were becoming an increasingly important consideration. The ethics of research, indeed research itself (when such a large percentage of it was conducted with federal funding), was almost entirely institutionalized. When Stevenson wrote *The Strange Case of Dr. Jekyll and Mr. Hyde*, the movement toward a scientific academy was in its infancy. Whereas Dr. Frankenstein and Dr. Van Helsing, in their many film portrayals, were placed into all sorts of situations completely unlike the printed source material in which they were created, Dr. Jekyll's tale was almost always told in ways that deviated only slightly from Stevenson's book. Part of the reason was to maintain the ability of the narrative to describe the state of the scientific community over the twentieth century. We see a century in which professional organizations are rising in influence, public intellectuals are in decline and are voluntarily confining themselves in institutions of higher learning, more of the science is being funded with public (rather than private) money, and the ethics of scientific research are becoming codified. It is in precisely this climate that Stevenson's story would resonate most. In fact, as the century progressed, the terror of the research scientist working on unethical experiments in his own private lab becomes more harrowing.

The Jekyll of the 1968 version, again, is not squeaky-clean and is not exactly the victim of his own obsession or ego; he is a criminal. Jekyll premeditatedly and intentionally turns himself into Hyde so that Hyde can commit murder for him. Eventually, Jekyll does have some remorse. He falls on his knees and prays when the deed is done—and he destroys his lab equipment. "I'm finished with scientific exploration," he says. "I'm going back to help the sick." Here, in order for his sins to be forgiven, Jekyll throws himself headfirst into his work with the academy (including the teaching of anatomy, no less). When trying to make up for his life of heresy and crime, Jekyll falls back on teaching. He is a very good teacher. Nine of his student papers are commended for their excellence by the academy. He also works around the clock doing volunteer medical work. Jekyll is the smallest threat and of the greatest benefit when he accepts his role within the scientific academy and applies his theoretical mind to practical (rather than experimental) work.

Deviations

The blaxploitation film *Dr. Black, Mr. Hyde* (1975) represents a deep contrast to the rest of the films discussed here. The nature of blaxploitation films makes this Dr. "Jekyll" an odd figure. With the end goal of raising the status of African Americans in mind, this doctor is a respected member of the medical community. He won a major medical award in 1971, and he does research on cellular regeneration at a major medical hospital. This is the first (and potentially only) film in which Jekyll is a researcher at a scientific institution and does his research under the ethics rules of a governing body.

This "Jekyll" is a better man than most of them. He is not self-aggrandizing. Morally, he is above reproach. He donates his time at a free clinic in the inner city. He uses his position as a respected physician to try to improve the African American community. Even his "Hyde" is not exactly an id-monster. He is not the expression of Dr. Black's desires, but a dark implementation of retribution triggered by the doctor's moral sense.

Dr. Black's research has been inspired by the death of his mother from cirrhosis: "My mother died, remember that. People standing around, doing nothing." Because of this, Black errs on the side of doing something. He begins to experiment on his terminal patient with the drug. The results are not good. His patient gets up and strangles the nurse, her skin pigment noticeably changed. When the results of this experiment point to failure, he tries it on himself, looking on with disgust as his skin turns powdery white after the injection. Henry Pryde (Black's alter-ego) is a raving monster, not unlike Blacula, who uses violence to clean up the streets. Pryde exacts revenge for the death of Black's mother. He does so in a way that seems to have societal benefit. The blaxploitation Jekyll and Hyde tale (despite the lagging production qualities) is, in many ways, more complex in its moral and ethical attitudes than the more direct translations of Stevenson's novella.

At a certain point in the film, Dr. Black thinks to use a prostitute Mr. Pryde has befriended as a participant in his experiment. She is unwilling to become involved in the research, not quite the answer that Black/Pryde was hoping for. "What if I insist?" he asks. The use of involuntary test subjects means something very different within the African American community than the culture at large. This is especially true of sex workers. The entire scenario uncomfortably channeled the Tuskegee syphilis experiments. If the function of the Jekyll and Hyde narrative became more powerful over the course of the century, this was eminently so for African Americans. The horrors of the Tuskegee experiments were a major impetus for the development of modern research ethics. An African American doctor willing to violate those ethical rules created a highly charged situation in the film.

The film ends with Mr. Pryde climbing a construction site and being shot down by a helicopter. Here, the film makes an obvious visual allusion to King Kong. This is interesting for a variety of reasons. One, Stevenson's Jekyll and Hyde tale has always had a heavy undercurrent of Darwinist thought (with Hyde frequently being described as "ape-like"). Visually, Hyde—with his ape-like features, body hair, and the like—is frequently depicted on film as a return to a previous evolutionary state. The use of evolutionary arguments to defend the institution of slavery was another unfortunate by-product of the rise of early Darwinist thought in the second half of the nineteenth century. Elizabeth Young's wonderful book, *Black Frankenstein: The Making of an American Metaphor*, delineates the ways that the Frankenstein narrative was embraced by the African American community to turn the tables on this misguided Darwinist argument. Little research has been done in the African American reception of the story of Dr. Jekyll, but in certain ways Mr. Pryde is more like Frankenstein's monster than a traditional Mr. Hyde. Pryde rips doors off hinges in angry rampages. In order to put an end to one of those episodes, the police send dogs after him—in a scene with distinct echoes of the use of dogs to track runaway slaves. The finale of *Dr. Black, Mr. Hyde* turns Jekyll into a composite of Hyde, Frankenstein's monster, and King Kong. Visually equating the black man with King Kong is especially powerful. *King Kong* is a tale of slavery and rebellion—the African captured and brought across the ocean against his will, only to break out of his bonds. In this film, Dr. Black is the victim of the monster of his own creation. *Dr. Black, Mr. Hyde* uses *The Strange Case of Dr. Jekyll and Mr. Hyde* as a lens through which to examine racial politics, including the history of medical research involving African American participants.

As the 1970s waned and nearly all of the public intellectuals had been successfully institutionalized (I am not entirely sure if I intended this pun), the cultural forces that kept the Jekyll narrative relatively close to its source text dissipated too. *Dr. Hekyl and Mr. Hype* (1980) featured an ugly podiatrist who took a serum that made him attractive—and a jerk. Unlike Drs. Frankenstein and Van Helsing, who had long been consigned to all sorts of outlandish scenarios, like *Dracula vs. Frankenstein* and *Frankenstein Meets the Space Monster*, the story of Dr. Jekyll was told and retold for 70 years with only minor variations, largely, I argue here, because suspicious cultural attitudes toward the scientific community and the public intellectual lingered as the site of scientific research became increasingly institutionalized. Even *Abbott and Costello Meet Dr. Jekyll and Mr. Hyde* (1953), for all its slapstick silliness, maintains a closeness in characterization, narrative structure, and theme to its source material—especially if considered against a comparison of *Abbott and Costello Meet Frankenstein* to Shelley's novel.

Dr. Jekyll, the Outsider and the Monster Within

One of the central features of the Jekyll and Hyde narrative is the idea that Hyde serves as a metaphor for the failed respectability of Jekyll. This consideration was far more important than even Dr. Jekyll's occupation. Over the course of the century, Dr. Jekyll was portrayed on film as a chemist, a psychologist, an alchemist, a virologist, an anatomist (who taught college-level courses on the subject), and even a hepatologist. While Jekyll was always a scientist, his area of specialty was rather inconsequential to the larger point the Jekyll films were trying to make about the role of the scientist in society. Jekyll's workroom was indifferently a chemical laboratory or a dissecting room, and "in [Victorian] culture . . . literary as well as scientific writers were able to make serious contributions to debates,"[5] an ability that was hampered precipitously as we moved further into the twentieth century. Twentieth-century filmic versions of the Jekyll narrative were an attempt of popular culture to add to the debate over the role of the scientist in society in an era that was increasingly pushing nonscientists out of that discourse. As a corollary, no scientific explanation is *ever* given (in any of these numerous films) as to how Jekyll's formula works. There are the trappings of science, but no real science. Even theoretical science cannot provide a forced explanation for the efficacy of Jekyll's potion. Social science makes a sort of appearance (at least in the form of psychology) and, of course, religion often plays a central role. As scientific inquiry became further removed from the casual understandings of nonscientists, Dr. Jekyll became a figure that allowed the general population to critique the role of the scientist in a culture that had relegated the discourse of science to the university community. That Dr. Jekyll himself embodied the last of the scientists refusing to accept his new role in the academy made him a powerful example of why the college laboratory was the proper space for scientific research, regardless of the area of specialization.

Bibliography

Davis, Michael. "Incongruous Compounds: Re-Reading Jekyll and Hyde and Late-Victorian Psychology." *Journal of Victorian Culture* 11, no. 2 (Autumn 2006): 207–225.
Halberstam, Judith. *Skin Shows: Gothic Horror and the Technology of Monsters*. Durham, NC: Duke University Press, 1995.
King, Charles. "Dr. Jekyll and Mr. Hyde: A Filmography." *Journal of Popular Film and Television* 25, no. 1 (1997): 9–20.

Filmography

Baker, Roy Ward, dir. *Dr. Jekyll and Sister Hyde*. Hammer Films, 1971.
Barbera, Joseph, and William Hanna, dirs. "Dr. Jekyll and Mr. Mouse." MGM, 1947.
Bass, Jules, dir. *Mad Monster Party*. Videocraft International, 1962.
Cain, William, dir. *Dr. Black, Mr. Hyde*. Dimension Pictures, 1975.
Curtis, Dan, dir. *The Strange Case of Dr. Jekyll and Mr. Hyde*. Canadian Broadcasting Corporation, 1968.
Fisher, Terence, dir. *The Two Faces of Dr. Jekyll*. Hammer Films, 1960.
Fleming, Victor, dir. *Dr. Jekyll and Mr. Hyde*. MGM, 1941.
Freleng, Isadore Fritz, dir. "Dr. Jerkyl's Hyde." Warner Bros., 1954.
———. "Hyde and Go Tweet." Warner Bros., 1959.
Griffith, Charles B., dir. *Dr. Heckyl and Mr. Hype*. MGM, 1980.
Henderson, Lucius, dir. *Dr. Jekyll and Mr. Hyde*. Thanhouser Company. 1912.
Lamont, Charles, dir. *Abbott and Costello Meet Dr. Jekyll and Mr. Hyde*. Universal Pictures, 1953.
Mamoulian, Rouben, dir. *Dr. Jekyll and Mr. Hyde*. Paramount Pictures, 1931.
Reisner, Allen, dir. "Dr. Jekyll and Mr. Hyde." *Climax!*, Season 1, Episode 34. Instor/Parasol Television, 1955.
Robertson, John S., dir. *Dr. Jekyll and Mr. Hyde*. Paramount Pictures, 1920.
Weeks, Stephen, dir. *I, Monster*. Amicus Films, 1973.

Chapter 4

Student Bodies: The School as Locus of Trauma in American Horror Films of the 1970s and 1980s

Unable to stay awake during the discussion of fantasy and reality in Shakespeare's *Hamlet* and *Julius Caesar*, *A Nightmare on Elm Street*'s (1984) heroine, Nancy, falls asleep in her English class. Her recently deceased friend Tina appears to her in a blood-smeared body bag. In an instant, the body bag disappears, and Nancy follows a trail of blood down the school hall. Eventually, she catches up to the body bag to find it being dragged by an invisible entity. As the pace of her chase begins to quicken, Nancy approaches a hall monitor, dressed in the same ratty red and green striped sweater worn by a man who has haunted many of her recent dreams. She ominously warns Nancy, "No running in the halls." Nancy follows the blood trail into the school boiler room where a severely burned man wearing a glove with razor blades attached to the fingertips accosts her. Fearing for her life, Nancy exits her dream by pressing her arm against a boiling hot pipe. She wakes up screaming in her English class with a blistered wound on her arm.

Whether it was falling asleep in class, solving word problems,[1] finding a date for the prom,[2] or teenage pregnancy,[3] there were few school-related anxieties that were not mined by American horror films of the 1970s and 1980s for their fear-inducing potential. High school was a verdant location for developing terror in horror film audiences; between 1968 and 1992, dozens of films in the horror genre either contained major scenes taking place in school or chose high schools as their primary (or sometimes sole) setting. Throughout the era, the audience for these films became increasingly teenaged. In the years following 1968, scary movies represented the first major, coordinated affront to the prevailing image of the innocence of childhood. Over the course of the period, filmmakers also became increasingly likely to set their films in familiar (rather than exotic) locations. The confluence of these three trends made the high school a favorite site for staging shocking physical, mental, and emotional trauma.

Sowing Bad Seeds: Changing Conceptions of Childhood in American Horror

Alfred Hitchcock's *Psycho* (1960) presaged a dramatic shift in the way that horror film would deal with the image of the American family. Norman Bates's preserving his mother's corpse through taxidermy as a means of assuaging his guilt for committing matricide represented a psychotic perversion of the family unit. In the ensuing decades, there was a distinct trend in horror film to depict the "destruction of the family."[4] In George Romero's *The Crazies* (1973), the devastation of the family unit—in this case due to madness caused by chemical warfare—served as a microcosm and metaphor for the confusion and instability in society resulting from the incident. The horror genre would become peppered with families who committed murder (*The Hills Have Eyes* [1977]) and engaged in cannibalism together (*The Texas Chainsaw Massacre* [1974]).

This trend corresponded closely to a change in the image of the child in American horror film over the same period. William Golding's *Lord of the Flies* (1954) epitomized a mid-twentieth century shift toward a less sentimental view of the child. In horror, a genre in which the child had been the perennial victim, audiences witnessed the advent of the child monster with the release of *The Bad Seed* in 1956.[5] While there are a few minor examples of child monsters in the intervening period,[6] the transformation of child as victim to child as monster was solidified by Romero's *Night of the Living Dead* (1968).[7] Romero's film depicts a deathly ill young girl named Karen whose family sought shelter from attacking zombies in the basement of a lone farmhouse. Borrowing from the traditional attitude of horror depicting children as victims, much of the conflict in the film derives from the family's attempts to get their daughter to the safety of a hospital or shelter. Unable to save her, the daughter joins the ranks of the walking undead, repeatedly stabs her mother with a trowel, and devours the flesh of her father. Made all the more horrifying because of the well-established tradition in horror of the innocent child victim, *Night of the Living Dead* represented a fundamental shift in the way children would be depicted in American horror film.

The winter of 1968 was an iconoclastic season. *Night of the Living Dead* was released within months of Roman Polanski's *Rosemary's Baby*. In conjunction with Romero's zombification of little Karen, Polanski's tale of a young woman giving birth to the child of Satan removed the assumption of innocence in children in horror film and established a new model for future child monsters.[8] The child who was born evil or possessed by demons became the standard icon of the child in a horror film. In fact, the metamorphosis of the child into this sort of monster became "the defining feature of horror films of the 1970s."[9] Horror film audiences experienced a veritable flood of evil children throughout the following decade: *The Other* (1972), *The Omen* (1976), *Damien: Omen II* (1978), *It's Alive* (1974), *It Lives Again* (1978), *It's Alive III* (1987), *The Brood* (1979), *The Exorcist* (1973), *Exorcist II* (1977), *Alice, Sweet Alice* (1976), and *Audrey Rose* (1977).

In the end, the effects of this shift in the image of the child within the context of horror were vastly important. Prior to the nineteenth century, children rarely figured into literature. Changes toward a harsher social climate in the nineteenth century as a result of industrialization made childhood seem "like heaven."[10] As a result, child characters began to figure more prominently in literature, most obviously with the work of Charles Dickens in England and Mark Twain in the United States. A complex image of the child was established in mid- to late nineteenth-century literature; childhood was a time of dependency and helplessness, danger and victimization, and innocence. Each of these themes presented the life of the child as providing an alternative to dominant cultural values. As a result, children were "othered," seen as fundamentally different from adults and dwelling outside of adult society. Adults found the image of the innocent child the most persuasive, and this became the predominant cultural attitude toward childhood for more than a century.[11]

The dominant cultural image of the child remained without serious challenge until the horror films of the late 1960s and 1970s. In place of nostalgic innocence, the makers of horror films began to project monstrosity, menace, and repulsion onto the idea of childhood. While youth had consistently been coded as "other" throughout the literary and film world, horror monsters had always embodied the darker aspects of the human psyche; children had been their ultimate victims. By upsetting long-standing stereotypes of children, horror filmmakers established a new layer of terror. In so doing, however, they worked against mainstream, bourgeois attitudes toward children and took the genre in a subversive direction.

Science fiction and horror film theorists have pointed out that there is a strong relationship between childhood and the way texts within these genres are received by readers. Science fiction returns the audience to the status of a child, forcing them to make sense of a newly discovered world. Even so, a sense of fear is implicit in this return: "The key emotion of childhood is fear, a fear we learn to live with through the process of finding our context and relating the self within to the world without."[12] By projecting the audience's fears onto a monstrous "other," horror films externalize internal conflicts, and they force their audiences to try to make sense of them. In this sense, they force their audiences to take a childlike approach to the film's monsters, searching for context and relating external monsters to inner demons. For this reason, horror films tend to be told from the perspective of a child, whose "absolute belief" in the "magic" of a situation is a necessary precondition to "absolute horror."[13]

If science fiction and horror are viewed from the perspective of a child, the advent of the "child as monster" paradigm within horror represented an even more radical shift in the genre. In effect, by turning the child into a monster, horror filmmakers were encouraging their audiences to see the world through the eyes of a monster. Instead of identifying with the victims, modern horror began to encourage audiences to identify with the monsters, and the line between predator and victim began to blur.

Horror Comes Home: The Suburbanization of Setting

The characterization of children as monsters was only one part of the American horror film renaissance of the 1970s and 1980s. Character, plot, and setting all underwent major revision over those two decades. Studios had worked for many years establishing audience familiarity with characters (e.g., mad scientists and suave vampires), plots (e.g., alien invasions and mysterious voyages), and settings (e.g., laboratories and ancient castles).[14] In a sense, however, this standardization worked against horror films' raison d'être: to frighten audiences. While horror is perhaps the most oversaturated of all the film genres, the aim of the films is to "generate suspense," a function that requires a certain level of freshness.[15] For this reason, American horror film sank into serious decline in the 1950s and 1960s.[16]

In order to regain their ability to frighten audiences, horror directors began to experiment with setting, taking the action out of dark castles, mad scientist labs, and gypsy trains.[17] Just as Hitchcock's *Psycho* heralded a dramatic shift in the conception of family in horror film, it also prefaced a trend toward a more quotidian setting. While horror films in the 1950s might have taken place in a world that had some connection with 1950s America (i.e., they frequently dealt with fears surrounding "the Bomb" or communist paranoia), they did so in a way that clearly marked them as fantasies (e.g., featuring giant insects attacking the planet). Hitchcock, setting *Psycho* at a roadside motel, presented audiences with a world that had evident commonality with their own.[18] Unlike the Universal horror films of the 1930s (*Dracula* [1931] and *Frankenstein* [1932], etc.) and the alien invasion films of the 1950s with their exotic locales and otherworldly monsters, *Psycho*'s ability to frighten audiences was facilitated by settings and characters that did not seem like fantasy.[19]

Just as *Rosemary's Baby* and *Night of the Living Dead* marked a new beginning for the depiction of children in horror film, they also spearheaded the movement toward a more "ordinary" setting. *Rosemary's Baby* used the everyday setting of a New York brownstone as a deliberate counterpoint to the supernatural terrors that were occurring inside.[20] A familiar backdrop made the unusual satanic rituals seem even more insidious. The setting for *Night of the Living Dead* was drastically different from that of *Rosemary's Baby*. The bulk of Romero's film took place in an average American farmhouse, and only two of the people who participated in the film were professional actors. The result of these directorial decisions was the establishment within the film of a palpable fear of the ordinary. The legacy of these two films was to move horror from a Transylvanian past into an American present.

While *Night of the Living Dead* was set in a rural farmhouse and *Rosemary's Baby* in a major metropolis, the drastic population shift to suburbia gave rise to the most prolific setting for horror films of the 1970s and 1980s. Romero again had a major impact on this movement. By choosing to set his film *Dawn of the Dead* (1978) in a shopping mall, Romero used zombiism as a metaphor for consumer culture. Nevertheless, it was John Carpenter's *Halloween* (also 1978) that made suburbia the setting for a whole new subgenre of horror movies—the slasher film. The premise of a homicidal madman escaping from the asylum and returning to his suburban boyhood home to murder teenage babysitters brought horror into direct contact with the everyday experience of audience members. In Carpenter's own words, it worked to undermine the "white flight" sense that "nothing could hurt you in suburbia."[21]

Picking up on this brand of terror caused by the "sustained and systematic destruction of the apparent fixity and solidity of small town life," Wes Craven's *Nightmare on Elm Street* series became the third major horror franchise to adopt suburbia as the center of action.[22] From the release of *Halloween* in 1978 to the end of the first wave of slasher films (signaled by the release of the final *Nightmare on Elm Street* movie, *Freddy's Dead: The Final Nightmare* in 1991), the suburbs reigned as the most popular setting for American horror film. In the end, it was this newfound ability to produce terrifying experiences organically rising from the day-to-day lives of the audience that positioned the American suburb at the geographic center of horror film.

The Victim Is the Viewer: The Horrified Audience

Horror films of the 1970s and 1980s were unique in the homogeneity of their audience. For marketing purposes, the movie industry since the late 1960s has seen the target demographic as males under the age of 25.[23] This marketing was largely successful. Horror filmmakers were able to exploit the new teen film market by aiming the genre at youth to the exclusion of their elders.[24] The audience for horror film did indeed become predominantly teenaged. Many scholars have noted that, for the last decades of the twentieth century, the viewership of scary movies had been *almost exclusively* youthful.[25] Beyond this, teenage audiences were extremely devoted to the genre with most people attending obsessively or not at all.[26]

Many adults were less than thrilled with the rise in youth attendance of horror films. Within months of the release of *Rosemary's Baby* and *Night of the Living Dead*, the Motion Picture Association of America established the G, M, R, and X rating system.[27] *Night of the Living Dead* became the first film to receive an X ("No children under seventeen admitted.") rating based solely on violent content.[28] Throughout the period, film reviewers spoke out against the danger of allowing young people to watch these films. *Variety* magazine wrote of *Night of the Living Dead*, "[it] casts serious doubts upon the integrity and social responsibility of its Pittsburgh-based makers, distributor Walter Reade, the film industry as a whole, and exhibitors who book the picture."[29] In a review of *Halloween*, one writer asked what made the film "morally superior to Nazi war relics?"[30] Others bemoaned the genre's "popularity with teenagers eager to test their mettle" by watching "pornographic" bloodbaths that "debase[d] both movies and audiences."[31] In 1980, Gene Siskel and Roger Ebert even devoted an entire episode of the PBS series *Sneak Previews* to speaking out against the negative influence of contemporary horror films.[32]

Keeping adolescents away from horror films was, in the end, a losing battle. In the 1960s, preventing children from accessing violent films was much easier than in the following decades. Broadcast television standards prohibited films like *Psycho* from being aired. The advent of the videocassette recorder and cable television in the late 1970s and early 1980s changed this. VCRs and cable TV gave adolescents who would have been denied entry into those films in the theaters the opportunity to see them in their own homes. Additionally, horror films provided fledgling cable stations cheap airtime "filler."[33] Mail-order horror film clubs also began to do brisk business. Concerns over American horror films ("video nasties") like *The Driller Killer* (1979), *I Spit on Your Grave* (1978), and *The Evil Dead* (1981) circulating to children through the Royal Mail led directly to British legislative action.[34] The avenues for adolescents to acquire and view graphic horror films, however, had become too numerous for such efforts to make much of an impact on distribution of these films to their target audience.

The animosity of film critics and legislators was eminently logical. Horror films, particularly slasher films, were "drenched in taboo" and lay well "beyond the purview of the respectable (middle-aged, middle class) audience."[35] This was the attraction of adolescent audiences to these films; the movies represented "a rebellious rejection of adult values" entwined with "a titillating glimpse of the forbidden."[36] Watching horror films became an act of teenage rebellion, but it extended well beyond mere rejection of middle-class adult values. As will be discussed in greater detail later, horror films in the 1970s and 1980s tended to *depict* teenagers resisting dominant cultural codes and taking control of situations that sources of adult authority could not or would not help them with; the films themselves were about teenage rebellion and young adults finding their way in the world.[37]

Feminist critics and scholars have frequently accused horror films of the 1970s and 1980s, especially those of the slasher variety, of sexism because of frequent depictions of graphic violence against women. At the same time, other critics have been less eager to denounce the movies based solely on that violence, arguing that the heroines of horror film "de-victimize" themselves by violently overcoming their attackers and upsetting gender roles (women as victims) present in the genre since its inception.[38] Whether young women were victimized or de-victimized by slasher films, it is clear that a substantial portion of their audience was female. Although the films were marketed to young males, half of the audience (or more) was female. Marketing research from the mid-1990s indicated that 27 percent of girls (aged 13 to 18) named horror films their favorite film genre, compared with 14 percent of boys.[39] For those espousing the feminist critiques, horror was "far more victim-viewed" than the standard view would have it.[40]

Horror, more than any other film genre, depends on audience participation. That is, in order to scare people, films have to convince their audience that the threats in the film are, on some level, real.[41] Psychologically speaking, horror filmmakers must be in touch with the fears of their audiences. Young children are apt to fear supernatural monsters and their own personal injury. Although adolescents continue to fear their physical destruction, political, economic, and especially social fears, including those surrounding school, begin to appear at this age.[42] As a result, the shift in the age of horror film audiences led directly to a change in the settings of the films and the types of scares they sought to elicit.

Additionally, as the audience for horror film become solidly composed almost exclusively of adolescents, some of the social functions of horror became more obvious. When film critic Janet Maslin observed that teenagers flocked to horror films to "test their mettle," her observation was rooted in one of the deep social truths regarding the function of fear and the social purpose of horror film. More than any other genre, sexuality has played a central role in horror film, and modern horror is "uniquely tailored to the psyches of troubled adolescents."[43] A recent psychological study showed that men enjoyed horror films most in the presence of a fearful female, while women enjoyed horror films least in the presence of a fearful male. Scary movies, therefore, provided young adolescent males the opportunity to show other males they were not cowards and females that they could assume the role of "protector."[44] For some adolescents, watching horror films played an important social function.

More than this, however, horror films are the "re-embodiments of secret fears and desires, of monstrous hungers and frightful lusts" of their audiences.[45] In the words of one sympathetic critic of horror films of the 1970s, the movies were made popular by the "twin thrills" of "overt violence" and "covert sexuality," which granted their audiences "the most sensuous and personal of pleasures: the experience of fear in a safe place."[46] Less sympathetic critics likened the films to "sexual pornography," a distinction that still acknowledges the close relationship between the films and the lusts of their audiences but repudiates the idea that the films had positive cathartic effects.[47] This book seeks neither to justify horror film as a "safety valve" nor to denounce it as sadistic hedonism. Rather, it takes the position that this debate "recognize[s] symptoms and ignore[s] causes," while also acknowledging that the horror film renaissance of the 1970s and 1980s "points to serious emotional problems, frustrations, and anger" in increasingly teenaged horror audiences.[48]

"The Killer Is Coming": Bullying and Revenge as Archetype

The horror film was in an era of great flux throughout the 1970s and 1980s. The image of the child in horror film became more sinister. The setting became less extraordinary and increasingly suburban. Moreover, audiences became even more predominantly teenaged. The net effect of these three trends in horror film led directly to the creation of a new iconic setting for terror. In order to attract the attention of teenage viewers and anchor the movies in their social fears, the films began to feature teenage "monsters" in their natural habitat: the school. Educational institutions of all varieties (e.g., summer camps, colleges, and universities) saw a great increase in attention from horror filmmakers, but the high school became the favorite setting for horror in the era. This chapter looks exclusively at films released between 1968 and 1992 taking place entirely (or nearly entirely) within the walls of the American high school,[49] prominently featuring the high school as a setting,[50] or providing comic satires of such films.[51]

The first significant American horror film in the era to take place in high school was De Palma's *Carrie* in 1976. In many ways, *Carrie* set up the character and plot archetypes that would become standards for the genre. Based on the novel by Stephen King of the same name, the film told the story of a young girl who experienced constant, mean-spirited teasing at the hands of her classmates. In one of the early scenes in the film, Carrie White is mocked mercilessly when she panics in the gym shower at the sight of the blood of her first menstrual period. She is pelted with feminine products, and the other girls chant "Plug it up!" at her. The scene culminates with Carrie shattering a light bulb with her mind and discovering she has telekinetic powers. As both the seriousness of the teasing by her peers and the strength of her powers increase, Carrie begins to lose control. When several of her classmates hatch a plot that involves drenching Carrie in pig's blood at the prom, she exacts violent revenge on the entire student body.

In certain ways, *Carrie* is a transitional film. It bridges the Romantic "child as victim" image and the "child monster" archetype.[52] Blurring traditional lines of protagonist and antagonist, the bullying of her classmates establishes Carrie as a victim, but her violent response indicates that she has metamorphosed from a "White" innocent into something grotesque. In order to find meaning in the violence, the audience needs to feel for Carrie and needs to want her to get her revenge, but she becomes too violent, harming even those people who tried to help her. The audience, once tempted to see Carrie's classmates solely as villains, soon watches as Carrie creates her own victims by using her powers to hurt them. The whole narrative becomes morally ambiguous, but it is clear that bullying by peers created a monster.

The shocking effect of the final scene of the film depends upon an audience desire for the survivors to have pangs of conscience for their treatment of Carrie. In the concluding scene, one of Carrie's bullies awakes from a nightmare in which Carrie's hand reaches up from the grave to drag her down. The tormentor is, in the end, as scarred as her victim. Following *Carrie*, bullying and retribution became a major theme in nearly every horror film that took place inside a high school for the next two decades.

King, who began writing horror in high school, based his character Carrie on a pair of young girls he knew in high school. One, whom he met when he was 14, wore the same clothes to school every day. She was bullied, as King describes, with "Kick Me Hard" signs. She eventually killed herself. The other, an epileptic girl who lived near him in high school, died of an epileptic seizure. For King, the writing of *Carrie* became a way to explore the effects of his own experiences with the trauma associated with high school bullying.[53] In King's own words, "Carrie's revenge is something that any student who has ever had his gym shorts pulled down in phys. ed. or his glasses thumb-rubbed in study hall could approve of."[54]

Jennifer and *The Spell*, two *Carrie* knockoffs, were released on the heels of De Palma's film. Both featured bullied females with supernatural powers exacting revenge on the people who picked on them.[55] *Jennifer* differed from the other high school horror films of the era in that it was one of only two such films to take place in a private school. More than most of the other high school horror films from the era, Jennifer's social class motivates her classmates to ostracize her. Her status as a scholarship student, her thick Southern accent, and her unusual religious beliefs (including snake handling) mark her as different and inspire her classmates to treat her poorly.

While Carrie was treated cruelly, the bullying in *Jennifer* was extremely serious and potentially deadly. In physical education class, one of the girls holds Jennifer underwater in the school pool in an attempt to drown her. The same girl kills Jennifer's pet cat and leaves the carcass in her locker. One girl who tries to stick up for Jennifer is raped as punishment for her kindness.

Jennifer slowly discovers that (as a result of a spiritual experience she has while handling serpents) she can mentally communicate with and has the power to control snakes. Ultimately, she uses her newly discovered power to have snakes attack her tormentors. While some of the bullies meet grisly ends trying to get away from the serpents, giant snakes swallow the rest. Jennifer overcomes her tormentors and decides to stay in school so that she can finish the job "the Lord appointed her to do."

Jennifer was not the only figure from a private high school who felt impelled by religious zealotry to avenge the victims of bullying.[56] One of the opening scenes of *The Redeemer* (1978) depicts a severe episode of bullying in which a kid pulls a knife on another child for not laughing at a joke: "I told a joke; you didn't laugh." The film then cuts to a priest preaching a homily warning of "eternal damnation" and the return of "Sodom." In the course of the movie, the priest fakes a high school reunion to get a group of people with whom he attended high school to return, and he slaughters them one by one for perceived moral transgressions, including bullying.

Unlike all the other films examined here, the links between the transgressions and reason for revenge in *The Redeemer* were never made fully clear. At times, the killings seemed unmotivated. Even the victims remained unaware of the reasons for their deaths:

"Revenge? What for? What did I do?"
"It could be anything, something we did to someone back in school."
"I don't remember doing anything to anybody."

Carrie, Jennifer, and the other films examined here encouraged audiences to identify with the monsters. They establish pathos by linking the "monster's" violent acts to their own victimization. In *The Redeemer*, the murders were not personal. Rather, they were committed for more abstract religious reasons.

The killer sums up the motivation for his violence in simple, theological terms: "Those who have sinned have met with the angel of the Lord's vengeance." In this respect, *The Redeemer* stood in stark contrast to the other high school films of the era, which tended to be deeply connected to the social fears of young audiences.

Even so, the final scene of the film reaffirmed one of the central conflicts of high school horror films. In the final scene, the boy who was bullied at the beginning of the film was seen holding a bloody pocketknife. The boy began speaking with one of the priests who told him not to worry and that "everything will be okay." The final shot of the film shows the bully's dead body with a slashed throat being carefully hidden in the trunk of the priest's car. The final sentiment of the film was that, through violence, the victims were able to overcome the tyranny of their attackers.

Slaughter High (1985) stole its premise directly from *The Redeemer*. In the subgenre's most formulaic entry, *Slaughter High* featured another set of fake high school reunion invitations being sent to yet another group of high school bullies. The bullies are then murdered one by one in extraordinarily elaborate and creative ways. Unlike *The Redeemer*, however, each of the killings is obviously motivated by a very specific antecedent bullying episode. Mass murder in *Slaughter High* was grounded in unambiguous social anxieties, and abstract moralistic arguments were entirely absent. As such, *Slaughter High* is perhaps the most representative of the high school horror films of the period.

The bullying in *Slaughter High* was more extreme than any other film from the period. The film took place on April Fool's Day, when a group of popular teenagers plotted a series of pranks on one of their intellectually talented, but socially awkward, classmates, Marty. One of the girls from the group convinced Marty to follow her into the girls' locker room, strip, and go into the shower. The rest of the group then opened the shower curtain and filmed as they poked and prodded Marty, sexually humiliated him, electrocuted him with a cattle prod, and shoved his head in a toilet. Two more of the conspirators tainted marijuana and offered it to Marty, who became violently nauseated after smoking it. While Marty was in the restroom vomiting, another student switched the labels on the bottles in the chemistry lab. When Marty returned to his experiments, he used the incorrect chemicals and was burned beyond recognition by both fire and nitric acid.

In the second part of the film, which took place a few years later in the newly abandoned high school, Marty hatched his plot for revenge. As Marty murdered each of his former classmates, he did so in ways that mimicked and formed ironic comments on his own experience being bullied. Just as he was sexually humiliated by electrocution, Marty wired the box spring of a bed to shock a couple of his former bullies as they committed adultery. Echoing his own head being shoved into a toilet, Marty threw one girl into a septic tank and left her to die. Another girl had her flesh eaten away by a nitric acid bath. Reminiscent of the toxic marijuana, one boy's stomach exploded after drinking a beer that Marty had poisoned. Each murder had a direct analogue in the bullying Marty experienced.

Horror, relying so heavily on audience participation in order to perform its social function, found bullying to be a teenage social anxiety easily exploited for scares. The films built tension by depicting increasingly horrendous mistreatment of their protagonists. Filmmakers eased that tension by showing the downtrodden overcoming their aggressors. Some of the films indirectly marked themselves to audience members as wish fulfillment fantasies for bullied young people.[57] *Slaughter High* did so directly. In the final scene, the audience discovered that none of the vengeful murders had actually occurred. Marty, still in the hospital, was merely fantasizing about his revenge. The film ended with Marty breaking out of the lunatic asylum, bent on realizing his fantasy.[58]

The *Prom Night* series represents an important, if disjointed, institution in the history of high school horror films. *Prom Night* (1980) proved another financially successful slasher film entry for *Halloween* star Jamie Lee Curtis.[59] The first film maintained the tradition of the bullied youth seeking his revenge. In yet another scene taking place in an abandoned school, the film began with a group of children playing a variation of hide-and-seek called "The Killer Is Coming." A group of children chased the loser of the game around the vacated building chanting, "The killer is coming." Terrified by her peers, the girl accidentally fell to her death out of a second-story window. The remainder of the film was standard slasher fare with the girl's brother sequentially killing each member of the group on the night of their senior prom.

The second and third installments in the *Prom Night* series offered variations on the bullying theme. *Prom Night II* (1987) introduced the character Mary Lou Maloney, a popular girl who treated her peers with disdain and disrespect. On prom night, a jilted boyfriend sought his revenge on her by planting a "stink bomb" to detonate during her prom queen coronation. The "stink bomb" accidentally set Mary Lou ablaze, and she died in the resulting fire. Despite Mary Lou's previous status as a bully, *Prom Night II* and *Prom Night III* (1990) feature her possessing the bodies of mild-mannered students in attempts to commit violent acts of revenge: "Places to go. People to kill. Vicki doesn't live here anymore." The central conflict of these two films then became youth battling to prevent their bodies from being possessed by a bully for evil purposes.[60] Usually these attempts were unsuccessful.

This theme of bodily possession for vicarious revenge would be revisited by Robert Englund's film *976-EVIL* (1989). In that film, a young man nicknamed "Hoax" was bullied. Other students forced his head into the toilet, threw him into a dumpster and beat on the sides of it, and emasculated him when he went out on a date. Hoax discovered a phone number for a self-help line, called it, and, in so doing, became the vessel for an evil spirit who granted him supernatural powers that would enable him to achieve his revenge. In the end, the audience discovers that the message machine for 976-EVIL that answered young people's calls was built by a man who claimed, "I built this myself. I used to live in Radio Shack when I was in high school." The phone service encouraged Hoax to kill other students so that he would stop being seen as a wimp. The film ends with a role reversal, with the formerly bullied student standing over one of his own bullies, spitting on him, a direct inversion of a scene near the beginning of the film.

The progenitor of the slasher genre, *Halloween*, helped solidify the bullying motif that would run through nearly every horror film to take place in a high school for more than a decade. In Carpenter's film, audiences were presented with a scene in which some children were making fun of a weaker student, bullying him, pushing him, breaking his Halloween pumpkin, and taunting him with a refrain of "The bogeyman is going to get you." When the young boy finally got away from his bullies, he raced around the street corner and ran into the masked, psychotic killer Michael Myers. The same boy, later in the film, told his babysitter when she tried to protect him from Michael Myers that "you can't kill the bogeyman." From the perspective of that little boy, the bullying of his peers brought an indestructible bogeyman to life. That bullying caused permanent damage to the psyche and created violent, vengeful monsters became the overriding message of the subgenre of horror films that took place in school.

"Now Do You Believe Me?": Adult Authority, Adolescent Rebellion

Adults in horror films of the 1970s and the 1980s generally fit into one of three categories: (1) the killer, (2) the wise elder offering advice, or (3) the ineffectual or apathetic caretaker.[61] In most of the horror films taking place in school, adults tended to fit into the third category. Film after film featured teenagers whose lives were in danger and adults who were unwilling or unable to do anything about it. Traditional authority figures were rendered impotent in modern horror films. Most remained unaware there were even threats against the young in their communities. Even when teenagers informed them of the dangers, adults rarely believed the youth. And those adults that knew of the problems ignored them or were powerless to do anything about them.[62]

In part, this portrayal of the relationships between teenagers and adults was intimately related to the advent of the "child monster" as a new horror icon. Bourgeois society's response to the youth movements and drug culture of the late 1960s and early 1970s was resoundingly negative. Those sentiments had clear effects on horror film. The number of cannibalistic, murderous, selfish, and even overtly sexual children depicted in horror film rose significantly, and the relationships between youth and adults portrayed in horror film demonstrated severe deterioration.[63] Horror films, which openly displayed many of society's taboos, established themselves as antithetical to the values of genteel society.[64] The children and teenagers depicted in horror film (even or especially the evil ones) actively resisted adult society. British horror filmmaker Peter Sasdy openly discussed the conflict between adults and youth in his films, describing his films as "a way [for] the younger generation [to] punish the older generation for their hypocrisy."[65]

Having been aimed at teenage audiences, many horror films dealt with the growth of teenagers into adulthood. As a result, many stalker films were built around significant rites of social passage.[66] After the success of *Halloween*, filmmakers searched for other holidays that could be exploited in their films; some literally took out a calendar and searched for unused holidays and other special calendar days (coming up with *Friday the 13th* [1980], *Happy Birthday to Me* [1981], *My Bloody Valentine* [1981], etc.).[67] By the mid-1980s, there were not many holidays or important rites of passage that had been overlooked as the setting for at least one horror film.[68] Because of the common use of schools as a backdrop, many of the films were set on important days on the school calendar, especially prom nights, class reunions, and graduation days. As anxiety-producing rites of passage, each of these days was exploited for the social fears it produced in their teenage viewers.

Graduation day represents a monumental change and a powerful source of anxiety in the lives of young people. The makers of *Graduation Day*, in an effort to promote the film, had dozens of students attend the premiere wearing caps and gowns and buttons that read, "I Survived *Graduation Day*." "I'm not ready for the shock; that's why I got the graduation day blues," a group of students in the film sang. Much of the conflict in the film derived from students' inability to let go of the people they love.

The film began with a track-and-field montage depicting a coach who pushed a female runner too hard. She collapsed on the track and was declared dead. After the dead girl's sister returned from her naval station on Guam to attend the funeral, a masked assailant began murdering other members of the track team. At the end of the film, the audience discovered that the deceased girl's boyfriend was actually committing the murders.[69] He intended to kill the coach and each member of the track team to avenge his girlfriend for the stress they put her under that had led directly to her death.

Graduation Day contains the most powerful artistic symbol in any of the slasher films discussed here. As if he were coaching or officiating a track meet, the killer timed each chase and subsequent murder with a stopwatch. The link was, therefore, clearly established between the stopwatch and death. The stopwatch's association with the fatal track meet, however, created a metaphorical association with the failure of the young girl to meet adult expectations, despite her extreme efforts to do so. That these murders took place among students who were anticipating high school graduation related graduation to their eventual demise. The stopping of the clock with each murder made the stopwatch a pregnant symbol, embodying fear of graduation, failure to meet adult expectations, and death.

The students in the film had no respect for adult authority, nor should they have. The principal was a womanizer. A deputy sheriff serving as a school resources officer confiscated, then smoked, the students' marijuana. Several teachers had affairs with students. Completely oblivious to the fact that his students were being murdered, the principal responded to the telephone calls of concerned parents by saying: "Today is graduation day. Those kids are getting kicked out of the nest, so to speak. From now on, it's fly or fall. They're probably just out raising hell." The police inspector sent to investigate the disappearances agreed with the principal's assessment, adding that the missing children were "a bunch of inconsiderate kids about to fly out of the nest and shit all over the rest of us." The adults, entirely unaware of the danger the children in their charge were experiencing, belittled the students' emotional turmoil caused by the impending graduation. The prevailing adult attitude toward the student body was stated most clearly by one of their teachers, "Animals! I swear to God they get worse from year to year."

Certainly, *Carrie* presented a deep conflict between youth and adult authority. Carrie's principal was unable to remember her name and called her "Cassie" throughout the movie. Her English teacher mocked her contributions to class. However, the twin rites of passage of a girl's first menstrual period and prom night represented the most serious rift between youth and adulthood. Carrie's mother was a religious zealot who proselytized to her neighbors. She was unable come to terms with her daughter's coming of age, deeming the telekinetic powers Carrie received with the coming of her first period "witchcraft." Carrie's burgeoning sexuality was a source of maternal punishment.

For socially awkward Carrie, the prom was another world: "It's like being on Mars!" Prom was a symbol of youthful sexuality, which was itself a rite of passage. When Carrie had pig's blood dumped on her head during prom queen coronation, it was symbolic of a complete break with the authority of her mother. For Carrie, the pig's blood was associated with both her menstrual blood and the blood of Christ. Being doused with the blood of a pig deepened an internal conflict. It became a symbol for both her bodily changes and her repudiation of her mother's religious values. Carrie responded by committing mass murder and crucifying her mother with kitchen knives. The only way for Carrie to embrace her own adult identity was a complete (and deadly) renunciation of her mother.[70]

The overwhelming majority of the other films in the sample have a similar attitude toward adult authority. In *Halloween*, the policeman blamed "kids" for the theft of Halloween masks and knives, oblivious even to the danger presented by the real thief to his own daughter. Hoax, in *976-EVIL*, told his mother, "If you value your life, I suggest you leave," and killed his mother (who spent much of her time watching televangelists) when she failed to do so. Adults in *Prom Night II* and *III* were apathetic or clueless and received no respect from youth. With blatant disrespect for religious authority, Mary Lou Maloney in *Prom Night II* went to confession, itemized each sin in lurid detail, and finally admitted to "loving every minute of it." Regarding one of the murders he committed, *Prom Night III*'s Alex (possessed by Mary Lou Maloney) diminished its importance by saying, "It wasn't a person. It was a guidance counselor." Despite the seriousness of the situation, Alex's principal said of the "so-called high school assassin" that he would not "allow the actions of a single homicidal student to ruin the fun of the others." Time after time, teenagers in high school horror films respond to the adult world with rebellion and derision. These actions are justified by parents' and teachers' refusal to acknowledge the seriousness of their children's concerns or the validity of their fears.[71]

In no film is this phenomenon clearer than in Craven's *A Nightmare on Elm Street* series. In the first film, Elm Street's children were left to pay for the sins of their parents. The district attorney, because of a legal technicality, was unable to secure the conviction of school custodian Freddy Krueger, a murderer of 20 children from the neighborhood. The parents from Elm Street, in the spirit of vigilante justice, burned the man alive for his crimes. Freddy then sought revenge on them by haunting (and killing) the next generation in their dreams.[72] Each film featured a group of young people afraid to fall asleep for fear of being brutally murdered by Freddy.

When confronted with their stories of a man attacking teenagers in their dreams, "parents, teachers, psychiatrists, and police are all unable to give any credence to the young people's stories."[73] For Nancy, the sole surviving female of the first film, living through the nightmares became a passage to both adulthood and ideological awareness.[74] Nancy rejected her mother's view that Fred Krueger was dead. "He's dead," Nancy's mother said. "He's dead because mommy killed him." As a result of this ideological viewpoint, Nancy's mother was unable to see her daughter's need for help and unwilling to aid in the struggle. She installed a keyed lock on the inside of the door to the house, tried to force her daughter to sleep, and took away the support of her peers. In one interaction with her mother, Nancy screamed, "The guy is after us in our dreams." Her mother responded by saying, "That just isn't reality, Nancy." Nancy's reaction was a complete denunciation of her mother's world: "Maybe I should just grab that bottle and 'veg' out with you and avoid everything that is happening to me." Nancy's fight against Krueger allowed her to develop her own independent identity and was the defining moment in her transition to adulthood.[75]

In 1991, *Freddy's Dead: The Final Nightmare* essentially ended the American horror renaissance that had begun in 1968 with *Night of the Living Dead* and *Rosemary's Baby*.[76] By the sixth film in the series, Freddy's revenge was nearly complete. He had killed all but one of the descendents of those who had murdered him. The town was devoid of children, and the adults had descended into madness. One teacher stood in front of an empty classroom delivering a lesson on the history of Freddy. The refusal of adults to acknowledge the problems of youth had led to its logical conclusion within the context of high school American horror films: apocalypse.

Some Concluding Remarks: Armageddon and Education

As we have seen, three distinct trends in the horror film genre—the development of the "child as monster icon," the rise of suburbia as a setting, and the juvenilization of the horror film audience—had the effect of creating a new subgenre of horror: the high school horror film. In order to provide audiences with scares that reflected their own anxieties, these films tended to focus on bullying and revenge and the transition from adolescence to adulthood. These two motifs were present in a staggering number of American horror films in the 1970s and 1980s.

The number of student protagonists and monsters in 1970s and 1980s horror films who overcame their aggressors in extraordinarily violent ways gave life to the idea that "violence only makes sense in the perverted mirror of hope."[77] Ultimately, films like *Carrie* bemoaned the kind of world that allowed good people to be tormented and turned into monsters.[78] In this way, horror films provided a way for young people to search for the meaning of their own anxieties and insecurities. The violence in the films was simultaneously destructive and part of a process of yearning for an easier transition to adulthood.

The apocalyptic vision of the final *Nightmare on Elm Street* film hinted at a shift in the emphasis of horror film. Very few horror films in recent years have featured high school as a prominent setting. Vengeance for bullying motivated Eric Harris and Dylan Klebold's mass murder of their fellow students at Columbine High School in Littleton, Colorado, on April 20, 1999. Until very recently, no significant horror film has been made featuring the previously ubiquitous theme of bullying and revenge.[79] Even the 2008 remake of *Prom Night* removed the deadly bullying, instead featuring an escaped mental patient as the killer, and did not contain a single scene that took place in a high school. In these post-Columbine days it is difficult to see a studio producing a film like *Return to Horror High* (1987), which was about a film crew making a horror film at a high school that had formerly been the scene of a series of school killings. Herb Freed, director of *Graduation Day*, stopped making horror films altogether after watching the reactions of the audience to the violence in his film. "It was good," he said, "but it was good that it *was*."

The recent American horror films that have depicted schools in any prominent way have provided an extremely bleak vision. In *Resident Evil: Apocalypse* (2004), the school was populated by hordes of virus-infected zombie children. Science fiction/horror film *Children of Men* (2006) presented a world in which humans were unable to procreate. Schools were depressing wastelands devoid of children altogether. The setting for *Silent Hill* (2006) was a desolate town whose school was vacant of any children, but rather was filled with incredibly graphic and disturbing images (like cadavers in the lavatory hog-tied with barbed wire). Horror films have historically served an important social function for young audiences. Films like *Halloween* and *A Nightmare on Elm Street* provided audiences with models of young people battling their way into adulthood. Films like

Carrie and even *Slaughter High* were hopeful, despite (or even because of) their vivid images of violence. Craven once said, "The ghost of *Carrie* haunts us all."[80] In this chapter, I have tried to outline the historical need that such a haunting served. If Columbine was a turning point in the development of a new style of high school horror film, more scholarly attention needs to be paid to the social function of contemporary horror films.

Bibliography

Brophy, Philip. "Horrality—The Textuality of Contemporary Horror Films." *Screen* 27, no. 1 (Jan–Feb 1986): 2–13.

Cantor, Joanne, and Mary Beth Oliver. "Developmental Differences in Responses to Horror." In *The Horror Film*, edited by Stephen Price, 224–241. New Brunswick, NJ: Rutgers University Press, 2004.

Cherry, Brigid. "Refusing to Refuse to Look: Female Viewers of the Horror Film." In *Identifying Hollywood's Audiences: Cultural Identity and the Movies*, edited by Melvyn Stokes and Richard Maltby, 187–203. London: British Film Institute, 1999.

Chute, David. "King of the Night: An Interview with Stephen King." *TakeOne* (January 1979): 33–38.

Clover, Carol J. *Men, Women, and Chain Saws: Gender in the Modern Horror Film*. Princeton, NJ: Princeton University Press, 1992.

Derry, Charles. "More Dark Dreams: Some Notes on the Recent Horror Film." In *American Horrors: Essays on the Modern American Horror Film*, edited by Gregory A. Waller, 162–174. Urbana, IL: University of Chicago Press, 1987.

Dike, Vera. "The Stalker Film, 1978–1981." In *American Horrors: Essays on the Modern American Horror Film*, edited by Gregory A. Waller, 86–101. Urbana, IL: University of Chicago Press, 1987.

Dillard, R. H. W. *Horror Films*. New York: Simon and Schuster, 1976.

Doherty, Thomas. *Teenagers and Teenpics: The Juvenilization of American Movies in the 1950s*. Philadelphia: Temple University Press, 2002.

Evans, Walter. "Monster Movies: A Sexual Theory." *Journal of Popular Film and Television* 2, no. 4 (1973): 353–365.

Foote, Bud. "Getting Things in the Right Order: Stephen King's *The Shining*, *The Stand*, and *It*." In *Nursery Realms: Children in the Worlds of Science Fiction, Fantasy, and Horror*, edited by Gary

Westfahl and George Slusser, 200–209. Athens: University of Georgia Press, 1999.

Frank, Allan. *The Horror Film Handbook*. Totowa, NJ: Barnes and Noble Press, 1982.

Heba, Gary. "Everyday Nightmares: The Rhetoric of Social Horror in the 'Nightmare on Elm Street' Series." *Journal of Popular Film and Television* 23, no. 3 (Fall 1995): 106–115.

Hefferman, Kevin. *Ghouls, Gimmicks, and Gold: Horror Films and the American Movie Business, 1955–1968*. Durham, NC: Duke University Press, 2004.

Jones, Darryl. *Horror: A Thematic History in Fiction and Film*. London: Oxford University, 2002.

Lewis, Frances Deutsch. "The Humpty Dumpty Effect, or Was the Old Egg Really All It Was Cracked Up to Be: Context and Coming of Age in Science Fiction and Fantasy." In *Nursery Realms: Children in the Worlds of Science Fiction, Fantasy, and Horror*, edited by Gary Westfahl and George Slusser, 20–28. Athens: University of Georgia Press, 1999.

Maslin, Janet. "Bloodbaths Debase Movies and Audiences." *New York Times*, November 21, 1982, H1.

Muir, John Kenneth. *Horror Films of the 1970s*. Jefferson, NC: McFarland, 2002.

Oliver, Mary Beth, and Meghan Sanders. "The Appeal of Horror and Suspense." In *The Horror Film*, edited by Stephen Price, 242–257. New Brunswick: Rutgers University Press, 2004.

Paul, William. *Laughing Screaming: Modern Hollywood Horror and Comedy*. New York: Columbia University Press, 1994.

Petley, Julian. "The Monstrous Child." In *The Body's Perilous Pleasures: Dangerous Desires and Contemporary Culture*, edited by Michael Aaron, 87–107. Edinburgh: Edinburgh University Press, 1999.

Pirie, David. "New Blood." *Sight and Sound* 40, no. 2 (1971): 73–75.

Rockoff, Adam. *Going to Pieces: The Rise and Fall of the Slasher Film, 1978–1986*. Jefferson, NC: McFarland, 2002.

Rockoff, Adam, writer. *Going to Pieces: The Rise and Fall of the Slasher Film*. ThinkFilm, 2006.

Rosenbaum, Jonathan. "*Halloween*: Suspense Is Generated by Waiting for a Woman to Be Torn Apart by a Maniac." *TakeOne* (January 1979): 8–9.

Samuels, Stuart. "The Age of Conspiracy and Conformity: Invasion of the Body Snatchers (1956)." In *American History/American*

Film: Interpreting the Hollywood Image, edited by John E. Connor and Martin A. Jackson. New York: Continuum, 1988.

Schlobin, Roger C. "Children of a Darker God: A Taxonomy of Deep Horror Fiction and Film and their Mass Popularity." *Journal of the Fantastic in the Arts* 1, no. 1 (1988): 25–50.

Sobcheck, Vivian. "Bringing It All Back Home: Family Economy and Generic Exchange." In *American Horrors: Essays on the Modern American Horror Film*, edited by Gregory A. Waller, 175–194. Urbana, IL: University of Chicago Press, 1987.

Springhall, John. *Youth, Popular Culture, and Moral Panics: Penny Gaffs to Gangsta-Rap, 1830–1996*. New York: St. Martin's Press, 1998.

Stoizer, Charles B. "Youth Violence and the Apocalyptic." *American Journal of Psychoanalysis* 62, no. 3 (September 2002): 285–298.

Talalay, Rachel. *Freddy's Dead: The Final Nightmare*. New Line Cinema, 1991.

Telotte, J. P. "Faith and Idolatry in the Horror Film." In *Planks of Reason: Essays on the Horror Film*, edited by Barry Keith Grant, 21–37. Metuchen, NJ: Scarecrow Press, 1984.

Tudor, Andrew. *Monsters and Mad Scientists: A Cultural History of the Horror Movie*. Cambridge, MA: Basil Blackwell, 1989.

Waller, Gregory A., ed. "Introduction." In *American Horrors: Essays on the Modern American Horror Film*, 1–13. Urbana, IL: University of Chicago Press, 1987.

Wolf, Leonard. "In Horror Movies, Some Things Are Sacred." *New York Times*, April 4, 1976, D1.

Wood, Robin. *Hollywood from Vietnam to Reagan . . . and Beyond*. New York: Columbia University Press, 2003.

Wood, Robin. "Returning the Look: *Eyes of a Stranger*." In *American Horrors: Essays on the Modern American Horror Film*, edited by Gregory A. Waller, 79–85. Urbana, IL: University of Chicago Press, 1987.

Filmography

Boorman, John, dir. *The Exorcist II: The Heretic*. Warner Bros., 1977.

Borris, Clay, dir. *Prom Night IV: Deliver Us from Evil*. Norstar Entertainment, 1992.

Carpenter, John, dir. *Halloween*. Compass International Pictures, 1978.

Cohen, Larry, dir. *Full Moon High*. Orion Pictures, 1981.

———. *It Lives Again*. Warner Bros., 1978.
———. *It's Alive*. Warner Bros., 1974.
———. *It's Alive III: Island of the Alive*. Warner Bros., 1987.
Craven, Wes, dir. *The Hills Have Eyes*. Vanguard, 1977.
———. *A Nightmare on Elm Street*. New Line, 1984.
Cronenberg, David, dir. *The Brood*. MGM, 1979.
Cuaron, Alfonso, dir. *Children of Men*. Universal Pictures, 2006.
Cunningham, Sean, dir. *Friday the 13th*. Paramount Pictures, 1980.
Daniel, Rod, dir. *Teen Wolf*. MGM, 1985.
De Palma, Brian, dir. *Carrie*. United Artists, 1976.
Donner, Richard, dir. *The Omen*. 20th Century Fox, 1976.
Dugdale, George, Mark Ezra, and Peter Litten, dirs. *Slaughter High*, 1985.
Englund, Robert, dir. *976-EVIL*. Cinetel Films, 1989.
Ferrara, Abel, dir. *The Driller Killer*. Navaron Productions, 1979.
Freed, Herb, dir. *Graduation Day*. Legacy Entertainment, 1981.
Friedkin, William, dir. *The Exorcist*. Warner Bros., 1973.
Froehlich, Bill, dir. *Return to Horror High*. New World Pictures, 1987.
Gans, Christophe, and Chris Sikorowski, dirs. *Silent Hill*. Sony Pictures, 2006.
Gochis, Constantine S., dir. *The Redeemer*. Enterprise Pictures, 1978.
Haines, Richard W., and Michael Hertz, dirs. *Class of Nuke 'Em High*. Troma Entertainment, 1986.
Hitchcock, Alfred, dir. *Psycho*. Universal Pictures, 1960.
Hodges, Mike, and Don Taylor, dirs. *Damien: Omen II*. 20th Century Fox, 1978.
Hooper, Tobe, dir. *The Texas Chainsaw Massacre*. Dark Sky Films, 1974.
Hopkins, Stephen, dir. *A Nightmare on Elm Street 5: The Dream Child*. New Line Cinema, 1989.
LeRoy, Mervyn, dir. *The Bad Seed*. Warner Bros., 1956.
Lynch, Paul, dir. *Prom Night*. MGM, 1980.
Mack, Brice, dir. *Jennifer*. Orion Pictures, 1978.
Mihalka, George, dir. *My Bloody Valentine*. Canadian Film Development Corporation, 1981.
Mulligan, Robert, dir. *The Other*. 20th Century Fox, 1972.
Oliver, Ron, and Peter R. Simpson, dirs. *Prom Night III: The Last Kiss*. Norstar Entertainment, 1990.
Pallenberg, Rospo, dir. *Cutting Class*. April Films, 1989.
Phillips, Lee, dir. *The Spell*. Charles Fries Productions, 1977.

Pittman, Bruce, dir. *Prom Night II: Hello Mary Lou*. MGM, 1987.
Polanski, Roman, dir. *Rosemary's Baby*. Paramount, 1968.
Powell, Michael, dir. *Peeping Tom*. Anglo-Amalgamated Film Distributors, 1960.
Raimi, Sam, dir. *The Evil Dead*. Renaissance Pictures, 1981.
Romero, George A., dir. *The Crazies*. Blue Underground, 1973.
———. *Dawn of the Dead*. Starz/Anchor Bay, 1978.
———. *Night of the Living Dead*. Elite Entertainment, 1968.
Shea, Katt, dir. *The Rage: Carrie 2*. Red Bank Films, 1999.
Sole, Alfred, dir. *Alice, Sweet Alice*. Henstooth Video, 1976.
Thompson, J. Lee, dir. *Happy Birthday to Me*. Canadian Film Development Corporation, 1981.
Wise, Robert, dir. *Audrey Rose*. MGM, 1977.
Witt, Alexander, dir. *Resident Evil: Apocalypse*. Sony Pictures, 2004.
Zarchi, Meir, dir. *I Spit on Your Grave*. Cinemagic Pictures, 1978.

CHAPTER 5

FINAL EXAMS AND GREEK TRAGEDIES:
COLLEGES AND UNIVERSITIES IN
AMERICAN HORROR FILMS OF THE
1970S AND 1980S

The Vietnam War was at its apex in the summer of 1966, when, on August 1, trained ex-Marine sharpshooter Charles Whitman stood atop the tower of the University of Texas at Austin and shot 16 people dead and wounded another 31 before being dispatched by two Austin police officers. This event and a series of suicide jumpers forced the closure of the UT Austin Tower and made it a powerful symbol of violence on American college campuses.[1]

The 1970s opened with a high-profile act of violence against student protesters. The infamous shooting of four students on May 4, 1970, by the Ohio National Guard at Kent State brought images of violence on college campuses into the national consciousness again. The onslaught on student protests brought on by the Cambodian incursion and subsequent shootings at Kent State brought student demonstrations to more than a third of all US college and university campuses.[2]

In 1974, young women began disappearing from college campuses in Washington and Oregon. By the time Ted Bundy was convicted of 3 murders in 1979, it was likely that he had also committed another 47. Before he was executed for his crimes in 1989, his story had been told in countless articles, five books, and a made-for-television movie.

In the 1970s and 1980s, horror filmmakers frequently set their films in educational institutions: high schools, summer camps, and, of course, colleges and universities. While the Columbine shooting in 1999 essentially ended the subgenre of horror films set in high schools, the high-profile acts of violence taking place on college campuses in the 1960s and 1970s did more to inspire bloody, violent films than quash them.

This chapter examines the depictions of violence in college and university horror films of the 1970s and 1980s, breaking them into three fundamental categories. First, there were several films such as *Sisters of Death* (1977) and *Waxwork* (1988) that used colleges as merely backdrop sets, convenient locations to find a congregation of young victims for a monster or killer. There was also a set of films in which university life was fully integrated into the movies; among these films were *Splatter University* (1984), *Final Exam* (1981), *The Dorm That Dripped Blood* (1982), and *Satan's School for Girls* (1973). Finally, the largest set of college horror films consisted of films in which fraternities and, especially, sororities figured prominently (e.g., *Black Christmas* [1974], the *Sorority House Massacre* series [1986 and 1990], *The House on Sorority Row* [1983], and *Sorority Babes in the Slimeball Bowl-O-Rama* [1988]).

Horror and the College Student

The 1981 horror *Final Exam* made direct reference, both visually and in dialogue, to the UT Austin killings. Before administering the final for his course, one professor warns his students not to copy each other's answers: "I get enough wrong answers without having to deal with the duplication." The professor also refers to his grading assistants as "snipers in the tower" set there to "take care of cheaters." One of the students compares the professor to Charles Whitman, "anxious to bag a few students." Mere moments later, the test is interrupted by a group of gunmen jumping out of a van and gunning down students in the quad. The scene is really uncomfortable—far more unsettling than any of the more intimate murders that would follow. Dark fantasy violence (even of the anonymous and motiveless variety) is easier to handle than more believably real violence. Even though it turns out to be a staged fraternity prank, there is no humor in it. One shaken student shouts, "It's happening! The psychopaths are here." He runs off to telephone emergency services.

Radish, the young man who was so disturbed by the fraternity prank, becomes obsessed with random killings, and he turns to the bottle for comfort. "People are killed every day for no reason," he muses. In a sly anti-Reagan joke, he talks about how serial killers get up, go to work, go about their day, and even (apparently) vote. After warning all the people he cares about to lock their dorm room doors, he winds up being the victim of a serial killer. One of his friends finds the body and thinks it is another prank: "I want you to move," she begs. "C'mon, smile!" Slowly, she realizes this is not a joke and her friend is actually dead. This is not amusing slapstick violence. It is not grandiose action violence. It is gritty, bloody violence with real emotional effects. In *Final Exam*, we never discover the killer's identity or motivation—his killings lack even the semblance of justification or explanation, leaving the audience with no easy answers regarding humanity's relationship to violence. While the film may have its fundamental flaws, the experiences of Radish do an excellent job establishing the "random killer" leitmotif.

In *Girls School Screamers* (1986), an elderly gentleman dies and leaves his estate to the nearby Catholic girls' college. The head nun gives the best and brightest girls an opportunity to travel to the estate and catalog its contents for auction. The girls decide to play a game of manhunt in the old house. Jackie, one of the girls invited to the manor, hides under a desk in a bedroom and discovers an old journal. It is the diary of a girl named Jennifer who was a junior at Trinity 30 years before when her parents died in a plane crash. She was invited to stay at the estate by its owner, her Uncle Tyler. Her uncle began to make romantic overtures, which she was conflicted about until he became insistent. We later discover that when she refused his advances he murdered her by pushing her down a flight of stairs. In a rare instance of historical research being depicted on film, Jackie's boyfriend digs through a stack of old newspapers at his father's office and finds an article describing Jennifer's death. In the newspaper is a photograph of the murdered young lady, which bears an eerie likeness to Jackie. Upon arriving at the manor, he discovers that Jennifer's spirit has taken possession of Jackie and is seeking to avenge her death.

The overarching theme of all these films is the inability of violence to stay buried in the past. Memories of violence constantly invade the present. In horror films, past trauma is personified in the form of a killer. That killer revisits the horrors of the past upon people in the present. Often, the aim is revenge upon those people responsible for historical violence, but sometimes the emptiness of the cycle is highlighted by bloody retribution exacted randomly.

The Last Refuge of the Mad Scientist

The decades of iterations of Drs. Frankenstein, Van Helsing, and Jekyll had given way to a new era of horror film. The mad scientist, especially the one operating independently of institutions of higher education, was an extremely endangered creature. Even in horror films of the 1970s and 1980s set in institutions of higher education, the character of the intellectual had changed considerably. Underlying the mad scientist narratives of early twentieth-century horror films was the idea that the institutionalization of the scientist in the university system would lead to corralling of aberrant research agendas. In a certain sense, some horror films in the 1970s and 1980s seemed to be trying to answer the question of what would happen to a mad scientist who had become a college professor.

At times, the "madness" of the university scientist is manifested in teaching methods that demonstrate mental instability. In the 1989 horror film *After Midnight*, a professor who teaches a course in the psychology of fear takes to faking his own suicide in front of the class and holding guns to students' heads in order to create abject terror in their minds. He states his professional opinion that fear cannot be found in a textbook and that to truly understand fear one must experience fear. *After Midnight* certainly belongs to the category of films in which the college serves as a backdrop. The film itself is a framed story set in this psychology of fear class, but most of the film comprised a series of vignettes unrelated to the school told by the students in the class in order to elicit fear in their classmates. Still, the film does provide a picture of what might happen to a mad scientist who had been co-opted into working in the university system.

At other times, it is the mad professor's research agenda that serves as the horrific backdrop of the story. In *Nightwish* (1988), a research professor is heavily involved in a research project based on the old idea that it is impossible for someone to die in his or her own dream—but if you *did* die in your dreamworld, then you would die in the real world as well. Thus, the scientist is trying to create a dream in which the dreamer dies. Of course, his research poses a danger to himself and others. Some of his research assistants have died in the past as a result of his research, and the film uses this research project as a way to explore the anxieties of graduate students.

Examples of horror films in the 1970s and 1980s that depict academic research scientists as a threat, though, are very few. Moreover, such examples as do exist are frequently balanced by film portrayals in which scientists at least try to use their resources as academicians to tackle real-world problems. Take, as an example, Carpenter's *Prince of Darkness* (1987). The film is something of an anomaly among higher education horror films—having a supernatural threat. The alignment of sun and moon is causing strange behavior in people, who, for instance, stand unmoving in fire ant mounds, staring at the sun. The film contains zombie-like folks eating maggots and people nailing pigeons to crosses. One of the odd folks, played by Alice Cooper, even kills a poor lab assistant with the rusty post of a bicycle. The madness of these people presages the arrival of the Antichrist.

At first glance, this is a film about scientists learning to think like men of faith, taking a leap of faith, and throwing away the trappings of their academic thinking. This seems to be the crux of the matter when the film asserts that the ancient monks sealed away the evil until scientists were capable of proving the truth in what Christ was saying. One of the graduate students says that "faith is a hard thing to come by these days."[3]

In this way, *Prince of Darkness* is, at its core, about the inadequacy of the higher education system to tackle important issues. If the scientist fails to develop a successful plan for addressing the threat, faith, too, in this film feels powerless. When science and faith both fail, solving important problems becomes a matter of brute force—in the case of this film bludgeoning people with two-by-fours. Higher education is depicted as intelligent, but not wise, asking questions whose answers are irrelevant to aid in the immediate problems. Religion is depicted as wise, but not intelligent, understanding the important questions that need answering but being unable to answer them. In any event, the tensions represented by scientific inquiry in this film were much different from those of previous decades. At times, horror films of the 1980s contained scientists who were fundamentally good people, like those working for the Helping Hands program training monkeys to assist the handicapped in Romero's *Monkey Shines* (1988)—even if the results of that program, by pure cinematic happenstance, placed vulnerable people at risk.

High School II: The College Years, College as Horrific Sequel to High School

When it came to creating sequels of horror films that took place in high school, the common production choice was to set the second film at a college. While *976-EVIL* was the epitome of the bullied high school student seeking revenge on his tormenters, *976-EVIL 2* (1991) did little to upset the motifs established by the original. Typically, college and university horror films have their own structure and themes, however *976-EVIL 2* reuses many high school film devices. Narrative decisions, like casting the college dean as a suspicious character (as many of the high school films did with principals) and focusing heavily on adult mistrust of youth, contributed to making the community college setting of the film feel more like a high school.

In the same way, there was little discernible difference between Tromaville High in *Class of Nuke 'Em High* and Tromaville Institute of Technology (T.I.T.) in *Class of Nuke 'Em High 2: Subhumanoid Meltdown* (1991). Some of this sequel does make clever commentary on college education, insinuating that college provides "liberty and charge cards for all" and that attending college frees people from work. For the most part, however, the sequel is set in a college not because of any particular narrative considerations that lend themselves to that setting but because, seemingly, the next logical step after making a high school film is making a college film. Even a film franchise like *Teen Wolf* opted to ditch the high school setting in *Teen Wolf Too* for a college backdrop without any compelling rationale for doing so.

For the most part, college and university films were very different in theme and tone than their high school counterparts. Certainly, there were films that used the themes common to high school horror films and placed them in a college setting. *The Dorm That Dripped Blood* (1982), for instance, deals with closure and takes place immediately before the semester break. The students are having a dorm party on the last night before they tear down the dormitory and convert another building into apartments for student housing. A group of students has agreed to stay behind to clean, clear, and board up the building. The closing of the dorm and the proximity to the semester break serves several functions. First, it reduces the number of students present—leaving fewer behind to find help, notify authority, or protect each other. Second, it seems to be playing on end-of-semester final exam anxieties. Third, it is easy to explain the mysterious disappearances once the students start dying: "Oh, her parents must have come to get her." Moreover, the closing of the dorm represents an end to a certain aspect of student life. Here, the bulldozing of the student residence seems to mirror the end of a certain portion of their lives (or the final end, if the killer gets his way). End-of-an-era tales and finding emotional closure are two anxieties highly typical of high school horror films, while the college and university horror films tended to deal with anxieties surrounding social class and the development of meaningful personal and professional connections.

BROTHERS AND SISTERS IN VIOLENCE

By far the largest subset of horror films set in colleges and universities focuses on fraternities and sororities. Certainly, fraternities and sororities are prominent institutions on many college campuses, but they form the geographical center of horror film after horror film. There are several reasons college Greek systems receive a high level of emphasis in horror film. Most slasher films follow a similar narrative pattern. A group of young people are brought together for an important event; a killer with nebulous motives is introduced into the situation; the young folks struggle against the killer but are murdered one by one; a solitary, usually female character overcomes the killer and is able to survive. The sorority or fraternity house, as a gathering place with limited supervision or interference by adult authority, provides a logical space for this narrative type. By portraying fraternities and sororities as institutions that provide mechanisms through which upper and upper middle class college students could build business and personal connections designed to maintain their social class status, horror films could use the setting not only as a gathering place for young people but specifically for privileged young people. As such, the selection of the fraternity or sorority as setting gave means by which horror film directors could use their films to craft arguments about the perpetuation of social class. Relatedly, fraternities and sororities are not open interpersonal spaces; one must be invited to join the group—often through a process involving real or simulated emotional or physical violence. As a result, this choice of setting provided the makers of scary movies with the opportunity to explore common school anxieties, such as social rejection, in a social setting with distinct violent undertones.

Another reason so many horror films are set in fraternities and sororities is the importance of the film *Black Christmas* in the development of slasher films as a subgenre of horror.

Predating Carpenter's *Halloween*, the 1974 movie *Black Christmas* was heavily instrumental in developing the film grammar of slasher movies. The film is set during the Christmas season and opens with the Christmas carol "Silent Night" playing. A series of shots show the Pi Kappa Sigma sorority house decorated for Christmas. Inside, the holiday scene is jarringly broken up when the phone rings with an obscene call from a man who has apparently called the house before. The young women in the house who have dealt with this harassment before call the man the "moaner." One girl, clearly distressed by the latest call, loses her patience and calls the "moaner" a "fucking creep." The moaner's response is simple: "I'm going to kill you." One by one, the girls are brutally murdered, one being suffocated with dry cleaner's plastic and another stabbed by the horn of a crystal unicorn. These killings represent the quintessence of the random act of violence. The killer's motivations, beyond a reaction to the emotional response of the girl on the telephone, are never explained in the film. The "madman on a killing spree" trope would become a central one to the slasher genre, and *Black Christmas* was one of the first modern horror movies to use it. Other slasher films, having borrowed heavily from the narrative structure of this film, also frequently borrow its setting.[4]

While the killings in *Black Christmas* were portrayed as lacking in true motivation (or, at least, a disproportionate response to a highly justified slight), there is little randomness behind the murders in the 1986 film, *Sorority House Massacre*. A young lady with a recent history of night terrors, seemingly exacerbated by being in her new sorority house, is trying to decide whether she wishes to formally join Phi Omega Phi. In a party over the special weekend, the girls and few party-crashing boys decide to tell scary stories by the fire. One of the boys, in a moment of very poor judgment, tells a story about a boy who killed his family with a pickaxe, the last family to live in the house before the sorority purchased the property. In a formulaic trope stolen wholesale from Carpenter's *Halloween*, the boy (who has since grown into a man) escapes from his mental institution and returns to the last house he knew before he was locked away in an attempt to finish the job by killing his last living sister—the sorority's newest pledge.

In adding the sorority element to the narrative, however, the film makes serious claims about the social function of violence. In particular, it deals with how a group of young ladies become a sisterhood. The other girls being hunted by the psychopath do not understand the killer's motivations. "We're not his sisters," they offer as a reason for being exempted from his rampage. Before each murder, the young man calls each of the sorority members by the name of one of his dead sisters. In this film, the girls metaphorically become sisters because of trauma. These murders represent a perversion of the sorority initiation. The killer brings the girls together as members of his psychotically imagined family, and he provides the trial that forges that sisterhood.

College and university horror films exhibit a preoccupation with the violence of sorority initiation rituals. This provides an interesting way for filmmakers to explore the social function of violence. On the one hand, these films depict violent initiation ceremonies, frequently taking the form of an initiation prank gone wrong and the ensuing revenge. This allows filmmakers to examine the dual function of violence. In the other hand, the violent ritual serves the function of uniting people. By going through the violent rite of passage, people are accepted into the group. The violence serves to foster group unity. When this rite fails and unity is not achieved, however, the memory of that violence becomes an event that serves to separate and exclude people. When a deranged killer is thrown into (or created by) the scenario, the dual nature of violence is reflected. Initially, the killer's violence serves to unify the group against a common threat, but as the numbers of surviving group members dwindle, the stress of the violence serves to separate people—who, by and large, make the poor choice to split up and lose that group unity. The fraternity/sorority initiation ritual provides the storyteller with a rich tableau for demonstrating the complexities of the effects of violence on interpersonal dynamics.

In the case of *Sorority House Massacre*, even the girls' coursework and school environment are spaces heavily steeped in brutal violence. This film openly discusses issues of campus violence. One girl wears a whistle around her neck, at the insistence of her mother, after a vicious rape took place on campus the month before. Even without the escaped mental patient stalking people, this college campus is not a paragon of safety for the girls. Inside one of the classes, a student discusses an experiment that showed the psychic connection between cats. The reactions of a mother cat, separated from her children, were observed as the kittens were murdered. Emotional reactions registered at the moment of her babies' deaths. This study mirrors the plot of the film, in which a vicious murderer remains psychically connected to the only sister who survived the murderous rampage in which he killed the rest of his family. However, it is important to note that the film creates the image of the university as a space wherein one grapples with the issues surrounding the psychology of violence. Certainly, *Sorority House Massacre* is one of the more literate of the films in this sample. It is a film in which characters have conversations about dream symbolism, muse over the psychology of violence in man, and acknowledge the knife as "phallic symbol"—all of which make the filmmakers seem keenly aware of the type of text they are crafting.

In *Sorority House Massacre*, the arrival of the killer serves the function of a violent sorority initiation. *Terror Train* (1979) features a fraternity/sorority initiation more typical of this type of horror film, one in which the initiation goes horribly wrong. The film begins at a fraternity/sorority winter bonfire. The new recruit, Kenny Hampson, is in the midst of his fraternity initiation. "You're going to be wearing that beanie all year if you don't get laid tonight," one of his would-be brothers says. This challenge sets the stage for a horrific episode of sexual humiliation (rather akin to the humiliation scenes in *Slaughter High* discussed in the previous chapter). One of the fraternity brothers has stolen a corpse from the medical school and placed it in a bed. Kenny walks in, and a girl hides behind the headboard coaxing him into the bed. Kenny has a breakdown when he discovers the dead body and ends up in a mental ward, and thankfully the film cuts away from the whole unpleasant scene.

The film continues during spring break at a costume party on a train, which is serving as the site of the soon-to-be-graduating students' "last big college party." The costume party is a convenient little quirk of this film—as it helps mask the identity of the killer. The rest of the film takes place on the train and has Kenny stalking and killing those responsible for the initiation prank gone wrong, dismembering their bodies and posing them in grotesque ways, acts somewhat akin to the way that Kenny's tormentors had treated the corpse they had stolen. The only one who expresses real remorse for what has happened is the one who survives—but, again, only because she is willing to commit yet another act of violence. In this film, as in nearly all horror movies, there is no isolated act of violence; violence is part of a cycle. Any violent act serves simultaneously as an echo of earlier violence and as the inception point for further violence.

Sisters of Death begins with another failed initiation ceremony. In the rite, two girls on their knees, pledging with a sorority, a "secret society of sisters," both proclaim that they "wish to be bound" to the group and begin the final test: the test of courage. They play an augmented game of Russian roulette. One of the sisters puts a pistol to the girl's head and pulls the trigger, trusting that the other sister has placed a blank in the chamber. The first girl survives and receives her sorority pendant. The second takes a bullet to the head—someone switched the blank with live ammunition.

Seven years later, each of the girls in the sorority receives an invitation to a reunion (a trope also used in several of the previously discussed high school films, including *The Redeemer* and *Slaughter High*). Most of the girls have clearly had a difficult time following their would-be sister's death. One has taken to prostitution and has a severe alcohol problem. Another has chosen to live on a hippie commune. A third hitchhikes around the American Southwest. The girls reconvene at the place specified on the invitation, and a strange car takes them to a manor in the middle of nowhere with a killer willing to use deadly means to determine which girl switched the bullet for the blank.

The film provides no easy answers for questions about violence. We find before the end of the film that Elizabeth, the girl who died, had had a hard childhood. The audience is led at one point to the highly plausible belief that Liz staged her own suicide to escape from the overbearing aspirations that her father had for her—pushing her into the life of a classical musician. Time and time again in these films, the violent actions of the past refuse to stay buried, and, again, this is another horror film that explores the emotional consequences of violence. The message of these films is clear: the ripple effect of violence is inescapable.

In *Final Exam*, a fraternity pledge is required to break into a professor's office and steal his final exam as the next step in his initiation. To the members of the fraternity it seems like a fitting trial; after all, "Does he want his brothers to have to study?" They believe in "studying the old-fashioned way: stolen tests." The initiation trials continue after the test is stolen. His brothers ominously tell him that he may just make it into the fraternity if he "make[s] it through the night." The fraternity members lash him almost naked to a tree, pour ice down his underwear, and spray him with a fire extinguisher. The campus police see him there and refuse to untie him, instead pouring alcohol into his underpants, giving him a shot "on the rocks." He never makes it into the fraternity—killed by the implement a homicidal maniac uses to unbind him. None of the fraternity members who left the young man tied to the tree survive the night.

Sorority Babes in the Slimeball Bowl-O-Rama, for all its silliness, still does not deviate too drastically from the attitudes toward hazing and the function of violence in the creation of group cohesion of the other fraternity/sorority horror films. This movie begins with the girls wearing black robes and preening themselves for their sorority initiation ceremony—which initially consists of a near-naked paddling.[5] After the first round of spankings, one of the girls seeks to quit the initiation, saying, "I'm not putting up with any more torture."

The sorority girls concoct a plan in which in order to complete the initiation the girls must break into a local mall, enter the bowling alley, steal a large bowling trophy, and make it out safely. There is seemingly little danger in this prank, as the father of one of the girls owns the shopping mall. Again, we see that the sorority girls are depicted as girls of means, and the horror of the situation places them in real trials for the first time in their lives. While less obvious, and vastly less artistically satisfying than Romero's *Dawn of the Dead* (in which zombiism stood as a relatively effective symbolism for the mindlessness of consumer culture), this film seems to be making a comment on the consumer culture of the 1980s—there is evil lurking in the mall.

Stealing the trophy unleashes the imp that had been trapped inside. From this point on, the film's tongue-in-cheek approach becomes even more pronounced. The demon is a Muppet-ish wisecracking imp with strong African American linguistic overtones who grants wishes. The imp transforms the girls, one by one, into demons who kill each other. In the end, the imp's games are an inversion of the sorority initiation. The girls' solidarity is compromised as one girl after another is turned against the group. It is "a nasty lesson, for a nasty [set of] girl[s]," the imp opines.

It is, however, a lesson that one group of young men and women after another would learn during their own fraternity and sorority hell weeks. In *Satan's School for Girls* (1973), a group of Salem Academy's select young ladies even "sacrifice their mortal souls, willingly" to get into an unholy sorority formed by the devil himself. In *The Initiation of Sarah* (1978), a film that functions much like a *Carrie* clone set in a sorority, Sarah's especially violent initiation ritual awakens some latent magical powers within her that she uses to hurt or kill her tormenters. In *Hell Night* (1989), new fraternity and sorority recruits are made to spend the night in a house that had been the site of a murder only to be terrorized, first by taunting members of the fraternity, then by the evil they awaken in the house. *Girls Nite Out* (1982) has an initiation that involves a scavenger hunt in which clues are announced over campus radio; a killer waits at the location of the next scavenger hunt item and murders its finder. In *Night of the Creeps* (1986), two male pledges steal a corpse, only to have to deal with both an escaped mental patient *and* brain-sucking invaders from another planet. Instead of a haunted house, the sorority pledge in *One Dark Night* (1982) must spend the night in a mausoleum where a famed parapsychologist was recently laid to rest in a vault. Instead of just leaving the pledge to sleep in the mausoleum on her own, the other girls break in to torment her, and the parapsychologist uses telekinesis from beyond the grave to scare (or, yes, kill) the girls. Unsurprisingly, the hazing ritual Delta Rho Chi uses in *The Initiation* (1984) does not go well. A rich young lady, Kelly, is required to do anything the existing members tell her to, no questions asked. The group of new pledges must go to Kelly's father's department store and steal the night watchman's uniform. Again, a mental patient stabs his nurse with a garden implement and escapes, killing the young women locked in the department store one by one. Even in the horror comedy *Vamp* (1986), which plays like an exceptionally crass *Teen Wolf*, a hazing ritual involving nooses hung around the young fraternity pledges' necks malfunctions, and the two young men who laugh at the failure are sent to find a stripper for the fraternity party as their alternate initiation. They wander into a vampire-infested strip club.

Taken together as dozens of horrific little puzzle pieces, I think, these films create a picture of an almost uniform attitude toward the use of violence in hazing and initiation rituals. Violence can be used to create group solidarity, but it also functions as a means of isolating and scarring individual members of the group. In so doing, it creates monsters whose memories of violent trauma cause them to use violent means to undermine group unity and create a sense of terrifying solitude in their victims.

By taking groups of privileged young ladies (and to a lesser extent men) and removing their social status by turning them all into the victims of heinous acts of violence, often precipitated by secrecy and solidarity surrounding hazing rituals and pranks that went too far, these films use violence as a great equalizer—allowing young people to form blood bonds, while graphically depicting the horrible consequences resulting when the simulated violence used to create them crosses into reality.

These films represent a type of education for these sorority girls. They are born, as one of the members of *The House on Sorority Row*'s (1983) Pi Phi says, with a "silver spoon in their nose." These battles with psychotic killers represent a trial for those whose lives have been up until now superficial and untested. The higher education these girls receive is, to run the risk of using a cliché, from the school of hard knocks (but I only use it because it sounds nicer than the school of deep stabbings).

Even after the bonds of sisterhood have been formed, group solidarity is frequently presented as planting the seeds of future violence. In *The House on Sorority Row*, the girls are planning a graduation party at the sorority house. A group of seniors spend the night drinking and plotting: "I'd like to thank you for helping me become what I am today: wasted!" The plan for an elaborate graduation party is opposed by the extraordinarily strict (and altogether creepy) house mother, Mrs. Slater, whose aghast response, "How could you even think of having a drunken spree in my house?" does little to dissuade the girls from their covert plot. In fact, the desire to get even with the "house mother to end all house mothers" takes the form of a "good, old-fashioned sorority prank." One girl, Katie, is uncomfortable and does not want to go along with the plan—at this moment it becomes obvious who the sole surviving female of the film will be.

The prank the young women devise is sick and depraved. The girls take Mrs. Slater's cane and place it on a flotation device in the middle of a murky, slimy, long out-of-commission pool, and force her to dive into the pool to retrieve it. When she refuses, one of the girls pulls a gun on her—which accidentally goes off. Mrs. Slater dies, and instead of calling the proper authorities, the girls sink the body to the bottom of the pool and proceed with their party plans.

During the party, the electricity goes out, and one of the sisters is sent to the basement to check the fuse. She is bludgeoned to death by the old woman's cane. The other girls sense their own peril: "For God's sake, we're in this together." As sisters, they share the blame for the violence—and the consequences of that violence. This is an ethical distinction that differentiates these films from their high school counterparts. In these films, solidarity is a cause of violence—not a means of combating it. Culpability is shared among the members of the sisterhood. Each of the girls' bodies is, one after the other, submerged in the pool. Once again, we see that in horror movies, one cannot keep the violent acts one has committed submerged in the past—like cadavers of sorority sisters in a pool, they will always resurface.

One of the defining characteristics distinguishing college and university horror films from the rest of the genre is the tension between group solidarity and individualism. On the one hand, group cohesion is necessary for survival. In horror films, generally, there is safety in numbers. Staying with a group serves as some protection against the threats of violence. In college and university films, especially those in the sorority/fraternity group, on the other hand, loyalty to the group is frequently the source of that violence, especially in the forms of hazing, mean-spirited pranks, and exclusionary practices. Individualism in horror films tends to come with inherent danger. The act of splitting up is an ominous sign (although this is often undermined by the iconic sole surviving female whose survival depends upon her individual qualities). In college films, group solidarity must be presented as implicitly dangerous, even as the dictates of the genre are that groups of young people must band together to survive. Using fraternities and sororities in horror films, then, adds another layer of tension—it is the source of the protection from violence that poses the threat. Frequently, the young woman who breaks the cohesion of the group, the one who speaks out against the group's actions, the one who expresses remorse for the violent and exclusionary practices, the pledge who has not been fully integrated, is the woman who survives and ends (often sadly temporarily) the cycle of violence.

Bibliography

Adamek, Raymond J., and Jerry M. Lewis. "Social Control Violence and Radicalization: The Kent State Case." *Social Forces* 51, no. 3 (March 1973): 342–347.

Gould, Lewis L. "Review: *A Sniper in the Tower.*" *Journal of American History* 84, no. 3 (December 1997): 1150.

Laverne, Gary M. *A Sniper in the Tower: The Charles Whitmore Murders.* Denton: University of North Texas Press, 1997.

Filmography

Carpenter, John, dir. *Prince of Darkness.* Universal Pictures, 1987.
Clark, Bob, dir. *Black Christmas.* Film Funding, 1974.
Cook, Bruce, dir. *Nightwish.* Vidmark Entertainment, 1988.
Day, Robert, dir. *The Initiation of Sarah.* MGM, 1978.
DeCoteau, David, dir. *Sorority Babes in the Slimeball Bowl-O-Rama.* Titan Productions, 1988.
Dekker, Fred, writer/dir. *Night of the Creeps.* Tristar Pictures, 1986.
De Simone, Tom, dir. *Hell Night.* BLT Productions, 1989.
Deubel, Robert, dir. *Girls Nite Out.* Aries International, 1982.
Finegan, John P., dir. *Girls School Screamers.* Troma Films, 1986.
Frank, Carol, dir. *Sorority House Massacre.* Concorde Pictures, 1986.
Haines, Richard W., dir. *Splatter University.* Vestron Video, 1984.
Huston, Jimmy, dir. *Final Exam.* Embassy Pictures, 1981.
Louzil, Eric, and Donald G. Jackson, dirs. *Class of Nuke 'Em High 2: Subhumanoid Meltdown.* Troma Pictures, 1991.
Mazzuca, Joseph, dir. *Sisters of Death.* VCI Video, 1977.
McLoughlin, Thomas, dir. *One Dark Night.* Liberty International, 1982.
Obrow, Jeffrey, and Stephen Carpenter, dirs. *The Dorm That Dripped Blood.* Wescom Productions, 1982.
Rich, David Lowell, dir. *Satan's School for Girls.* 20th Century Fox, 1973.
Romero, George, dir. *Monkey Shines.* Orion Pictures, 1988.
Rosman, Mark, dir. *The House on Sorority Row.* VAE Productions, 1983.
Spottiswoode, Roger, dir. *Terror Train.* 20th Century Fox, 1979.
Stewart, Larry, dir. *The Initiation,* Georgian Bay Productions, 1984.
Wenk, Richard, dir. *Vamp.* New World Pictures, 1986.
Wheat, Ken, and Jim Wheat, dirs. *After Midnight.* United Artists, 1989.
Wynorski, Jim, dir. *976-EVIL 2.* Cinetel Films, 1991.
———. *Sorority House Massacre II.* Concorde Pictures, 1990.

CHAPTER 6

SURVIVAL TRAINING: SUMMER CAMP AS EDUCATIONAL INSTITUTION IN SLASHER FILMS OF THE 1980S

In Nathaniel Hawthorne's "Young Goodman Brown," the American wilderness is depicted as a dangerous, menacing space with the potential of leading even the most faithful into the service of the devil:

> The whole forest was peopled with frightful sounds; the creaking of the trees, the howling of wild beasts, and the yell of Indians; while, sometimes the wind tolled like a distant church-bell, and sometimes gave a broad roar around the traveller, as if all Nature were laughing him to scorn.[1]

A little more than a century later, Frank Capra made a film in which an idealistic young politician heads to Washington, DC, to mount a seemingly impossible battle against corrupt politicians who sought to build a dam at the site promised for a national boys' camp. *Mr. Smith Goes to Washington* (1939) presents the summer camp as an institution that epitomizes the American experience. Sometime over the course of the century, a drastic shift in American attitudes toward wild areas had occurred.

After another 40 years, a hockey-masked, machete-wielding mass murderer stalking abandoned summer camps in search of his next victim became an icon of American horror film. The *Friday the 13th* saga, now in its thirteenth installment, adopted a darker view of the American wilderness much more akin to that of Hawthorne than Capra. Seeking to capitalize on the success of *Friday the 13th* (1980), a host of horror films borrowed the summer camp setting. Another major horror film series, *Sleepaway Camp* (1983–2008), prominently featured organized camps as its primary setting. Several more major films in the genre, including *The Burning* (1981), *Cheerleader Camp* (1988), and *Madman* (1982) were also set in camps. Even more films, such as *Don't Go in the Woods* (1981), *Campsite Massacre* (1983), and *The Forest* (1982) were set in other sparsely settled, wooded areas.

In such a saturated subgenre, it is little wonder Marcus Nispel, director of *Friday the 13th* (2009), would be asked why a remake of the original film would be needed. His answer, however, indicated a deep understanding of the nature of his work. Nispel responded that he was not remaking *Friday the 13th*, he was retelling "Hansel and Gretel," a story in which "kids off the beaten path get into trouble."[2] Nispel acknowledges that his film adopts an orientation toward the wilderness more akin to early nineteenth-century dark literature for children than to turn-of-the-twentieth-century summer camp reformers. In virtually all the summer camp slasher films, homicidal maniacs viciously murdered teenagers who engaged in morally objectionable behavior, like premarital sex and substance abuse. Only the paragons of moral purity survived. In this sense, the pedagogical intent of summer camp slashers ironically dovetailed with those of the founders of the earliest summer camps: lauding the influence of wilderness survival training on moral development. This chapter seeks to reconcile the image of summer camps as educational institutions as they were initially conceived with their depiction in slasher horror films of the 1980s.

The Closing of the Frontier, the Opening of the Camp

The rapid urbanization of the United States in the latter half of the nineteenth century drastically changed American attitudes toward the wild spaces of the country. The frontier spirit spurring westward expansion in the early nineteenth century implied a desire to see the wilderness tamed: settled, plowed, and cultivated. In 1893 Frederick Jackson Turner's *The Significance of the Frontier in American History* put forth the thesis that the closing of the frontier to further settlement would create a situation in which ever-increasing populations of impoverished masses would be unable to relocate from city slums. By this time, however, the view of nature as dangerous and threatening was already well on its way to being supplanted by a softer, more romantic notion.

The publication of Henry David Thoreau's *Walden* in 1854 had been a watershed moment in the history of the transcendental movement and incited Americans to adopt an idyllic view of nature. The effects of this movement on the way that (especially middle- and upper-class) Americans spent their ever-increasing leisure time were significant.[3] Indeed, the idea that contemplating nature could "refurbish souls" and "lift spirits" gave rise to a host of new recreational activities, including spending time at summer resort hotels, urban parks, newly formed national parks, health spas, and, of course, camps.[4] Transcendentalism had, in the last half of the nineteenth century, inspired the idea of camping as vacation.[5]

Because of the direct correspondence between the closing of the American frontier and the opening of American summer camps, many of the sentiments that gave rise to the idea of the summer camp were decidedly anti-Modernist in tone.[6] Camps were nostalgic institutions, formed under the auspices of recreating a lost American past.[7] In an era in which the effects of a diminishing frontier were being contemplated, summer camps were forming as simulations of that disappearing frontier.

It is important to note, however, that summer camps were not, in themselves, wild places; instead, they represented a controlled nature. Only rarely did summer camp leaders expect their charges to survive in the wilderness. Hunting was not a common activity, and even sleeping outside of the comfort of a cabin or large tent was rare.[8] Educational summer camping has from its inception been a form of playacting. Children and adolescents from the city are asked to voluntarily give up modern comforts and travel to a re-creation of the frontier.[9] As a result, early summer camps manufactured a version of the wilderness that would meet the expectations of the campers and, more importantly, their parents.[10] Parents sought camps that would provide their children with nostalgia for an era they had never experienced—or, perhaps, that had never really existed. The backbreaking labor, dangers of hunger and disease, and clashes with the native inhabitants experienced on the frontier were romantically translated into fishing, cooking on an open fire, and crafting.

Summer camps developed as an attempt to take young people away from the pernicious influences of city life during their summer vacations. In the closing years of the nineteenth century, child labor laws in conjunction with mandatory schooling laws had created the summer vacation. As the United States became increasingly urban, the number of children involved in agricultural labor from the home was also in decline. As a result, children were left with a block of free time in the summer. Many parents, afraid of the moral dangers to their children presented by spending long periods of time in the anonymity of city life, sought a rural alternative. The summer camp developed in response to a perceived gap in the moral education of youth.[11]

While a large part of the raison d'être of the summer camp may have been for city youth to pass their summer leisure hours in morally sound recreation in the wilderness, the closing of the frontier represents only one piece of that puzzle. Equally important to the formation of the summer camp were the ideas of psychologist and educator G. Stanley Hall. Modern life represented not only a moral danger but also a danger to manhood itself. According to Hall, civilization had an effeminizing influence on the male population, the end result of which would be the degeneration of the human race. The problem, as outlined by Hall, was even more acute for whites than for other races, as their higher level of civilization made them even more vulnerable to the effeminizing effect of modernity. Using Hall's line of reasoning, leaving the city for a period of time each year throughout childhood to engage in physical activities close to nature could stave off the negative effects of a sessile adulthood in the city.[12]

Proponents of summer camping were hardly shy about justifying their institutions by linking them to Hall's recapitulation theory. Henry Wellington Wack, in his report on summer camping for *Red Book* magazine, quoted liberally from Edward Carpenter's *Civilization: Its Cause and Cure*, borrowing his hypothesis that civilization was a disease that needed a cure, and that a part of that cure could be found in the summer camp.[13] Wack lamented the decline of the human race that was resulting from increased medical treatments allowing people with weak immune systems to survive into adulthood and procreate. He even alluded to the "race degeneracy" stemming from such developments in the field of medicine.[14] Along these very lines, Wack described how camps granted youngsters the opportunity to return to a premodern lifestyle by giving them a chance to playact at being members of a more primitive people: "Said one boy, 'Never mind the moral [of the story]. Tell us more about those cannibals!' Whereupon another chirped ravenously, 'Cage the cannibals! Tell us about ourselves.'"[15] By encouraging mostly middle- and upper-class white children to take up the trappings of Native American life, such as canoeing, archery, and building teepees and totem poles, the proponents of summer camps were directly applying the recapitulation theories of Hall.

In the end, the hypotheses of Hall and Turner were not mutually exclusive with respect to the development of summer camps. Without the presence of an open frontier, the effeminizing effects of modern society were inescapable. The problem of recapitulation, then, was compounded by the loss of wild spaces. Advocates of the summer camp sought to alleviate both problems by providing spaces that mimicked life on the frontier so that young men could rediscover their masculine energy.

Origins of the Summer Camp

The movement to send children to summer camp was spearheaded by the *New York Herald Tribune* in 1877. The idea of removing children from the city for a vacation in the countryside seems to have been the brainchild of Reverend William Parsons. Assigned to a parish in the Lower East Side of New York City, Parsons served an impoverished congregation containing many young people. In 1877, Parsons moved out of the city to serve a new congregation in Sherman, Pennsylvania. Shortly thereafter, he conceived of the idea of bringing some of the children from his previous parish to Sherman to get them out of the city for a few weeks in the summer.

This program was not, strictly speaking, a summer camp program. The children did not move into camping facilities with tents or bunkhouses. Rather, the children were assigned to the homes of local families, and they spent their summers helping the volunteer families with agricultural work. The purpose of the program was not, it seems, to give children a taste of frontier life. Instead, Parsons was motivated by a drive to give underprivileged youth a respite from the city slums for a few weeks.[16]

Welfare agencies, terming the summer camp movement for the poor "fresh air work," deemed selecting, assembling, and sending of youth to the countryside an important part of their organized welfare programs.[17] Prominent magazine publishers established charitable funds whose donations would be used to send lower-class boys to camp. In addition to the aforementioned *Red Book*, *Life* magazine, in 1883, began the Fresh Air Fund. Their October 13, 1887, issue solicited funds from readers: "Three dollars will send a child to the country for a fortnight."[18] A follow-up article the next summer claimed "all the children we have sent to the country have gone to good places, mostly to farms."[19] Ultimately, as more funds became available for the program, the money was used to lease land for the establishment of a more permanent campsite. Other agencies, like the Children's Aid Society of New York, the Association for Improving the Condition of the Poor, and the City Mission Society, also began "fresh air" programs in the 1880s and 1890s. In the early days of the movement, summer camps for needy children were organized and funded in a decentralized way by a variety of charities. While certain organizations, notably the Fresh Air Federation of New York in 1916 and the Children's Welfare Federation in 1921, attempted to bring the disparate organizations together under a common mission, summer camping for the poor remained largely the province of individual charities.

Even as the poorest children in the northeastern United States were being sent out to area farms during the summer, the earliest proper summer camps were aimed at a much different clientele. In the 1880s, most of the summer camps that developed served upper-class Protestant boys.[20] Many of the early summer camps were formed by private boarding schools that saw summer camps as an extension of their mission to the upper class.[21] An example of such a camp was Camp Harvard, formed in the early 1880s by two students from the Cambridge Theological Seminary. One young camper wrote of his experiences at Camp Harvard in the children's literary magazine, *St. Nicholas*. He described the mission of Camp Harvard as "cultivat[ing] good habits" and "build[ing] up bodily strength,"[22] adding that by the end of the summer, "we were all healthily bronzed, and were as hardy as only life in the open air can make boys; and I am sure that camp life enabled us all to do better work at school during the winter."[23]

According to Hall's theories, members of the upper class would more acutely feel the loss of masculine energy. The sedentary nature of upper-class occupations sequestered upper-class males from the types of activities that could have recharged that energy. Certainly, shades of that rhetoric appeared in the *St. Nicholas* article; summer camps provided the exercise, sunlight, and open air that would sustain upper-class boys through their long hours of study in the winter.

Just as spending summers in city slums threatened the moral development of the poor, advocates for summer camps felt that idleness could have calamitous consequences on wealthy adolescents. Camp director Henry G. Gibson described the summer as "a period of moral deterioration with most boys . . . who have heretofore wasted the glorious summer time loafing on the city streets, or as disastrously at summer hotels or amusement places."[24] Wasting time was, in itself, a moral wrong, but idleness coupled with money in the wrong setting could lead to even greater sins. The "rich food, promiscuous companionship, late hours and feverish amusements" of summer resorts were not an appropriate sort of recreation.[25] Early advocates of the summer camp touted the camps' morally transformative ability: "some [boys] can even be turned from evil courses into good ones by graduating from a judiciously selected summer home in the woods."[26] With this in mind, summer camps for wealthy youth often focused their rhetoric on the power of interacting with nature to develop solid moral character.

Much of the early camp rhetoric regarding needy youth was of a much different character. Summer camp charities concentrated on the *physical* health benefits that summer camps offered youth. They touted the positive effects of extra rest on underweight and malnourished youth. "The aims" of welfare camps, in general, were "fresh air" and "increased weight."[27] For some camps, countering the effects of starvation was the measure of a camp's success: "A child goes home as soon as he has regained normal weight and health, and makes room for others."[28]

In any event, the summer camp movement in the last decades of the nineteenth century was an oddly diverse one. On the one hand, exclusive private boarding schools established their own summer camps as extensions of their educational missions, providing wealthy boys with a morally healthy alternative to a summer in the city or at a resort. On the other hand, ever-increasing numbers of impoverished young men were benefiting from charity work that allowed for a summer exodus out of the city slums for a breath of fresh air and regular meals. Nature, in the minds of summer camp advocates, did not discriminate based on social class—it provided physical and moral healing for any young man.

Camping for the Middle Class, Camping for the Urban

The infrastructure for getting the wealthiest and the poorest youth to summer camps developed well ahead of organizations aiming to bring the camp experience to middle-class youth.

The dangers of young men in the slums becoming physically and morally unhealthy and the young men in the elite boarding schools becoming effete drove the movement to cater to children on the extreme opposite ends of the social class spectrum. When summer camping for middle-class young men did began to develop, it did so for largely religious reasons. In 1880, Reverend George W. Hinckley of West Hartford, Connecticut, started the first church-sponsored boys' camp as part of the Muscular Christianity movement. With their emphasis on energetic evangelism and militant masculinity, the physical and moral health benefits alleged by proponents of the summer camp appealed strongly to Muscular Christians. Christian organizations such as the Young Men's Christian Association (YMCA) began to open summer camps of their own, and, by the turn of the twentieth century, such camps began to proliferate.[29] Said Walter M. Wood, superintendent of educational work at YMCA Chicago, summer camps "deliberately planned to educate the boy campers as to how to have a good time in physical, educational, social, and religious ways."[30]

By the early twentieth century, summer camps had broad appeal across the various social classes, but the movement was confined almost exclusively to cities in the Northeast. One million children went to camp in 1920; by 1930 this number had reached two million. In the late 1920s in Brooklyn, 25 percent of all boys and 17 percent of all girls had been to summer camp. In 1931, one thousand of the fifty thousand African American children in New York City attended summer camp. In 1930, more than half of all paying campers lived in the greater New York City area (within a day's journey of New York), but in a survey of one hundred children from the Midwest in the same year, not a single one had attended a summer camp.[31] As a romantic response to the pernicious effects of rapid industrialization, summer camps were highly successful at enlisting an incredibly diverse, yet predominantly urban, clientele. Each summer, New York City would experience a mass exodus of "tenement waifs and hearty young suburbanites, Boy Scouts and tiny cripples, state wards and scions of Park Avenue."[32]

For a long time, young girls were left out of this motley group of summer pilgrims. Anxiety about civilized young men becoming increasingly feminine drove wealthy young men to the simulated wilderness to playact at savagery. The Muscular Christian agenda of developing a more masculine faith was aided by sending young men back to nature for physical and moral training. This type of rhetoric could not be applied to justify sending young ladies back to nature; while using nature retreats to recharge the masculine energy of young boys may have been seen as a noble cause, the creation of more masculine young ladies was not a part of the camping mission. Even as YMCA camps were experiencing a meteoric rise, the YWCA did not begin a similar movement aimed at young women. Advocates of limited camping experiences for girls, such as Dr. Luther Gulick, who founded the Campfire Girls in 1911, were blunt with respect to gender: "We hate manly women and womanly men."[33] In the interwar years, as American culture became increasingly secular (especially in the Northeast where most of the summer camps were located), the ideas of the Muscular Christians and G. Stanley Hall that had propelled the summer camp movement found themselves in decline. All the while, the numbers of female campers gradually increased over the same period so that, by 1930, two-thirds of girls entering Vassar College had attended a summer camp.[34] The Progressive Era eventually created the sort of female campers who would "be a vivacious companion to their husbands and energetic mothers to the next generation of boys."[35] Thus, the camping mission was expanded to include members of the fairer sex in ways that could be justified as gender-appropriate and would remain so until the end of the Second World War.

The Cold War further changed the gender dynamic with respect to summer camps. The promotion of nuclear families, imagined to be a bulwark against the evils of communism, necessitated a reevaluation of the sex-segregated camp. Coeducational camps responded to adult concerns about the heterosexual development of children. Adult leaders increasingly felt that the comingling of males and females was less likely to create "manly women" and "womanly men" and more likely to produced young adults with healthy (hetero)sexual identities. Through the 1950s and into the 1960s, most new summer camps were coeducational.[36]

With females making up an ever-increasing portion of the summer camping population, camping had transcended class, race, *and* gender lines.[37] The *New York Times* reported a noticeable increase in attendance at artistic and cultural events. It attributed this rise to the wealth of parents having a "belated or second honeymoon" because a "son or daughter has gone to camp."[38] Even as large numbers of youngsters were escaping the evils of city life, their parents were able to enjoy all that modern urban attractions had to offer.

By the interwar period, summer camps had become an important part of the educational landscape of the American Northeast. Even so, the summer camp establishment remained incredibly diverse. Four different varieties of summer camp, privately run (often operated by boarding schools), charity run (maintained by organizations like the Children's Aid Society of New York), religiously run (associated with individual churches or dioceses), and youth organization run (such as YMCA and Girl Scout camps), had all become entrenched. As the movement transitioned from adolescence to adulthood, the miscellany of summer camps made developing a unified educational mission difficult. Camps were trying to develop "from a mere escape from city life, . . . aiming at a status beside the school."[39] Camp directors made some overtures toward aligning their missions with the tenets of Deweyan progressivism, placing special emphasis on Dewey's argument for the pedagogical importance of environmental interactions.[40] Even so, trying to distill the mission of the summer camp into a succinct mission statement proved difficult. Ultimately, when what amounted to a camp director's creed was issued at the March 1929 national conference of the Camp Director's Association in Atlantic City, New Jersey, it painted the mission of the summer camp with incredibly broad strokes: "The essential functions of the Camp are education for: Physical Health, Emotional integration, An Understanding of the primitive processes, Enlightened social participation, The acquisition of taste and appreciation, and

Spiritual growth."[41] The educational aims of summer camp directors were both broad and high.[42]

Children's Folklore and Scary Stories

As many children's first experience away from their homes, their parents, their immediate families, and their neighborhoods, summer camps were also often the sites of a child's first experiences of homesickness. Located in spaces that were private, secluded, and intentionally removed from civilization, feelings of loneliness could be all the more acute. At times, summer camps could be emotionally and physically dangerous places. Being sequestered from parental oversight, scenes of child molestation at summer camps were not uncommon. In the summer of 1930, several campers at Lake Cohasset in New York were victims of serial rape and physical assault.[43] While there may have been moral and physical health benefits to being in close proximity to the wilderness, summer camps were also locations extremely vulnerable to predators, both from within and without.

However, being worlds unto themselves, summer camps were also places where vibrant children's folklore could and did develop. While some children's culture is established and passed on inside the family institution, usually through older siblings, with larger numbers of children in close proximity to one another, residential institutions like summer camps are fertile sites for the emergence of expressive culture for children.[44] Gathering around the campfire in the evenings, children and supervising adults engaged in what would become a strong tradition of storytelling. Given the anxieties associated with the environment in which the stories were told, scary campfire tales naturally began to develop.

"Scary stories" are an important, but underexamined, segment of the folk tradition. Folklorists tend to be disinterested in scary stories because they are fabrications; they are usually created by individual storytellers or are unique to specific institutions. Each tale is not, generally, a variation of a tale told in a broader context—and is sometimes considered to be the intellectual property of the individual storyteller who created it (who also has exclusive, if unstated, permission to retell the tale).[45] Horror stories told at camp are also, frequently, an intermediate form of folk narrative; while fiction, the tales are usually presented as though they were true. In order to inspire fear in the mind of the person hearing the tale, the storyteller attempts to convince the listener of the possibility that the tale might actually have happened or could actually happen. As a result, "such narratives are neither 'real' legends nor tales, but narratives deliberately designed to fit the gray area between."[46] Interestingly for the purposes of this study, one scholar noted that the scary campfire tale arouses the "entertaining kind of fear one feels watching John Carpenter's *Halloween*."[47] Campfire tales, like slasher films, derive their capability to terrify from their plausibility.

Stories at children's camps come in three varieties: stories by staff for staff, stories by children for children, and stories by staff for children. The latter variety often takes the form of a scary story or ghost tale, which frequently allow adults to exercise indirect control over the behavior of the campers. By relating narratives in which tragedy befalls a child who did not follow the rules of the camp, the directions of the camp counselor, or the dictates of a moral code, adults at camps sometimes use the scary story form as a cautionary parable.[48]

As extensions of the campfire tale, mock ordeals and legend trips became important parts of the folklore of summer camps. Mock ordeals are interactive tales in which a group of campers and counselors venture out into the woods or surrounding wilderness with the intent of confronting some sort of supernatural being or legend and then returning to the safety of the camp. In the usual format, more experienced members of the group tell newcomers to the camp of a reputedly haunted place. The group travels to that spot and performs a ritual to invoke the supernatural. The group then returns to safety to discuss the uncanny events they perceived.[49]

Hiram Camp outside of Cleveland, for example, occasionally holds a "Majaska Hunt."[50] According to the tale, Majaska was an orphan raised by wild dogs after Hermit Dan murdered his parents in the forest. Upon reaching adulthood, Majaska exacted his revenge, murdering Hermit Dan and becoming cursed to wander the woods as a terrible, violent ogre. In the mock ordeal, a group of campers goes out into the nighttime woods in search of Majaska, calling out his name and trying to track him down. Upon returning to camp, the group discusses any "evidence" that Majaska was near they may have experienced.[51]

Bill Ellis writes, "The Majaska campfire story that proceeds and informs the Hunt is framed as a conscious fantasy . . . more typical of märchen than legends."[52] In effect, scary campfire stories like "Majaska" are closely connected to the dark fairy tales of the early nineteenth century, such as "Hansel and Gretel" and "Little Red Riding Hood," which warned of the dangers of the forest to the young. While the educational function of the summer camp may have been spiritual growth attained by spending time in proximity to nature, the tales that were told in the camps themselves tended toward a pre-transcendentalist mindset. Slasher films set in summer camp seem to be channeling the same types of narrative. One scholar claimed the *Friday the 13th* films "dramatically render adolescent legends wherein the penalty for sex is mutilation by a crazed monster."[53] Ultimately, as cinematic renditions of adolescent legends, summer camp slashers are inheritors of a rich tradition of dark, violent tales for youth.

Origins of the Slasher Film

What exactly constitutes a "slasher" film can be difficult to ascertain. The slasher was a subgenre of the horror film that rose to prominence in the late 1970s. Commonly, slasher films featured a psychopath, whose pathology frequently stemmed from some sort of mental trauma (which was not always fully depicted or explained), who murdered a series of generally teen-aged victims. The genre obtained its moniker from the method the killer used to carry out his violent acts; teenage victims were slashed or stabbed by whatever sharp metal implement the killer happened to have on hand.[54] Slashers were horror film's graphic, brutally violent cousin.

While the subject matter of summer camp slasher films feel derived from scary campfire tales, the formula developed from a different sort of text. Most scholars consider Hitchcock's *Psycho* (1960) the progenitor of the slasher film.[55] Very loosely based on the case of serial killer Ed Gein, *Psycho* tells the story of Marion Crane (played by Janet Leigh), a young woman who steals $40,000 from her boss and has the misfortune of stopping at a motel operated by a young man named Norman Bates. Haunted by memories of matricide, Bates, in one of cinema's most famous scenes, dresses as his mother and stabs Crane repeatedly in the shower. In the end, Bates's mother, whom he has preserved by taxidermy, is discovered in her cellar, and he is arrested for his transsexual killing spree.

Psycho established many of the hallmarks of the slasher film. First, just as Norman Bates dressed as his mother before committing murder, many films in the subgenre featured a killer whose gender was ambiguous. Likewise, in many films in the slasher filmography, females, like Marion Crane, who committed sexual transgressions (such as premarital sex or adultery) eventually became victims of the killer. Additionally, the murders in slasher films were, like Bates's murders, almost exclusively bloody stabbings or slashings by hand-wielded, metal weaponry.[56] Though far removed from its successors in terms of both graphic violence and body count, many of the very strict conventions of the slasher genre were inherited directly from Hitchcock's groundbreaking film.

Although the American horror film experienced a great rebirth several years later, rejuvenated by 1968's *Rosemary's Baby* and *Night of the Living Dead*, the slasher film lay dormant for a period. Some waves were made when Tobe Hooper released his grisly *The Texas Chainsaw Massacre* in 1974,[57] but the slasher film found its greatest success with *Halloween* (1978). Carpenter's film is the tale of a deeply troubled child who murders his sister, is sent to a sanitarium, escapes, and returns to his hometown after 15 years to stalk and kill a group of babysitters, including Laurie (played by Janet Leigh's daughter, Jamie Leigh Curtis). Suspenseful and well constructed, *Halloween* was released to some critical acclaim (including the boisterous support of film critic Roger Ebert). It became a great financial success, grossing more than $50 million on an investment of less than $300,000.[58] With huge profits to be made on small investments, studios and independent filmmakers let loose a flood of similar films, in which a superhuman killer commits a sequence of grotesque murders, over the course of the next decade.

While the audiences of horror films were predominantly teenaged, audiences for slasher films were almost exclusively adolescent.[59] As such, the films were frequently set in locations familiar to young adults, such as high schools and, shortly thereafter, summer camps.[60] Film studios, eager to profit from the success of *Halloween*, began snapping up distribution rights to many new slasher projects. Desiring to be among the new wave of horror filmmakers, director Sean Cunningham, who had previously been involved in a combination of small films for children and soft-core pornography, placed an advertisement in *Variety* magazine for "the scariest movie ever made" when he had only a title: *Friday the 13th*. Without a script, a cast, or financing, Cunningham gambled that his title alone would garner attention of backers. His gamble worked; he was flooded with telephone calls asking about his film. The advertisement touched off a bidding war that was ultimately won by Paramount Pictures for a price of $70 million.[61]

Paramount's capital outlay proved to be a good investment. *Friday the 13th* went on to become the second highest grossing film of the summer of 1980. Much to the consternation of many film critics, *Friday the 13th* was at the vanguard of a resurgence of the B-movie:

> B-movies are enjoying a measure of financial success they haven't known since the mid-1950s. Mr. Cunningham's *Friday the Thirteenth*, for example, grossed $31 million in its first six weeks of release . . . Only *The Empire Strikes Back*, the sequel to *Star Wars* did better. Not bad for a movie starring Betsy Palmer on a budget of $600,000.[62]

Huge profits ensured that Hollywood film studios would continue to exploit the newly discovered market. *Friday the 13th* was a harbinger of the saturation of the slasher film market by endless (and cheap) copycats and sequels.

The success of Cunningham's *Friday the 13th* established the summer camp as a new setting for horror film. *Friday* was followed by a long bloody trail of sequels, but it also inspired more than a handful of other summer camp films, including the *Sleepaway Camp* trilogy, *The Burning*, *Madman*, and *Cheerleader Camp*. *Friday the 13th* had ensured that the summer camp would become an iconic setting for violent horror films.

After three years of *Halloween* imitations, critics were beginning to tire of the slasher film. On film, *Psycho*'s Norman Bates only kills two people. *Halloween*'s Michael Myers murders six, but, as the slasher film movement gained momentum, the number of victims per film kept rising. In the later entries of the *Friday the 13th* series, Jason Voorhees killed more than a dozen teenagers per film.[63] Barney Cohen, writer of *Friday the 13th: The Final Chapter* (1984), compared the writing of a slasher film to writing a musical: "You can't go too long without a song or kill." Some filmmakers kept a very strict formula. Adam Marcus, director of *Jason Goes to Hell* (1993), made sure his film featured a "death" or "fresh pair of breasts" every seven minutes. This represented an upward adjustment from Danny Steinmann's (director of *Friday the 13th Part V: A New Beginning* [1985]) deliberate formula of a "big jump" or kill every eight or nine minutes.[64]

As the murders became more frequent, bloodier, and more outlandish, critics became increasingly vicious as well. One film reviewer, titling his review of *Friday the 13th Part VII: The New Blood* (1988) "More of the Shame," declared, "Those reviews of 'Friday the Thirteenth' movies that come out on Saturday the Fourteenth could never be as mindless and brutal as the films themselves."[65] Critics began to dismiss the entire subgenre, describing Paramount Pictures as "the studio that backed [the *Friday* filmmaker] in his exploitation," and longing for the period in horror's history when films were "demure, suspenseful, [and] discrete," instead of the "graphic, overt, gut-wrenching stuff" that had overtaken the genre.[66] Gene Siskel's patience for the genre had expired at least three *Friday*'s before that, declaring that the fourth entry was indicative of a series that had become merely a "bloody, awful, unrelentingly sadistic, series . . . featuring gruesome murders by a vengeful young man."[67] Siskel, reviewing *Sleepaway Camp* in the same issue, appeared tired of both the genre and the setting. The entirety of his review simply stated "more teenage murders in a summer camp setting."[68]

Teenage Murders in a Summer Camp Setting

Friday the 13th opens with a flashback to the summer of 1958 with a group of coeducational campers sitting around the fireplace in a cabin singing religiously themed folk songs: "The river Jordan is deep and wide/Alleluia/Milk and honey on the other side/Alleluia." Two campers leave their singing friends behind, retreat to their bunks with the intention of fornicating, and are brutally murdered. This scene sets the tone for the entire summer camp slasher lexicon. The summer camp is as it was intended to be, a retreat from city life to the morally restorative wilderness. Those who bring corruption with them are punished.

Flashing forward 20 years, a group of young camp counselors is being brought to Crystal Lake with the intent of reopening the camp. One young counselor, Annie, arrives in the town of Crystal Lake and hitches a ride to the campground. The driver looks at her with incredulity when she says she wants to go to Camp Crystal Lake: "Camp Blood—they're opening that place again? . . . You'll never come back. It's got a death curse." When asked why anyone would want to reopen the camp, Annie, citing altruistic motives reminiscent of turn-of-the-century Fresh Air workers, claims the "campers will be mostly, like, inner-city children." Annie never makes it to the campground. After she is dropped off, she is chased through the woods and murdered by an anonymous killer.

Ralph, the town drunk, prophetically warns the remaining children to end their attempts to reopen Camp Crystal Lake: "You're doomed if you stay here. This place is cursed. It's got a death curse. God sent me . . . Go, go!" While the camp counselors may have seen their work, trying to bring kids out of the inner city for some fresh air in the woods, as a noble cause, the film repeatedly undermines that view of the forest. The wilderness is a place where people are hunted like animals. It is a place populated by the vicious and mentally unbalanced. The counselors are, in the estimation of the owner of the camp, merely "babes in the woods." A moral failing in each of them is inevitably followed by a slaughter. In one spectacularly grotesque death scene, Jack (played by a young Kevin Bacon), post-coitus, relaxes on a cot, smoking a marijuana joint, and has an arrow forced through his trachea. The moral lesson is made perfectly clear.

Near the end of the film, the audience discovers the true identity of the killer. Mrs. Voorhees, the mother of a young, mentally challenged boy named Jason who drowned in the lake 20 years prior while his counselors left the boy alone when they went off to have sex, hatched a plot to prevent Camp Crystal Lake from reopening by murdering the people who were working to renovate it.[69] "They were making love while my boy drowned," Mrs. Voorhees exclaims, in defense of her actions. While sex leading to death had been a theme in slasher films since *Psycho* established the tradition, few films in the subgenre had made so explicit the reason for the punishment.

Friday the 13th, for all its B-movie qualities, bears a strong kinship to *Psycho*. In fact, the story of Jason and his mother is, in many ways, an inversion of the story of Norman and his. While Norman cross-dressed as his mother to commit murders at the urging of his dead mother, Mrs. Voorhees dressed as a man and committed murders at the behest of her dead son. Just as Hitchcock chose a secluded, off-the-beaten-path motel as the setting for his film, Victor Miller, writer of *Friday the 13th*, sought to "create a world in which teenagers could not be helped by adults." The summer camp seemed a good candidate.[70]

Friday the 13th: Part II (1981) makes the link between the summer camp slasher and the scary campfire story explicit for the first time. This *Friday* uses a scene of a group of camp counselors gathered around a campfire to explain the events of the first film as though Jason and his mother were characters in a scary story.[71] This same technique would also be used in *Sleepaway Camp II: Unhappy Campers* (1988) to relate the events of the first film. An augmented version of this tactic would also be effectively used in *The Burning* (also of 1981); the film ended with a group of campers telling the story of the killer with a new chapter added—a reencapsulation of the film the viewer just watched. *Madman* (1982) takes the idea even further. In taking a group of children out into the woods to tell the story of Madman Marz (a man who killed his entire family with an ax, walked into a bar, placed the bloody implement on the counter, and ordered a drink) at a location that is literally a stone's throw away from the Madman's "abandoned" house, the film codes itself as a sort of mock ordeal; the audience has come to the film in order to bear witness to terrifying events before returning to the safety of the lobby. Makers of slasher films set in summer camp seem keenly aware of the scary story tradition that makes up an important aspect of the summer camp experience, and they seek to portray themselves as heirs of that tradition.

While *Friday the 13th* depicted camp counselors trying to reopen an abandoned camp, *Friday the 13th: Part II* took place in a nearly operational one. The counselors arriving at Crystal Lake came to attend a training center for camp counselors. Setting the film at an institution like this solved a potential problem for the filmmakers. Horror directors have a difficult time using child actors because of the ethical and legal obligation to shield young children from the graphic violence and gratuitous nudity that typify the genre. Setting a film at a summer camp creates a certain expectation that children will need to be present on set. For *Friday the 13th: Part II*, it seems, the filmmakers solved the problem of maximizing the number of teenage counselors while minimizing the number of children present by creating an institution attended solely by teenagers.

In any event, the second installment of the series was one of only three of the films in the *Friday* cycle that featured an operational camp. *Friday the 13th: Part II* was also one of the few films that actually addressed the curriculum of the camp; counselors would learn survival training, first aid, archery, and swimming at their training center. Like the first film, the curriculum of this camp also included moral training. After five years, Jason Voorhees, who died as a child in the first film, has returned on a murderous rampage and (for completely inexplicable reasons) is now a grown man. He continues his mother's educational work, pinning a pair of lovemaking counselors to their mattress with a spear and giving a paraplegic young man a swift machete blow to the face after an encounter with a female counselor that was laced with sexual innuendo and included marijuana use.

While the following two entries in the series are both set on Crystal Lake, the next *Friday the 13th* film attempting to reopen a camp there is *Part V: A New Beginning* (1985). In the fourth installment, Jason was hacked, presumably to death, by a young man named Tommy Jarvis (played by teen heartthrob Corey Feldman). The fifth film opens with Jarvis on his way to the Unger Mental Health Institution. The trauma he experienced at the hands of Jason was manifesting itself as nightmares about a hockey-masked figure. Eventually, he ends up at Pinehurst Youth Development Center, a camp established to help mentally troubled youth reenter society and, as the poster in his camp administrator's office loudly announces, "destroy a family tradition" of violence.[72] Emphasizing the freedom of the rural setting, the head doctor at the camp describes it as a relaxing retreat in the woods that differs drastically from traditional mental institutions: "We don't have any guards here. No one's going to tell you what you can do and what you can't do. Basically, you're your own boss." The camp administrators' view of the psychologically restorative properties of the setting differs substantially from those of the film. The country is not depicted as a place of high moral standing. The locals are polluted: slow-witted, quick to anger, and prejudiced. Neither do the campers find the site relaxing. Shortly after Jarvis arrives, one camper, annoyed by one of his fellow inmates as he is chopping wood, murders him with the ax. The film presents an image of the failure of the camping experiment; the young men and women go into the woods, but they find no healing.

Friday the 13th Part VI: Jason Lives (1986) contains the only example of an operational summer camp for children in the series. Camp Forest Green, formerly known as Camp Crystal Lake, has had its name changed because of the history of grotesque violence at the site. The mission of the camp, however, remained largely in the tradition of the best Progressive Era summer camps.[73] A series of signs lining the thoroughfare into the camp greeted arriving campers; the camp sought to instill Friendliness, Sportsmanship, Integrity, Courage, Self-Reliance, and Tolerance.

Little camping actually takes place at Camp Forest Green. Tommy Jarvis, in an attempt to convince himself that Jason Voorhees is dead, digs up the corpse—which is accidentally reanimated by a lightning strike.[74] Jason then continues his mother's quest to prevent a summer camp from ever reopening at Crystal Lake. While the counselors and children discuss all the fun activities that *will* occur, none of them materializes—as both children and counselors are preoccupied with the resurrected Jason. This film seems to break one of the unspoken taboos of the summer camp slasher film. In only two summer camp slashers of the era were children threatened with serious violence. This film, however, eased the tension with comic relief. As the group of children cowers under their bunks, hoping to be hidden from the view of a machete-wielding maniac, one boy says to another, "So, what were you going to be when you grew up?" The confrontation with the wilderness led the youngsters to rue for what modern life once had to offer them, a decidedly different view of the transformative power of the forest from that of the founders of the summer camp movement.

The camp was more effective at fulfilling its religious mission. One little girl, when confronted by the predator, followed her counselor's advice, closed her eyes, "said a prayer and everything scary went away." Having learned the traditional "Now I Lay Me Down to Sleep" bedtime prayer, Jason's appearance prompts the girl to close her eyes and chant the prayer over and over. When she opened her eyes, the physical embodiment of her fears had disappeared, as though her act of prayer had signaled to Jason that this was a girl who was not in need of the moral training he had to offer. For this young girl, the trip to the forest taught her the power of prayer.

In no film is the contrast between the city and the forest starker than in *The Burning* (1981). Before becoming a major Hollywood film producer, Harvey Weinstein wrote the script to this summer camp slasher, which tells the tale of Cropsy, a cruel camp caretaker who terrorizes the young men in his charge. The teenagers plan to pull a prank on Cropsy, but the prank goes wrong and Cropsy is severely burned and disfigured. After his release from the city hospital, the bitter and angry man wanders the city streets. The scene illustrates exactly the type of cityscape camps were established to save children from. The city is filled with peep shows, X-rated movies, and prostitutes. Cropsy's last act before returning to the summer camp is to kill a prostitute with a pair of scissors.

While Camp Blackfoot has closed as a result of the incident, Camp Stonewater has opened a little farther down the lakeshore. Cropsy brings his murderous rage back from the city with him. Interestingly, the ensuing slaughter does not occur at the camp itself. It is as though the ordered nature represented by the mess hall and bunkhouses was not the proper venue for a bloody massacre. Cropsy waits until several of the teenage campers go on an overnight camping trip in the wild. That night, he releases their canoes into the stream, and the carnage begins. Immediately after discovering the missing canoes, the campers realize they are stranded in the wilderness and, in what feels like a camp arts-and-crafts project on a grand scale, begin to build a makeshift raft. The attempted escape upriver ends badly, with a particularly sadistic mass murder with a pair of gardening shears. The wilderness serves as an interesting counterpoint to the city. The city is the scene of unrestrained carnal desire of the sexual variety; in the inescapable wilderness, such desire is held in check by unrepressed bloodlust.

Friday the 13th Part VIII: Jason Takes Manhattan (1989) contains a similar treatment of city life. The opening montage of the film depicts the evils of the city, such as intravenous drug use and vagrancy. The film then returns the viewer to Crystal Lake, where a group of graduating high school students is planning a trip up the river to New York. (Like *all* of the summer camps featured in the slasher films of the era, Camp Crystal

Lake is intended to serve youth from New York City.) Due to budgetary concerns, most of the film takes place aboard the ship *Lazarus* upon which a resurrected Jason slays a series of celebrating high school graduates as they anxiously await their arrival at the Big Apple.[75]

The group arrives in the city via New York Harbor, and the ship travels past the Statue of Liberty. Like the many immigrants who arrived in the city by boat before them, the sight of the New York City skyline is a symbol of hope and salvation for the passengers on the deadly cruise. That hope is short-lived. The first thing that happens when the group reaches the city is a mugging at gunpoint. One of the girls from the group is nearly raped after forced intravenous drug use but is ultimately saved when Jason runs her rapist through with his own syringe. In the city, and with his proclivity for punishing people's moral failings, Jason is less dangerous and more moral than many of the city's denizens.

Friday's Manhattan, awash in crime, graffiti, and toxic waste, is an anonymous place with no sense of community. While the site of the summer camp may have been a commonly chosen setting for a horror film because of its distance from civilization and lack of adult authority to help imperiled youth, the city is depicted in this film as being as isolated as the wilderness. No one on the subway shows even the slightest inclination to help the teenagers as they run screaming from Jason. In perhaps the most telling scene in the film, the girls run into the diner and scream, "You don't understand. There's a maniac trying to kill us." The jaded response from the waitress is a simple, "Welcome to New York." Ultimately, this is part of the downfall of the picture. At Crystal Lake, Jason Voorhees is a lone maniac protecting his unspoiled wilderness from the invasion from the city. In New York City, Jason is hardly the most colorful, or even dangerous, character. At the end of the film, Jason, chasing a teenage girl through the New York City sewer system, dies in a symbolic flood of toxic waste. He still has not learned to swim.

Carpenter's *Halloween* established the convention of the sole surviving female. One female, Jamie Leigh Curtis's Laurie, is able to survive Michael Myers's massacre. This convention was continued in nearly all slasher films, including the *Friday the 13th* films. Resourceful Alice summons the courage to decapitate Mrs. Voorhees at the end of the first film. In *Friday the 13th: Part II*, Ginny, who is majoring in child psychology, is able to survive Jason's wrath because she understands the boy's relationship with his mother; she masquerades as his mother, adopts a maternal voice, and tries to convince her "son" that he can stop killing, distracting Jason long enough for her to mount her machete-driven defense. In Carol Clover's estimation, the sole surviving female is neither fully feminine nor fully masculine. She can adopt feminine trappings (e.g., maternal instinct) when required, but, unlike the female victims, she is also adroit at more masculine endeavors (e.g., grappling energetically with her overpowered male attacker).[76] It is her ability to become a "manly woman" that, ultimately, enables her to survive in the wilderness.

Sexual dysfunction was the overarching theme of Robert Hiltzik's *Sleepaway Camp* (1983). The film opens with shots of an empty summer camp. From the outset, the summer camp scene takes center stage. Soon, busloads of children arrive at the camp to the leering eyes of a shady-looking staff. They are open with their pedophiliac tendencies. After making lewd comments about one of the young girls as she got off the bus, the cook defends himself by declaring, "Ain't no such thing as too young. You're just too old." Inevitably, a series of murders begin at the camp. After attempting to sexually molest a young girl named Angela in the pantry, the cook is the killer's first victim; he is boiled alive in a giant corn-cooking pot. Sexually inappropriate behavior involving adults and children seems an epidemic at Camp Arawak. The camp owner takes very seriously the murder of one of his female co-eds with whom he was having an implied affair. Camp administrators actively encouraged sexual innuendo from the teenaged counselors directed at them. While the killer stalked the camp in search of fresh victims, he was hardly the only predator loose on the camp.

Like many of the summer camp films of the era, including those that were not horror films, *Sleepaway Camp* deals with the theme of burgeoning sexuality in adolescence.[77] *Sleepaway Camp* is a simple cross-pollination of *Friday the 13th* and De Palma's *Carrie* (1976)[78]; it is the tale of a young girl at summer camp who brutally murders her bullies. Angela is the victim of a great deal of bullying. She is mocked for not having reached puberty or having had her first menstrual period. Some older girls, knowing of her inability to swim, throw her into the lake. After she is rescued, some of the camp's younger kids kick sand on her. Each of these tormentors meets a grisly demise. In the other example of violence against young children in summer camp slashers of the era, the children who kicked sand on Angela are depicted the following morning as a stack of bloody sleeping bags.[79] In one of the most disturbing scenes of the film, Meg, the most vicious of the older girls, dies after an implied use of a curling iron to penetrate her.

Angela's rage cannot be fully explained by her bullying. She is also clearly afraid of her growing sexual feelings. She refuses to give the boy upon whom she has a crush a second kiss goodnight. As the film progresses, it becomes increasingly obvious there is something different about Angela. Near the end of the film, a scene in which Angela and her new boyfriend are necking on the beach is intercut with a fantasy scene of two grown men engaging in homosexual lovemaking. This is prelude to the "surprise" ending in which a naked—and obviously male—Angela laughs maniacally as she holds the severed head of her young lover.[80]

Sleepaway Camp transcends many of the genre conventions upon which it so heavily relies. In this film, the sole surviving female is actually male, and "she" is able to survive by virtue of the fact that "she" is also the killer. However, the surprise ending tinges the whole film with homophobia. The transgender female is responsible for the murders because she has a sexual desire she cannot control or understand. While the homosexual love scene is portrayed honestly and tenderly, the true villain seems to be Angela's "aunt" who, after taking Angela in after her parents die, forces her to live as a girl for no other reason than she always wanted a daughter. The idea that a transgender parent would force a child into the same lifestyle, instilling such sexual identity confusion as to create a serial killer, seems too extreme to release the filmmakers from responsibility for what can only be interpreted as homophobia. In any event, the ending solidifies the central motif of the film: adults impressing their sexuality upon the young. Whether it is the pedophiliac staff member who gets boiled alive, the camp owner who develops a personal vendetta against the person who killed the counselor he was statutorily raping, or the transgender aunt who forces her sexual preference on her nephew, the film is peppered with adults who create serious sexual identity problems in youth under their charge—with deadly consequences.

The inevitable (and in most ways superior) sequel, *Sleepaway Camp II: Unhappy Campers*, features the return of Angela, this time played by rock musician Bruce Springsteen's sister Pamela. After spending several years in a mental institution, Angela is given a clean bill of mental health and, upon her release, she returns to the summer camp as a camp counselor. According to the mission of the summer camp laid out by early summer camp supporters, Angela was a model counselor. In a conversation with the owner of the summer camp, he bemoans the moral deterioration of his clientele, saying, "I used to brag that every good kid in New York came here. Now, I have difficulty filling the cabins with God knows who . . . What happened to all the good kids?" Angela's response is more optimistic: "Don't talk like that, Uncle John. There are lots of good kids. All we have to do is weed out the bad."

One teenage girl approaches Angela for some advice regarding a relationship with a boy at the camp. Lacking confidence, the girl expresses a fear that she will not be able to compete with another girl who is "more experienced." Angela assuages the girl's fears with her bluntness: "Which probably means she has a disease or two. Keep your morals straight, and you'll never go wrong." Angela is an upbeat counselor who hums "Kumbaya" and sings her own "Happy Camper Song," which ends with the rousing refrain: "And with the grace of God, we'll camp until we die."

Angela's song proves prophetic. Soon she is taking her camp counselor responsibilities a bit too seriously. She is trying to take a group of bad kids and help them succeed as campers. Unable to help the Schlitz sisters overcome their drinking problems, Angela takes the radical step of burning them alive. She drowns another girl in an outhouse for being a "shitty" friend, "pissing" away her life, and being a "leech." Although Angela gives each of the campers a second chance to change his or her ways, she kills them if they refuse to change. Over the course of the film, the killings become less motivated, and Angela loses control of her psychosis.[81] As a result, her definition of a mortal sin broadens. Seemingly aware of the morally educative properties of the slasher subgenre, one camper, Molly, asks Angela why she is being murdered: "What did I do? I didn't *do* anything." Angela's response is simple but weak: "You're going to tell." This is hardly the level of transgression that killed Molly's compatriots. Angela's compulsive desire to be the perfect camp counselor provides the source of the film's horror.

Angela returns to camp as a camper in *Sleepaway Camp III: Teenage Wasteland* (1989). Conventional and extraordinarily formulaic, even for a slasher, the era of the summer camp slasher film was effectively ended with the release of this film. Set in a summer camp that was "an experiment in sharing," Camp New Horizons set out to "promote sharing, love, harmony, and peace, and a better understanding between rich and poor." The camp brought together the "higher-class establishment and lower-class homes." In summer camp slashers, the wilderness was a great equalizer. Rich and poor, male and female, black and white, all were subject to the same moral retribution at the hands of the monster in the forest. There is no mystery behind Angela's motivations in this third installment. She has written herself a checklist: "Are you a cheerleader? Are you a virgin? Do you take drugs? Strike three!"[82] Comfortable and familiar, *Sleepaway Camp III* ended the era of the summer camp slasher, not with a bang, but with an enjoyable whimper.

Some Concluding Remarks

By 1989, the first wave of slashers had crashed and broken, and the fresh thrills of Carpenter's *Halloween* had devolved into endless iterations of already established film series. After *Friday the 13th Part VIII: Jason Takes Manhattan*, the *Friday* series continued but became increasingly outlandish, even hypothesizing about the kind of killing spree Jason could unleash in outer space.[83] Horror film is a rather unique genre insofar as it required the periodic infusion of fresh ideas in order to maintain its fundamental function—to shock and terrify. When I asked Doug Bradley, who played Pinhead in the *Hellraiser* series, what he thought about his series' tendency to experiment with setting, he responded by saying, "You can make any setting scary if you do it right, I think."[84]

Bradley's answer, while acknowledging the need for horror films to maintain novelty, ignores the fact that there are places that are implicitly unsettling. The summer camp had proved a perfect setting for tales of terror. It allowed filmmakers to gather a large group of teenage victims and sequester them from both civilization and the aid of adults. Wooded areas provided the killer with ample places to hide and jump out at unsuspecting youth. The campfire already had a long and deep association with scary stories, and it was a rich tradition from which filmmakers could borrow motifs. Moreover, Americans' relationship with the wilderness was long and complicated and filled with anxiety.

Because of the disproportionate number of teenagers who attend slasher films, the films tend to be primarily set in spaces familiar to teenagers that are capable of inspiring fear in that audience. Frequently, filmmakers opted to set their films in educational institutions. Summer camp slasher films exploited the mission of the summer camp for its potential for creating terror in their viewers. The films inverted the basic tenets of the camps. Progressive Era camp advocates tried to build a summer camp system that promoted physical health, emotional development, and spiritual growth. In horror film, summer camps were places of physical peril and severe emotional trauma. Moral lessons were taught alongside survival skills by crazed madmen who would administer cruel punishments for any infraction. When enlisted to write the screenplay for what was being billed as the scariest movie ever made, Miller may not have set out to craft a Victorian morality tale, but, by mixing the conventions of the slasher subgenre with a dark vision of a pre-transcendentalist wilderness, that is exactly what he did.[85]

Bibliography

Aron, Cindy S. *Working at Play: A History of Vacations in the United States*. New York: Oxford University Press, 1999.
Barnard, Eunice Fuller. "Young America Is Off to Summer Camp." *New York Times*, June 29, 1930, 14.
Boyles, Denis. "Hollywood's 'B's' Make the Box Office Buzz." *New York Times*, August 3, 1980.
"A Boy's Camp By One of the Campers." *St. Nicholas* 13, no. 8 (June 1886): 607–613.
Briefel, Aviva. "Monster Pains: Masochism, Menstruation, and Identification in the Horror Film." *Film Quarterly* 58, no. 3 (Spring 2005): 16–27.
Buckley, Tom. "A Potboiler of Gold at the End of His Rainbow." *New York Times*, January 23, 1981, C8.
"Cable TV Movies." *Chicago Tribune*, October 26, 1986, J40.
Clover, Carol J. "Her Body, Himself: Gender in the Slasher Films." *Representations* (Autumn 1987): 187–228.
Dewey, John. *Democracy and Education*. Champaign, IL: The Gutenberg Project, 1916. Updated January 26, 2013. http://www.gutenberg.org/files/852/852-h/852-h.htm.
Eells, Eleanor. *History of Organized Camping: The First 100 Years*. Martinsville, IN: American Camping Association, 1986.
Ellis, Bill. "The Camp Mock-Ordeal: Theatre as Life." *Journal of American Folklore* 94, no. 374 (Oct–Dec 1981): 486–505.
———. "'Ralph and Rudy': The Audience's Role in Recreating a Camp Legend." *Western Folklore* 41, no. 3 (July 1982): 169–191.
Ferrends, Daniel, dir. *His Name Was Jason: 30 Years of Friday the 13th*. Anchor Bay Entertainment, 2008.
Hall, Gary. "The Big Tunnel: Legends and Legend Telling." *Indiana Folklore* 6 (1973): 147–153.
Hawthorne, Nathaniel. "Young Goodman Brown," 1835. http://www.netlibrary.net.
Herrington, Richard. "'Friday VII': More of the Shame." *Washington Post*, May 14, 1988, C3.
Maynard, W. Barksdale. "'An Ideal Life in the Woods for Boys': Architecture and Culture in the Earliest Summer Camps." *Winterthur Portfolio* 34, no. 1 (Spring 1999): 3–29.

Mechler, Jay. "Children's Folklore in Residential Institutions: Summer Camps, Boarding Schools, Hospitals, and Custodial Facilities." In *Children's Folklore: A Source Book*, edited by Brain Sutton-Smith, Jay Mechling, Thomas W. Johnson, and Felicia R. McMahon, 273–291. New York and London: Garland Publishing, 1995.

Mishler, Paul C. *Raising Reds: The Young Pioneers, Radical Summer Camps, and Communist Political Culture in the United States*. New York: Columbia University Press, 1999.

"The Movie Channel." *Washington Post*, July 19, 1987, TV48.

Norton, Charles L. "Summer Camps for Boys." *Christian Union* 38, no. 8 (August 23, 1888): 193.

Paris, Leslie. *Children's Nature: The Rise of the American Summer Camp*. New York: New York University Press, 2008.

Rockoff, Adam. *Going to Pieces: The Rise and Fall of the Slasher Film, 1978–1986*. Jefferson, NC: McFarland, 2002.

Rosenbaum, Jonathan. "*Halloween*: Suspense Is Generated by Waiting for a Woman to Be Torn Apart by a Maniac." *TakeOne* (January 1979): 8–9.

Sharp, Lloyd Burgess. *Education and the Summer Camp: An Experiment*. New York: Bureau of Publications, Teachers College, Columbia University, 1930.

Siskel, Gene. "Siskel's Flicks Picks." *Chicago Tribune*, May 14, 1984, D-A12.

"Summer Camps Boon to Parents." *New York Times*, July 15, 1923, E5.

Thigpen, Jr., Kenneth A. "Adolescent Legends in Brown County: A Survey." *Indiana Folklore* 4 (1971): 204–205.

Tillery, Randal K. "Touring Arcadia: Elements of Discursive Simulation and Cultural Struggle at a Children's Summer Camp." *Cultural Anthropology* 7, no. 3 (August 1992): 378.

Ulanoff, Stanley M. "The Organization and Development of Organized Camping in the United States, 1861–1961." Ph.D. diss., New York University, 1968.

Van Slyck, Abigail A. *A Manufactured Wilderness: Summer Camps and the Shaping of American Youth, 1890–1960*. Minneapolis: University of Minnesota Press, 2006.

Wack, Henry Wellington. *The Camping Ideal: The New Human Race*. New York: Red Book Magazine, 1925.

Werner, Laurie. "Film Horror Falls into the Hands of the Gore Corps." *Chicago Tribune*, August 24, 1980, D26.

Wood, Robin. *Hollywood from Vietnam to Reagan . . . and Beyond*. New York: Columbia University Press, 2003.

———. "Returning the Look: *Eyes of a Stranger*." In *American Horrors: Essays on the Modern American Horror Film*, edited by Gregory A. Waller, 79–85. Urbana, IL: University of Illinois Press, 1987.

Filmography

Buechler, John Carl, dir. *Friday the 13th Part VII: The New Blood*. Paramount Pictures, 1988.
Capra, Frank, dir. *Mr. Smith Goes to Washington*. Columbia Pictures, 1939.
Carpenter, John, dir. *Halloween*. Compass International Pictures, 1978.
Cunningham, Sean S. dir. *Friday the 13th*. Paramount Pictures, 1980.
Giannone, Joe, dir. *Madman*. The Legend Lives Company, 1982.
Heddon, Rob, dir. *Friday the 13th Part VIII: Jason Takes Manhattan*. Paramount Pictures, 1989.
Hitchcock, Alfred, dir. *Psycho*. Universal Pictures, 1960.
Hiltzik, Robert, dir. *Return to Sleepaway Camp*. Go2Sho Films, 2008.
———. *Sleepaway Camp*. American Eagle Film Corporation, 1983.
Marcus, Adam, dir. *Jason Goes to Hell: The Final Friday*. New Line Pictures, 1993.
Maxwell, Ronald F., dir. *Little Darlings*. Kings Road Productions, 1980.
Maylam, Tony, dir. *The Burning*. MGM, 1981.
McLoughlin, Tom, dir. *Friday the 13th Part VI: Jason Lives*. Paramount Pictures, 1986.
Miner, Steve, dir. *Friday the 13th: Part II*. Paramount Pictures, 1981.
———. *Friday the 13th: Part III*. Paramount Pictures, 1982.
Nispel, Marcus, dir. *Friday the 13th*. New Line Cinema, 2009.
Quinn, John, dir. *Cheerleader Camp*. Prism Entertainment, 1988.
Reitman, Ivan, dir. *Meatballs*. Canadian Film Development Corporation, 1979.
Simpson, Michael A., dir. *Sleepaway Camp II: Unhappy Campers*. Double Helix Films, 1988.
———. *Sleepaway Camp III: Teenage Wasteland*. Double Helix Films, 1989.
Steinmann, Danny, dir. *Friday the 13th Part V: A New Beginning*. Paramount Pictures, 1985.
Zito, Joseph, dir. *Friday the 13th: The Final Chapter*. Paramount Pictures, 1984.

Chapter 7

Some Concluding Thoughts

The history of horror film is broken into a series of natural eras. The initial silent film era's attempts at instilling fear in audiences produced some terrifying works of dark fantasy that would create a set of imagery and iconography that would both provide inspiration for successive generations of filmmakers and set the standard against which these films would be judged. *Nosferatu* (1922), *The Golem* (1920), *The Cabinet of Dr. Caligari* (1920), the films of Lon Chaney, Sr., and the early film depictions of Dr. Frankenstein and Dr. Jekyll made horror film a vibrant part of early film art. In the 1930s, Universal, an American film studio, set the great works of British Gothic to an atmosphere heavily steeped in German Expressionism and created the lexicon of horror film; Bela Lugosi's Dracula and Boris Karloff's Frankenstein's monster remain the two most enduring nightmarish figures in the history of cinema and have even supplanted the image of these figures from the original literary source material. More than 80 years later, children preparing for Halloween will grab their plastic pumpkins, throw on costumes meant to call to mind these film monsters, and go trick-or-treating. In the late 1950s, British studios, like Hammer and Amicus, brought these tales back across the Atlantic and gave them new life (or, perhaps, un-death). Shortly thereafter, visionary films in the 1960s, including Alfred Hitchcock's *Psycho*, Roman Polanski's *Rosemary's Baby*, and George Romero's *Night of the Living*

Dead would leave Transylvania behind and make horror an extension of the everyday lives of their audiences. This would lay the groundwork for 1970s auteurs to create an entirely new horror subgenre with a filmic language all its own. Bob Clark's *Black Christmas*, Tobe Hooper's *The Texas Chainsaw Massacre*, and John Carpenter's *Halloween*, with their preoccupations with bloody murder, gave life to the new slasher film.

For all of horror films' artistic achievements, there were periods of stagnation in the genre. As the Universal films series dragged on into the mid-1940s, they became pale imitations of the great films that had invented horror film in the post–silent film era. The collapse of the Universal horror film set the stage for a decade and a half of atomic age, creature feature B-movies. The British horror film would follow a similar trajectory, as Hammer's Technicolor triumph with *The Curse of Frankenstein* and *The Horror of Dracula* gradually gave way to *Dracula A.D. 1972*. While there have been a few examples of quality British horror films in the intervening years, that footing was never completely regained. By the mid-1990s, the *Halloween*, *Friday the 13th*, and *Nightmare on Elm Street* films had raised the body count and gratuitous nudity to nearly ridiculous levels to try to keep audiences who had become intimately familiar with the slasher formula interested in the seventh or eighth films in their series. Eventually, these films too collapsed under their own weight.

There is an inherent dilemma in the history of horror film. Horror films are frequently among the most formulaic of all the film genres. As the slasher film was gasping for breath, one of the few innovative film series keeping it from dying completely was Wes Craven's *Scream* movies—a deliberately humorous, yet bloody postmodern series built around the idea of a killer who was keenly aware of the genre considerations that were governing the murders he was committing on screen. While slasher films were likely more formulaic than the rest of the horror genre, horror films had always had an element of predictability. Certainly, Universal's monsters were no strangers to long, meandering film series with new entries that bore more than a slight resemblance to prior ones. In part, the late nineteenth-century penny dreadful had establish a literary tradition of heavy serialization. The Motion Picture Production Code that dictated the types of immoral acts that could be portrayed on screen and, at times, the consequences for on-screen violators of good moral sense added another layer of predictability on what had historically already tended toward formula. Given the way that film studios operated (and continue to operate), film producers were content to stick to a strict formula model for the production of horror films.

The other horn of that dilemma, though, is that horror (like comedy) requires a certain element of surprise in its audience to create the desired emotional effect. In order to effectively build tension, a film must establish a filmic space in which the audience is unsure, left wondering the identity of the killer, the location of the threat, or the secret motives of the film's key agents. The prolonged use of strict formulas undermines the ability of any given film within the genre to create this sort of tension. A seasoned viewer of slasher movies, for instance, can guess with a strong degree of accuracy and within a few minutes of the beginning of the film which of the characters in the film are going to die.

One of the effects of the horror film formula working against its raison d'être is to encourage filmmakers working in the genre to innovate along lines unrelated to the preestablished structure of their films. One of the ways that filmmakers commonly attempted this was to try to make the level of violence more shocking. Raising the film's body count was a common tactic. For instance, in the first *Halloween* film, Michael Myers kills 5 people; in the fourth movie, that number increased almost threefold to 13. Making the on-screen deaths more gory and gruesome was another tactic. These strategies, though, can only really work up to a point. Is 13 film murders scarier than 4? Or is 13 murders in an hour and a half more absurd and, hence, less frightening?

None of this discussion is meant to disparage the genre itself. It is merely meant to explain the periodic artistic declines horror films experience. New eras of horror filmmaking tend to begin with a fresh idea that is subsequently folded into existing formulas or establishes a new formula. Filmmakers try to keep audiences interested by aggrandizing the horrors of the film while following the strictures of the formula. Eventually, there becomes little that can be done to keep audiences interested while still maintaining the strict genre conventions.

Yet, throughout film history, while the horror genre has undergone artistic ebbs and flows, the genre has always been able to become relevant again. It has done so, not always by pushing the envelope of graphic violence and good taste, but by capitalizing on the personal and cultural fears of its audience. At times, these fears existed on a grand, geopolitical scale. Fears of the Cold War devolving into nuclear war were translated into body snatchers invading American small towns and giant insects destroying American cities. Other times, these fears were more intimate and personal. Many scholars have argued that James Whale's *Frankenstein* and *Bride of Frankenstein* explore themes of rejection and ostracism, feelings that must have been acute for the homosexual filmmaker working in a time in which his sexual identity would have alienated him from executives in the studio system and the public at large. Horror films capitalized on the political and cultural climate in which they were made. In so doing, they served as a metaphorical way for filmmakers to critique those political situations. Equally importantly, by building narratives around the cultural fears and personal anxieties of their audiences, horror films could create tension within the confines of relatively inflexible genre rules.

In terms of classical music, the structure of a fugue, while complex, is fairly rigid. Within this rigid form, there are ways for classical musicians to creatively explore themes and variations on that theme. There was a time, at the beginning of this project, that I wondered why people would continue to watch film after film when one began watching each movie already highly familiar with the plot structure. The slasher film, if one allows the analogy, is rather like listening to a fugue. One already knows all the elements of the piece's structure. The reason people listen to a fugue when they already know what the structure of the piece will be is to see how the composer creates his art within the confines of the strict form. The same

Some Concluding Thoughts

is true of horror movies; the audience already knows that there will be a monster, the monster will go on a rampage, people will die (and most people with more than a passing familiarity with the form will know which people), and the monster will eventually be overcome. What makes the film interesting is not the structure, it is how the filmmaker operates within the structure; audiences are interested not in who dies, but *how* and *why*. They know the monster will likely be overcome; what makes the film interesting is *how* the monster is defeated. The tension of the horror film is not built by the structure of the plot, rather it is imposed on the text as a superstructure built of personal and cultural anxieties.

These superstructures are precisely why horror films are interesting primary artifacts for historians. Because they do not necessarily arise organically from within the structure of the text, but are imposed from the outside of the narrative, by analyzing the superstructures, historians are able to determine the types of fears and anxieties that people were experiencing in their everyday lives outside of the theater.

With the advent of compulsory education laws at the end of the nineteenth century, formal schooling became a unifying aspect of culture in the United States. Enrollments in high school skyrocketed in the first half of the twentieth century, and postsecondary matriculation also grew at a steady rate over the same period. Formal education beyond the elementary school years went from being the exception to being a near-universal experience. In turn, this led larger numbers of well-educated intellectuals to work within the expanding educational system, especially the college and university systems. Increasing student enrollments and decreasing numbers of intellectuals operating outside of the university system created a host of new anxieties surrounding education.

Some of these were cultural anxieties produced by the struggle of people to adjust to the new educational landscape. As the number of intellectuals operating outside of the academy dropped, suspicion of those researchers who refused to make that transition grew. As the rate of technical advancement increased, so did the sense that the public needed the intellectuals working to protect them from the potentially devastating effects of these new developments. In the same way, as ethical rules for the treatment of people during the scientific research process were being codified, researchers operating outside of that context could be seen as a threat to the general welfare. These cultural anxieties, then, centered around the role of the intellectual in higher education. These anxieties would themselves form part of the superstructure of horror imposed upon scary movies throughout the first half of the twentieth century and would eventually result in the formation of the mad scientist as a symbol of the intellectual whose work was not conducted under the accountability provided by the academy.

Mandatory school attendance comes with its own set of personal anxieties. Fears about the inability to meet academic demands become commonplace. Compelling attendance places entire youth populations together under the schoolhouse roof, regardless of their social desire to associate with each other. Delaying a person's entry into the workplace until after completion also serves to prolong adolescence, and graduation becomes the rite of passage representing the beginning of adult life. The prolonging of adolescence in turn, changes adult perceptions regarding teenagers and affects the relationships between young adults and the adult figures in their lives. In other words, the ballooning in high school enrollments was not without its effects on the individual psyches of American youth. Of course, horror filmmakers could exploit these feelings of unease about school life.

When Dr. Van Helsing is pictured in his chair, poring over an arcane volume and developing a stratagem for defeating the evil count, the audience develops a sense that, even if he is not a swashbuckling action hero, nonetheless the intellectual is engaged in work that seeks to protect the innocent. When Dr. Frankenstein has begun killing young ladies for their organs, the audience is led to understand that clinical research ought to be conducted with robust oversight from the academic community. This fear is especially acute in an era in which people are learning of how intellectuals operating outside of such a context have committed atrocities. When Dr. Black pressures his other

African American patients to become subjects in his dangerous research, the mind of the viewer sees not only the frightening injustice Dr. Black is trying to commit but the history of the systematic injustices that kept African Americans from having even the basic right of control over what happened to their own bodies. These horror films provide an excellent opportunity for the historian to examine that superstructure of terror laid over these narratives and expose those cultural fears and historical traumas that created the films' emotional resonance with their audiences.

Likewise, these films also provide an opportunity to discover the individual and personal fears experienced by their teenaged audience members. When Freddy Krueger is murdering Nancy's friends, instead of lending a sympathetic ear or even believing in the legitimacy of her perspective, her mother tries to have her involuntarily drugged. When Carrie is mercilessly taunted and publicly embarrassed, the audience is torn between wanting to see her bullies receive justice for their treatment of her and balking at the extreme nature of her violent reaction. Undergirding these two films are the ideas that parents are unwilling to truly listen to their children and that bullies will even exploit the natural sexual development of one's body to further their torment. In examining these horror films set in high schools, historians can get a sense of the types of personal anxieties that horror filmmakers employed to invest the films with the ability to frighten their viewers.

Horror films also frequently deal with the nature of violence itself. Certainly in the case of *Carrie*, the issue of the role of violence in creating trauma from which one might not be able to psychologically recover represents a major theme of the film. Horror films set in college, however, tended to address different themes, as a postsecondary education was not a compulsory experience. More frequently, college films dealt with anxieties related to social class. However, in gravitating toward the fraternity and sorority house as their setting, horror films set in college frequently focused on hazing and initiation rituals. In particular, they built their narratives around the ways that violence could bring a sense of group cohesion or, given a slightly different context, could create a sense of crippling isolation.

Summer camps, with their mission of returning urban children to a wilderness environment in order to provide them with a setting for education outside of the anonymity and potential immorality of the city, created a sense of horror that substantially differed from either high schools or colleges. Sequestered from family and isolated by geography, the summer camp had the ability to create an entirely different type of fear in the youth who attended. The summer camp—having the tradition of the campfire tale—also already had its own native form of horror narrative that was designed to exploit those fears of isolation. Horror filmmakers, then, simply by virtue of choosing the summer camp as their setting, became a part of a rich scary story tradition and could tap into commonly held personal and cultural fears about the relationship between modernity, the wilderness, and moral education.

For the past century, horror films have been engaging in a dialogue with their audiences regarding educational fears. They have sought to build their stories around the cultural anxieties regarding the growth of educational institutions and the role of the intellectual in those institutions. Horror films have attempted to exploit the deep personal fears held by their audiences about their own role in the educational process, including feelings of academic inadequacy, emotional distance from adult members of the community, angst about the types of physical and emotional violence commonly experienced in schools and as part of school life, and concerns about the transition from school to life outside of academia. With the intellectual now solidly entrenched in the college and university environment, the modern era of horror film has seen the dwindling of depictions of the lone researcher operating outside of the academy. As the culture resolved that tension, it no longer provided an effective well of cultural fear from which to draw. However, personal anxieties about school life held by individual adolescents have certainly not gone away.

In this book, I briefly mentioned the idea that blaming horror films for violence is chastising the symptoms and ignoring the causes of the sickness. The violence and fear would exist, even if the films did not. The films merely provide a mirror in which to identify the fears that may have resonated or, if they were well constructed, did resonate with the people who watched them. The violent images get their power from the emotions that the spectators bring to their viewing. In the end, this is why analysis of horror films set in educational institutions is so worthwhile. Youth struggle on their path to adulthood and are frequently beset by difficulties. They do not escape childhood without becoming the victim of some degree of emotional or physical violence. Horror films set in schools show us the monsters that haunt youth and show youth the path to overcoming those monsters.

Notes

Chapter 1

1. Jeffrey Mirel, "The Traditional High School: Historical Debates over Its Nature and Function," *Education Next* 6 (2006): 14–21.
2. US Census Bureau, "Education Summary—High School Graduates, and College Enrollment and Degrees: 1900 to 2001," Historical Statistics Table HS-21, http://www.census.gov/statab/hist/HS-21.pdf.
3. Andrew Monument, dir., *Nightmares in Red, White, and Blue: The Evolution of American Horror Film* (Lux Digital Pictures, 2009).
4. Monument, *Nightmares in Red*.

Chapter 2

1. David J. Skal, *Screams of Reason: Mad Science and Modern Culture* (New York: Norton, 1998), 18–19. For a discussion of this more complex image of the mad scientist within the context of postwar film science fiction comedies, see also Sevan Terzian and Andrew Grunzke, "Scrambled Eggheads: Ambivalent Representations of Scientists in Six Hollywood Film Comedies from 1961 to 1965," *Public Understanding of Science* 16 (October 2007): 407–419.
2. Esther Schor, "Frankenstein and Film," in *The Cambridge Companion to Mary Shelley* (Cambridge: Cambridge University Press, 2003), 63; James A. W. Heffernan, "Looking at the Monster: Frankenstein and Film," *Critical Inquiry* 24, no. 1 (Autumn 1997): 136.
3. Russell Jacoby, *The Last Intellectuals: American Culture in the Age of Academe* (New York: Basic Books, 1987).
4. Richard Hofstadter, *Anti-Intellectualism and American Life* (New York: Knopf, 1963); Craig Howley, Aimee Howley, and Edwine D. Pendarvis, *Out of Our Minds: Anti-Intellectualism and Talent*

Development in American Schooling (New York: Teachers College Press: 1995); Merle Curti, "Intellectuals and Other People," *American Historical Review* 60 (1955): 259–282.
5. Andrew Tudor, *Monsters and Mad Scientists: A Cultural History of the Horror Movie* (Oxford, England: Basil Blackwell, 1989), 20, 61, 67, 83–84, 185.
6. There are a few counterexamples to this claim, most notably *Phantasmagoria*, the German collection of horror tales. Generally speaking, however, the bulk of the notable Gothic horror novels are English in origin.
7. E. Michael Jones, *Monsters from the Id: The Rise of Horror in Fiction and Film* (Dallas, TX: Spence, 2000), 8.
8. Ibid., 32–59.
9. The fragment of the story begun by Byron still survives and is available in any number of collections, including Alan Ryan, ed., *Vampires: Two Centuries of Great Vampire Stories* (Garden City, NY: Doubleday, 1987).
10. Jones, *Monsters from the Id*, 77.
11. Ibid., 95.
12. Skal, *Screams of Reason*, 33; Schor, "Frankenstein and Film," 63–83.
13. Rosemary Jackson, "Narcissism and Beyond: A Psychoanalytic Reading of *Frankenstein* and Fantasies of the Double," in *Aspects of Fantasy*, ed. William Coyle (Westport, CT: Greenwood Press, 1986), 43.
14. Ibid., 51.
15. Schor, "Frankenstein and Film," 63.
16. Frederick Wiebel, *Edison's Frankenstein* (New York: BearManor Media, 2010); Elizabeth Young, *Black Frankenstein: The Making of an American Metaphor* (New York: New York University Press, 2008), 160–163; Heffernan, "Looking at the Monster," 136.
17. While predominantly an invasion tale, the vampire tale, generally, is also a projection of demonic possession. Outside forces transform the victims of the vampire; something evil (that is not part of themselves) possesses their bodies. Van Helsing in this model, then, serves as the exorcist.
18. Tudor, *Monsters and Mad Scientists*, 90–93.
19. Ronald Foust, "Rite of Passage: The Vampire Tale as Cosmogonic Myth," in *Aspects of Fantasy*, ed. William Coyle (Westport, CT: Greenwood Press, 1986), 78.

20. Jones, *Monsters from the Id*, 105. In this sense, he is not unlike the Professor from *Gilligan's Island*, whose field of study is nebulous but seems to include various natural sciences (like chemistry and ethnobotany) and various social sciences, including the languages, religions, and cultural practices of Pacific Islanders.
21. Tudor, *Monsters and Mad Scientists*, 165.
22. Jones, *Monsters from the Id*, 124.
23. Quoted in Foust, "Rite of Passage," 79.
24. Jones, *Monsters from the Id*, 109.
25. Thomas Schatz, *The Genius of the System: Hollywood Filmmaking in the Studio Era* (New York: Henry Holt, 1988), 252.
26. Ibid., 87–88.
27. Ibid., 89–91.
28. Carl Laemmle, founder of Universal Pictures, was so sure of *Dracula*'s potential for success that he signed the deal to produce *Frankenstein* two weeks *before* the release of the first film.
29. The film even ended with a plea for the audience to purchase war bonds.
30. Schatz, *The Genius of the System*, 92.
31. Tudor, 133.
32. Whale's films are perhaps the only two *Frankenstein* films in which the term "protagonist" could be applied to Dr. Frankenstein. There are many films in which Frankenstein serves as the antagonist, and several in which he could be considered an antihero. The only other film in this sample in which one could possibly describe Frankenstein as the protagonist would be *Frankenstein Meets the Space Monster*.
33. As shall be discussed later, it is unimaginable that Peter Cushing's Frankenstein (Hammer Films) would express such feelings of conscience.
34. This theme would be revisited in Andy Warhol's Frankenstein picture, *Flesh for Frankenstein* (1973).
35. This is a trope that would be more thoroughly and artfully explored in several of the Hammer *Frankenstein* films.
36. Again, this is an idea that would be more fully explored in the Hammer *Frankenstein* cycle.
37. This breaks with the anti-intellectual assumptions that support most of these films. Ludwig assumes that if he puts the brain of a man of character and learning into the monster that the monster will become moral.

38. Schatz, *The Genius of the System*, 347.
39. Ibid., 465–466.
40. As Young points out in her brilliant book, *Black Frankenstein*, Shelley's Frankenstein was not created as a slave. That is, he is not forced to engage in unpaid labor (p. 44). This is also true for the first two films in the Universal *Frankenstein* cycle. The idea that the creation would obey his creator unconditionally is a development within film history, and it appears to find its genesis with Ygor's snake-charmer-like flute used to compel the monster to do his bidding in *Son of Frankenstein* and *Ghost of Frankenstein*.
41. David Pirie, *A Heritage of Horror: The English Gothic Cinema, 1946–1972* (New York: Equinox Books, 1973), 30.
42. American Dracula and Frankenstein films from the 1950s to the 1970s were isolated events, usually produced by small film studios specializing in drive-in movie fare and exploitation films.
43. Jonathan Rigby, *English Gothic: A Century of Horror Cinema* (London: Reynolds and Hearn, 2004), 48.
44. Ibid., 56–57. In one interview, Terence Fisher, director of several of Hammer's most prominent *Frankenstein* and *Dracula* entries, described his own interest in British source material, saying that he was brought up on Gothic horror tradition, "and I think we knew what it was all about; it may be something English. James Whale was English, I believe."
45. Gary A. Smith, *Uneasy Dreams: The Golden Age of British Horror Films, 1956–1976* (Jefferson, NC: McFarland, 2000), 53.
46. Ibid., 8.
47. Tudor, *Monsters and Mad Scientists*, 40.
48. Rigby, *English Gothic*, 57.
49. Pirie, *Heritage of Horror*, 73.
50. There was a Hammer *Frankenstein* film featuring Peter Cushing as the doctor between *The Revenge of Frankenstein* and *Frankenstein Created Woman*. It was entitled *The Evil of Frankenstein*. The character of Frankenstein is much different in this film, self-pitying and emasculated. Even the monster is different in both appearance and attitude from Christopher Lee's monster in the first film. Scholars and fans tend to view this film as distinctly out of step with the rest of the series. Likewise, *The Horror of Frankenstein* (1970), which was both a black comedy and the only Hammer *Frankenstein* film to use an actor other than Cushing for the title role, does not fit well within the broader Hammer *Frankenstein* context. For those reasons, and the interest of space, those two films will not be included in this examination.

51. Tudor, *Monsters and Mad Scientists*, 148; Smith, *Uneasy Dreams*, 90.
52. This particular sequence of the film is uncomfortably shocking. It might be helpful to see the scene within the broader context of the *Frankenstein* series. Dr. Frankenstein does not demonstrate the same level of misogyny in any of the other Hammer films. Coming right after *Frankenstein Created Woman*, however, the rape scene might best be read as Dr. Frankenstein's revenge against women for the "feminine" weakness that destroyed his creation in the previous film.
53. Within the context of Hammer horror films, this seems to have a social class element as well. Baron Frankenstein is able to do what he wants because he is an aristocrat.
54. The film seems to be making a visual allusion to Sherlock Holmes, a role also famously played by Peter Cushing.
55. Rigby, *English Gothic*, 66.
56. Ibid., 100.
57. *Dracula vs. Frankenstein* (1971) also featured a descendent of Dr. Frankenstein as one of its two title villains.
58. The backwards spelling "Alucard" was also an alias used by Dracula in the Chaney film *Son of Dracula*.
59. Rigby, *English Gothic*, 238.
60. Tudor, *Monsters and Mad Scientists*, 56–60.
61. Ibid.
62. None of the major film studios produced either *Dracula* or *Frankenstein* films. That having been said, several of the studios, including Universal and Paramount, inked deals to distribute Hammer *Frankenstein* and *Dracula* films.
63. Dan Curtis (who was also the creator of the vampire soap opera, *Dark Shadows*) directed what is perhaps the film in this sample that most closely resembles Stoker's novel. It does include a few elements not found in the novel, such as the love-never-dies motif involving Mina Harker—which would later be borrowed by Francis Ford Coppola in his *Bram Stoker's Dracula* (1992). Many scholars attribute the eternal love and reincarnation subthemes to Curtis. For more information on this, see Carrol L. Fry and John Robert Craig's "'Unfit for Earth, Undoomed for Heaven': The Genesis of Coppola's Byronic Dracula" (*Literature/Film Quarterly* 30 [2002]: 271–275). I am unconvinced of this claim. The 1973 film *Scream, Blacula, Scream*—in which the undead African prince meets his reincarnated true love in modern Los Angeles—deals with exactly the same themes. It is highly possible the two were

independent inventions and that Curtis's film was the stronger influence on Coppola's. Nevertheless, the sequel to *Blacula* originated (or at least predated Curtis's film in developing) the idea that the vampire's motivation was a quest to find his eternal love.

64. This movie was actually a made-for-television film that was produced by Universal for NBC. A condensed version of this film did receive a theatrical release in Great Britain. Because of some of the remarkable differences between this film and the book, including Frankenstein using solar power to animate the monster and making John Polidori the main villain, it is difficult to tell whether the title was meant ironically or if the production deviated from the artistic vision with which it began.
65. The vampire tale has always had a strong metaphorical association with sex. In this sense, the Universal and Hammer film series have an almost exclusively heterosexual bias. Bela Lugosi's Dracula never had a male victim (unless you count Renfield, Dracula's asylum-bound vassal). Christopher Lee's Dracula had to wait 14 years and more than half a dozen films before he bit his first male victim (and the film cuts away before the blood sucking). Blacula's victims were a fair mix of both men and women. He is even brought to Los Angeles when a gay couple buys Dracula's manor for its camp value and to sell the antiques it housed, including the coffin in the basement that unbeknownst to them contained the body of Blacula. The stereotypical and less than flattering portrayal of homosexual characters in the film juxtaposed with the bisexual nature of Blacula's blood sucking paints a complex sexual picture in desperate need of further scholarly examination.
66. Very few Frankensteins were American. Certainly, Universal's *Son of Frankenstein* and *Ghost of Frankenstein* featured American scientists. *Frankenstein Meets the Space Monster* also had an American doctor, but Dr. Steele was not, strictly speaking, a Frankenstein.
67. A version of this appendix appeared in Andrew Tudor's *Monsters and Mad Scientists*.

Chapter 3

1. Michael Davis, "Incongruous Compounds: Re-Reading Jekyll and Hyde and Late-Victorian Psychology," *Journal of Victorian Culture* 11, no. 2 (Autumn 2006): 208.
2. This technique would be revisited in the famous Steadicam shot opening John Carpenter's *Halloween*.

3. Judith Halberstam, *Skin Shows: Gothic Horror and the Technology of Monsters* (Durham, NC: Duke University Press, 1995), 76.
4. Ibid., 53–55.
5. Davis, "Incongruous Compounds," 207–208.

CHAPTER 4

1. The killer in *Cutting Class* (1989) selected one of his victims based on his inability to answer a word problem.
2. In *Prom Night* (1980), a girl received an obscene call from a murderer while waiting by the phone for a prom invitation.
3. Teenage pregnancy was the central conflict in *A Nightmare on Elm Street 5: The Dream Child* (1989). It was also a minor theme in *Class of Nuke 'Em High* (1986).
4. Philip Brophy, "Horrality—The Textuality of Contemporary Horror Films," *Screen* 27, no. 1 (Jan–Feb 1986): 7.
5. Julian Petley, "The Monstrous Child," in *The Body's Perilous Pleasures: Dangerous Desires and Contemporary Culture*, ed. Michael Aaron (Edinburgh: Edinburgh University Press, 1999), 91–92.
6. While the scope of this study is American horror film, there are several notable examples of child monsters from the well-established British horror film industry. Among these are *The Village of the Damned* series: *The Village of the Damned* (1960), *The Damned* (1961), and *Children of the Damned* (1964).
7. William Paul, *Laughing Screaming: Modern Hollywood Horror and Comedy* (New York: Columbia University Press, 1994), 261.
8. Kevin Heffernan, *Ghouls, Gimmicks, and Gold: Horror Films and the American Movie Business, 1955–1968* (Durham, NC: Duke University Press, 2004), 201.
9. Petley, "Monstrous Child," 94.
10. Ibid., 89.
11. Ibid., 88–89.
12. Frances Deutsch Lewis, "The Humpty Dumpty Effect, or Was the Old Egg Really All It Was Cracked Up to Be: Context and Coming of Age in Science Fiction and Fantasy," in *Nursery Realms: Children in the Worlds of Science Fiction, Fantasy, and Horror*, ed. Gary Westfahl and George Slusser (Athens: University of Georgia Press, 1999), 20–23.
13. Bud Foote, "Getting Things in the Right Order: Stephen King's *The Shining*, *The Stand*, and *It*," in *Nursery Realms*, 204.
14. Heffernan, *Ghouls, Gimmicks, and Gold*, 9.

15. Brophy, "Horrality," 5.
16. R. H. W. Dillard, *Horror Films* (New York: Simon and Schuster, 1976), 5.
17. As one very telling example, mad scientists figured in more than half of all horror films in the years leading up to 1960. By the 1980s, fewer than 15 percent of horror films featured them. Tudor, *Monsters and Mad Scientists*, 88.
18. Michael Powell's contemporaneous *Peeping Tom* (1960) was a groundbreaking horror film whose impact on the advent of the slasher subgenre was tremendous. It, too, heralded a new type of setting for the genre. Discussion of this film is excluded here. First, it was a British film, not an American one. Additionally, the controversial subject matter forced American distributors to present a heavily edited version in the United States. As a result, Powell's film made far less of an impact in the United States than on the other side of the Atlantic. An unedited version of the film was not available in the United States until the late 1970s when, championed by Martin Scorsese, it came to the attention of aspiring horror filmmakers.
19. J. P. Telotte, "Faith and Idolatry in the Horror Film," in *Planks of Reason: Essays on the Horror Film*," ed. Barry Keith Grant (Metuchen, NJ: Scarecrow Press, 1984), 23.
20. Allan Frank, *The Horror Film Handbook* (Totowa, NJ: Barnes and Noble Press, 1982), 120.
21. Adam Rockoff, writer, *Going to Pieces: The Rise and Fall of the Slasher Film* (ThinkFilm, 2006).
22. Tudor, *Monsters and Mad Scientists*, 177. Of the four most prolific horror series in American cinema of the 1970s and 1980s, *Halloween*, Romero's *Dead* sequence, and *Nightmare on Elm Street* made significant use of a suburban setting. The fourth major series, *Friday the 13th*, opted for the forested seclusion of a summer camp (see Chapter 6 for a discussion on summer camps).
23. Brigid Cherry, "Refusing to Refuse to Look: Female Viewers of the Horror Film," in *Identifying Hollywood's Audiences: Cultural Identity and the Movies*, ed. Melvyn Stokes and Richard Maltby (London: British Film Institute, 1999), 188.
24. Hefferman, *Ghouls, Gimmicks, and Gold*, 8; for a broader historical context of the rise of the film for teenagers, see also Thomas Doherty, *Teenagers and Teenpics: The Juvenilization of American Movies in the 1950s* (Philadelphia: Temple University Press, 2002).

25. Adam Rockoff, *Going to Pieces: The Rise and Fall of the Slasher Film, 1978–1986* (Jefferson, NC: McFarland, 2002), 10; Robin Wood, *Hollywood from Vietnam to Reagan . . . and Beyond* (New York: Columbia University Press, 2003), 173; Robin Wood, "Returning the Look: *Eyes of a Stranger*," in *American Horrors: Essays on the Modern American Horror Film*, ed. Gregory A. Waller (Urbana, IL: University of Chicago Press, 1987), 80.
26. Wood, *Hollywood from Vietnam to Reagan*, 69.
27. Hefferman, *Ghouls, Gimmicks, and Gold*, 221.
28. Darryl Jones, *Horror: A Thematic History in Fiction and Film* (London: Oxford University, 2002), 161.
29. Review of *Night of the Living Dead* (George A. Romero, dir.), *Variety*, October 15, 1968.
30. Jonathan Rosenbaum, "*Halloween*: Suspense Is Generated by Waiting for a Woman to Be Torn Apart by a Maniac," *TakeOne* (January 1979): 9.
31. Janet Maslin, "Bloodbaths Debase Movies and Audiences," *New York Times*, November 21, 1982, H1.
32. Interestingly, both Siskel and Ebert gave extremely positive reviews to *Halloween*, and their reviews may have been instrumental in helping the low-budget film achieve its phenomenal financial success—and, given *Halloween*'s enormous influence on the development of the slasher subgenre, may have had a major impact on the advent of the very films they were chastising.
33. Rockoff, *Going to Pieces*, 19; Paul, *Laughing Screaming*, 9.
34. John Springhall, *Youth, Popular Culture, and Moral Panics: Penny Gaffs to Gansta-Rap, 1830–1996* (New York: St. Martin's Press, 1998), 148–149.
35. Carol J. Clover, *Men, Women, and Chain Saws: Gender in the Modern Horror Film* (Princeton, NJ: Princeton University Press, 1992), 21. Much more research needs to be done with respect to the social class of horror film viewers. Some evidence suggests that the viewer's broader community and life situation played a role in enjoyment of horror films. Specifically, people who lived in poorer, more violent areas were more likely to watch them. In this sense, it seems that slasher films were literally a repudiation of middle-class values to the people who watched them. Mary Beth Oliver and Meghan Sanders, "The Appeal of Horror and Suspense," in *The Horror Film*, ed. Stephen Price (New Brunswick: Rutgers University Press, 2004), 249; Clover, *Men, Women, and Chain Saws*, 6.

36. Charles Derry, "More Dark Dreams: Some Notes on the Recent Horror Film," in *American Horrors: Essays on the Modern American Horror Film*," ed. Gregory A. Waller (Urbana, IL: University of Chicago Press, 1987), 163.
37. Gary Heba, "Everyday Nightmares: The Rhetoric of Social Horror in the 'Nightmare on Elm Street' Series," *Journal of Popular Film and Television* 23, no. 3 (Fall 1995): 109.
38. Ibid., 107. As has been argued in this chapter, the image of both women and children in horror film underwent significant change. While the phenomenon of the "sole surviving female" of moral purity may have presented a stronger vision of the woman, the "child as monster" represented a far more negative vision. Women were, in some sense, able to shed the mantle of victim, but children ended up adopting one of both victim and monster.
39. Cherry, "Refusing to Refuse to Look," 188–192.
40. Clover, *Men, Women, and Chain Saws*, 8.
41. Telotte, "Faith and Idolatry," 24.
42. Joanne Cantor and Mary Beth Oliver, "Developmental Differences in Responses to Horror," in *The Horror Film*, ed. Stephen Price (New Brunswick, NJ: Rutgers University Press, 2004), 230.
43. Walter Evans, "Monster Movies: A Sexual Theory," *Journal of Popular Film and Television* 2, no. 4 (1973): 354. Evans argues that film monsters tended to be isolated figures who had undergone radical psychological and/or physical changes. As such, they had a metaphorical link to the pubescent teenagers that made up the bulk of their audience. Teenage audiences were encouraged to identify with the films' monsters on a fundamental, deeply psychosexual level.
44. Cherry, "Refusing to Refuse to Look," 188.
45. Roger C. Schlobin, "Children of a Darker God: A Taxonomy of Deep Horror Fiction and Film and Their Mass Popularity," *Journal of the Fantastic in the Arts* 1, no. 1 (1988): 42.
46. Leonard Wolf, "In Horror Movies, Some Things Are Sacred," *New York Times*, April 4, 1976, D1.
47. Maslin, "Bloodbaths Debase Movies and Audiences," H1.
48. Schlobin, "Children of a Darker God," 45.
49. Among these films were *Carrie* (1976), *Jennifer* (1978), *The Spell* (1977), *Prom Night I, II, III*, and *IV* (1980, 1987, 1990, 1992), *Slaughter High* (1986), *976-EVIL* (1988), *Graduation Day* (1981), *Return to Horror High* (1987), *The Redeemer* (1978), *Cutting Class* (1989), and *Class of Nuke 'Em High* (1986).

50. These films included *Halloween* (1978) and *A Nightmare on Elm Street I, V,* and *VI* (1984, 1989, and 1991).
51. *Student Bodies* (1981), *Full Moon High* (1981), *C.H.U.D. II* (1989), and *Teen Wolf* (1985) are the four such films considered for those purposes. In fact, these films can, in many cases, tell us more about the genre than their "serious" counterparts. Contemporary horror film embraces its clichés, often causing a humorous undercurrent by overplaying them. Because the genre mimics itself mercilessly, it is difficult for the viewer at times to determine whether some scenes and films, even scenes in films of deep horror, are meant to be taken seriously. Because this type of humor requires the viewer to have an understanding of the genre formulas, scholars can learn a great deal about those formulas by viewing comedic interpretations of horror. Brophy, "Horrality," 3, 12.
52. In many respects, *Carrie* contains echoes of Frankenstein's monster. Carrie is thrust into a society she lacks the emotional capability to handle, and society's pressures create a monster.
53. David Chute, "King of the Night: An Interview with Stephen King," *TakeOne* (January 1979): 33–35; "Stephen King and the Writing of Carrie," *Carrie* (Special Edition DVD), MGM, 2001.
54. Jones, *Horror*, 117.
55. *The Spell*, a made-for-television film, was a sanitized reiteration of *Carrie* and recycled many of the same motifs. An overweight girl is forced to endure the taunts of her peers. As she discovers she has telekinetic powers, she begins to use those powers to get back at her tormentors. Over the course of the film, she discovers that she has become the one who treats her peers unfairly. Its status as a made-for-television movie made *The Spell* subject to content restrictions the theatrical releases did not have to negotiate. As a result, I have decided not to include a prolonged discussion of the film here. Even so, it is an interesting artifact in that it demonstrates the pervasiveness of the "victim of bullying seeking monstrous revenge" plot formula.
56. *The Redeemer* is perhaps the only horror film from the era to take place in a Catholic high school.
57. The situation may actually have been more complicated than this. It is, in fact, difficult to see school horror film audiences of the 1970s and 1980s being wholly composed of bullied youth. If the previously asserted premise that these films were far more "victim viewed" than the prevailing scholarship would have it, many of the audience members may have themselves been bullies.

The horror contained in the films would have been amplified for young people who were being confronted by some of the possible consequences of their own aggressive actions toward their peers. In any event, there was an element of social dysfunction present in both film and audience.

58. Simon Scuddamore (who played Marty in *Slaughter High*) was himself a haunted young man. He was unavailable on weekends during filming because he volunteered his services at a school for deprived children working to improve the lives of troubled youth. He died of an intentional drug overdose shortly after the release of the film.

59. Horror filmmakers have noted that Paramount's decision to make *Friday the 13th* instead of *Prom Night* may have been the only reason for the former's iconic (mainstream) status and the latter's relative obscurity. Rockoff, *Going to Pieces*, ThinkFilm.

60. Oddly, *Prom Night IV* does not continue the theme. Mary Lou is not featured in the film and very little action takes place in school. The killer in the film was an overzealous priest who punished a group of kids for their sexual immorality when they threw a house party on prom night while their parents were out of town. Part of the film's deviation from the established themes of the series may have to do with the period in which it was made. *Prom Night IV* was released in the early 1990s, at the tail end of the slasher era, and does not seem to share some of the unique markers of texts from the period (including setting).

61. Rockoff, *Going to Pieces*, 11.

62. Vera Dike, "The Stalker Film, 1978–1981," in *American Horrors: Essays on the Modern American Horror Film*, ed. Gregory A. Waller (Urbana, IL: University of Chicago Press, 1987), 91; Heba, "Everyday Nightmares," 114.

63. Vivian Sobcheck, "Bringing It All Back Home: Family Economy and Generic Exchange," in *American Horrors: Essays on the Modern American Horror Film*, ed. Gregory A. Waller (Urbana, IL: University of Chicago Press, 1987), 182.

64. The exception to this general rule was *The Exorcist*—which was an essentially conservative film that echoed the sermons of Cotton Mather. In Stephen King's words, "It was a movie for all those parents who felt, in a kind of agony and terror, that they were losing their children and could not understand why or how it was happening." Taking this posture may help explain the mass

popularity of *The Exorcist*, even among audiences who did not normally attend such films. Petley, "Monstrous Child," 98.
65. David Pirie, "New Blood," *Sight and Sound* 40, no. 2 (1971): 74–75.
66. Dike, "The Stalker Film," 96.
67. Rockoff, *Going to Pieces*, ThinkFilm.
68. Rockoff, *Going to Pieces*, 99.
69. In an allusion to Hitchcock's *Psycho*, the young man has used taxidermy to preserve the corpse of his girlfriend, and the two of them "live together" in his bedroom.
70. *Jennifer* took the opposite approach to the development of adult identity with respect to religion. Like Carrie, Jennifer was raised by an extremely religious single parent. She begins the film with a contentious relationship with her father—who, for example, tells her to be home "prompt" to cook his dinner. In resolution of the conflict, however, Jennifer embraces her religious heritage as a "snake handler" and gains power as a result. The film is unusual among horror films in its handling of adult/child relationships. Interestingly, the parent and child dynamic is not a source of conflict in *The Spell* either.
71. The horror comedies from the era indicate a similar attitude toward adult authority. In *Full Moon High*, on a trip to Eastern Europe, someone emptied a bedpan out the window and onto a young man who responded by saying, "I'll give my father the message." Even Michael J. Fox's *Teen Wolf* uses a family condition of lycanthropy as a metaphor for the generation gap.
72. While the violence was not perpetrated against school children by their peers, the *Nightmare* films also contained the theme of revenge as a clear undercurrent.
73. Heba, "Everyday Nightmares," 110.
74. Ibid., 115.
75. Some evidence indicates that Craven may have been using his film to deal with some of his own unresolved issues from his school days. In a belated act of revenge, Craven named Freddy after his worst junior high school bully.
76. Rockoff, *Going to Pieces*, ThinkFilm.
77. Charles B. Stoizer, "Youth Violence and the Apocalyptic," *American Journal of Psychoanalysis* 62, no. 3 (September 2002): 290.
78. John Kenneth Muir, *Horror Films of the 1970s* (Jefferson, NC: McFarland, 2002), 388.

79. While one could debate its significance, the lone exception appears to be *The Rage: Carrie II* (1999). Being a direct sequel following more than two decades after the original, its status as an anomaly is seriously questionable. Moreover, it was in production at the time of the Columbine killings. As a result, I have not included it here. That having been said, the Swedish film *Let the Right One In* (2008) and its American remake, as well as the 2013 remake of *Carrie*, deal with these themes and might be in the vanguard of a renaissance of this type of film.
80. Rockoff, *Going to Pieces*, 155.

Chapter 5

1. Gary M. Laverne, *A Sniper in the Tower: The Charles Whitmore Murders* (Denton: University of North Texas Press, 1997); Lewis L. Gould, "Review: *A Sniper in the Tower*," *Journal of American History* 84, no. 3 (December 1997), 1150.
2. Raymond J. Adamek and Jerry M. Lewis, "Social Control Violence and Radicalization: The Kent State Case," *Social Forces* 51, no. 3 (March 1973): 342–347.
3. The depiction of tension between faith and higher education is also explored in *Splatter University* (1984). In that film, another mental patient escapes from the asylum, and a person dressed as a priest roams St. Trinian's College murdering students. The visual association of the priest with the madman represents a great deal of the tension underlying the film.
4. This is true both in terms of time and space. While numerous films used the sorority house as the site of horrifying violent acts, many films also set their stories during important events on the calendar: *Halloween, Mother's Day, Happy Birthday to Me, Graduation Day*, and even *Friday the 13th*.
5. This follows the tradition established by *House on Sorority Row* and continued by *Sorority House Massacre*; both contain montages of girls dressing or putting on makeup.

Chapter 6

1. Nathaniel Hawthorne, "Young Goodman Brown," 1835, http://www.netlibrary.net.

2. Marcus Nispel, interview in Daniel Ferrends, dir., *His Name Was Jason: 30 Years of Friday the 13th* (Anchor Bay Entertainment, 2008).
3. Leslie Paris, *Children's Nature: The Rise of the American Summer Camp* (New York: New York University Press, 2008), 28–29.
4. Cindy Aron, *Working at Play: A History of Vacations in the United States* (New York: Oxford University Press, 1999), 230.
5. Ibid., 158.
6. Paris, *Children's Nature*, 18, 43; Abigail A. Van Slyck, *A Manufactured Wilderness: Summer Camps and the Shaping of American Youth, 1890–1960* (Minneapolis: University of Minnesota Press, 2006), xxiii–xxiv.
7. Paris, *Children's Nature*, 13, 258–260.
8. Aron, *Working at Play*, 157–158; Paris, *Children's Nature*, 9.
9. Bill Ellis, "The Camp Mock-Ordeal: Theatre as Life," *Journal of American Folklore* 94, no. 374 (Oct–Dec 1981): 486.
10. Van Slyck, *Manufactured Wilderness*, xx.
11. Van Slyck astutely points out that the advent in the germ theory of disease made city crowding seem dangerous and unhealthy. She argues that the view of the city as detrimental to one's health fostered the summer camp movement (p. 8).
12. Paris, *Children's Nature*, 19–21, 190–208.
13. Henry Wellington Wack, *The Camping Ideal: The New Human Race* (New York: Red Book Magazine, 1925), 30.
14. Ibid.
15. Ibid., 18.
16. Lloyd Burgess Sharp, *Education and the Summer Camp: An Experiment* (New York: Bureau of Publications, Teachers College, Columbia University, 1930); Paris, *Children's Nature*, 53–55.
17. Sharp, *Education and the Summer Camp*, 1.
18. "Fresh Air Fund," *Life*, October 13, 1887, quoted in Sharp, *Education and the Summer Camp*, 9.
19. Ibid.
20. Paris, *Children's Nature*, 3.
21. Van Slyck, *Manufactured Wilderness*, xxviii; Paris, *Children's Nature*, 79.
22. "A Boy's Camp By One of the Campers," *St. Nicholas* 13, no. 8 (June 1886): 607.
23. Ibid., 612.

24. Henry G. Gibson, quoted in Van Slyck, *Manufactured Wilderness*, xxiii.
25. W. Barksdale Maynard, "'An Ideal Life in the Woods for Boys': Architecture and Culture in the Earliest Summer Camps," *Winterthur Portfolio* 34, no. 1 (Spring 1999): 3–29.
26. Charles L Norton, "Summer Camps for Boys," *Christian Union* 38, no. 8 (August 23, 1888): 193.
27. See the *73rd Annual Report of the Children's Aid Society of New York*, June 15, 1926, Part II, 13 in New York Historical Society Museum, series III, subseries III.1, box 7, folder 10.
28. Ibid.
29. Paris, *Children's Nature*, 32–42.
30. Walter M. Wood, quoted in Van Slyck, *Manufactured Wilderness*, 47.
31. Paris, *Children's Nature*, 6, 11, 62.
32. Eunice Fuller Barnard, "Young America Is Off to Summer Camp," *New York Times*, June 29, 1930, 14.
33. Paris, *Children's Nature*, 48–49.
34. Ibid., 6, 235.
35. Van Slyck, *Manufactured Wilderness*, xxv.
36. Paris, *Children's Nature*, 271.
37. While significant numbers of African American children attended camps in the early nineteenth century, camps still remained disproportionately white. Many camps were de facto segregated because they were sponsored by all-white organizations (such as churches and fraternal organizations) and because the cost of summer camp proved prohibitive for African American families. Camps run by leftist organizations had a long legacy of racial integration, but such policies proved problematic in the 1930s, 1940s, and 1950s. In the end, large numbers of African American children were able to attend summer camp, often as a result of charity work, but their proportion was significantly smaller than that of the white population. Paul C. Mishler, *Raising Reds: The Young Pioneers, Radical Summer Camps, and Communist Political Culture in the United States* (New York: Columbia University Press, 1999).
38. "Summer Camps Boon to Parents," *New York Times*, July 15, 1923, E5.
39. Barnard, "Young America Is Off to Summer Camp," 14.
40. John Dewey, *Democracy and Education* (Champaign, IL: The Gutenberg Project, 1916. Updated January 26, 2013), 9–19.

http://www.gutenberg.org/files/852/852-h/852-h.htm;
Sharp, *Education and the Summer Camp*, 37–38.
41. Sharp, *Education and the Summer Camp*, 39.
42. The lack of a clear educational mission did much to solidify the view that the summer camp was a less important educational institution than the public school. Summer camps seemed more like recreational institutions than educational ones. This perception is largely a prejudice that historians of education have also adopted. Aside from the many histories of prominent organizations involved in formal summer camping institutions (such as the Boy Scouts and the YMCA) and those few other scholarly works cited herein, there is little scholarship from historians of education on summer camps. Eleanor Eells's *History of Organized Camping: The First 100 Years* (Martinsville, IN: American Camping Association, 1986) and Stanley M. Ulanoff's "The Organization and Development of Organized Camping in the United States, 1861–1961" (Ph.D. diss., New York University, 1968) notwithstanding, there are few examples of histories of summer camps as educational institutions.
43. Paris, *Children's Nature*, 187.
44. Jay Mechler, "Children's Folklore in Residential Institutions: Summer Camps, Boarding Schools, Hospitals, and Custodial Facilities," in *Children's Folklore: A Source Book*, ed. Brian Sutton-Smith, Jay Mechling, Thomas W. Johnson, and Felicia R. McMahon (New York and London: Garland Publishing, 1995), 273.
45. Bill Ellis, "'Ralph and Rudy': The Audience's Role in Recreating a Camp Legend," *Western Folklore* 41, no. 3 (July 1982): 169–170.
46. Ibid., 171.
47. Ibid.
48. Mechler, "Children's Folklore in Residential Institutions," 278.
49. Ellis, "The Camp Mock-Ordeal," 487; Mechler, "Children's Folklore in Residential Institutions," 282; Kenneth A. Thigpen, Jr., "Adolescent Legends in Brown County: A Survey," *Indiana Folklore* 4 (1971): 204–205; Gary Hall, "The Big Tunnel: Legends and Legend Telling," *Indiana Folklore* 6 (1973): 147–153.
50. Hiram Camp was formed at the turn of the twentieth century and served underprivileged youth.
51. Ellis, "The Camp Mock-Ordeal," 491–492.
52. Ibid., 496.

53. Mechler, "Children's Folklore in Residential Institutions," 288–289.
54. Rockoff, *Going to Pieces*, 1–9.
55. The importance of Michael Powell's film *Peeping Tom* (1960) is often overlooked. Released almost concurrently with Hitchcock's film, *Peeping Tom* tells the story of a young man whose experimental psychologist father deliberately traumatizes him as a child in order to study the effects on his son. As it turns out, the result of his father's experiment was to produce a son who experiences sexual gratification by filming young women as he murders them. Negative critical responses to the film effectively ended the filmmaking career of the great director.
56. These weapons were not always knives, but they came in a large number of varieties: machetes, chain saws, arrows, electric drills, corkscrews, and so on. Killers in slasher films, with only exceedingly rare exceptions (such as high school horror film *The Redeemer* [1976]), did not favor firearms.
57. This film was also an extremely loose adaptation of the history of Ed Gein.
58. Rockoff, *Going to Pieces*, 56. While *Halloween* had its champions among critics (notably both Gene Siskel and Roger Ebert), it was not universally acclaimed. One reviewer even went so far as to ask what made the film "morally superior to Nazi war relics?" Even as some critics acknowledged the importance of the film, others balked at its cold, graphic, and brutal violence. Rosenbaum, "*Halloween*," 9.
59. Rockoff, *Going to Pieces*, 12; Wood, *Hollywood from Vietnam to Reagan*, 173; Wood, "Returning the Look," 80.
60. Rockoff, *Going to Pieces*, 10.
61. Tom Buckley, "A Potboiler of Gold at the End of His Rainbow," *New York Times*, January 23, 1981, C8.
62. Denis Boyles, "Hollywood's 'B's' Make the Box Office Buzz," *New York Times*, August 3, 1980.
63. *Friday the 13th: Part III* contained no less than 14 victims. Carol J. Clover, "Her Body, Himself: Gender in the Slasher Films," *Representations* (Autumn 1987): 199.
64. Interviews contained in Ferrends, *His Name Was Jason*.
65. Richard Herrington, "'Friday VII': More of the Shame," *Washington Post*, May 14, 1988, C3.
66. To be fair, Laurie Werner had been a vociferous protester against the slasher film from her initial review of *Halloween*, and she was

certainly no fan of the original *Friday the 13th*, describing the film as "cheap, tawdry, amateurish... the acting was stiff, the dialog was silly, and even the... premise of the killer stalking camp counselors was trite." Laurie Werner, "Film Horror Falls into the Hands of the Gore Corps," *Chicago Tribune*, August 24, 1980, D26.

67. Gene Siskel, "Siskel's Flicks Picks," *Chicago Tribune*, May 14, 1984, D-A12.
68. Ibid.
69. Oddly, young Jason is the only child attending a functional camp depicted in the film.
70. Victor Miller, interview in Ferrends, *His Name Was Jason*.
71. The footage of the scary campfire story is reused in *Friday the 13th: Part IV*.
72. The poster represents an ironic comment on the violence of the mother/son dynamic in the series.
73. The Camp Crystal Lake sign that stood at the edge of the summer camp in the first film indicated that the original camp was established in 1935. This would have been an odd time for a camp to be opening, as many camps had difficulty staying in operation during the Depression. Even so, Camp Crystal Lake was founded solidly within the initial summer camp movement.
74. The lightning strike links Jason's reanimation to another famous work of horror; it is the precise method used by Victor Frankenstein to bring his monster to life. Both texts deal with the tension between nature and modernity.
75. Rob Heddon, director of *Friday the 13th Part VIII: Jason Takes Manhattan*, interview in Ferrends, *His Name Was Jason*.
76. Clover, "Her Body, Himself," 204. In a sense, this is an inversion of the gender ambiguity common among slasher film killers—those who, like Pamela Voorhees and Norman Bates, tended to disguise their sexual identities before committing murder.
77. Certainly this is a major theme in both *Little Darlings* (1980) and *Meatballs* (1979).
78. Carrie, like Jason's mother, was another female monster, an extremely common trope in horror films of the late 1970s and early 1980s. Aviva Briefel, "Monster Pains: Masochism, Menstruation, and Identification in the Horror Film," *Film Quarterly* 58, no. 3 (Spring 2005): 16–27.
79. In his commentary to the DVD release of the film, the director admits that this scene "may have gone too far." "Original audio commentary with writer/director Robert Hiltzik and star Felissa

Rose," *Sleepaway Camp* (Collector's Edition DVD), Shout! Factory, 2014.
80. Critics and periodical writers were kind in keeping the surprise ending a secret, even if it meant describing the film inaccurately. The cable television guide in the *Chicago Tribune*'s description of the film was simply a description of the setting: "Bunks and showers are a mad stalker's beat at a summer camp strictly for teens." Oddly, Camp Arawak was not "strictly for teens." In fact, it was one of the few camps in any of these films that allowed young children to attend. However, the description demonstrates the importance of the summer camp setting to this type of film. The *Washington Post* played very fast and loose with facts to cover up the ending: "An introverted teenager goes to a summer camp where she and fellow campers are menaced by a killer." It was nice of the caption writer to conceal the fact that the "introverted young girl" was actually an introverted young boy. What is a little strange, however, is that she is not menaced by the killer, but *is* the killer. Conveniently, these sorts of descriptions allowed reviewers to avoid the transgender themes of the film. "Cable TV Movies," *Chicago Tribune*, October 26, 1986, J40; "The Movie Channel," *Washington Post*, July 19, 1987, TV48.
81. Michael Simpson, director, and Fritz Gordon, screenwriter, state much of this directly in the DVD commentary to the film. "Audio commentary with director Michael Simpson and screenwriter Fritz Gordon," *Sleepaway Camp II: Unhappy Campers* (Special Edition DVD), Starz/Anchor Bay, 1988.
82. Cheerleaders fare no better in *Cheerleader Camp* (1988), which featured an aging, balding Leif Garrett trying to play a male teenage cheerleader. The premise of the film is that at Camp Hurrah there is a contest to see which of the attending cheerleaders would become the Camp Queen. The killer knocks off her competition one by one in her drive to be number one.
83. Jason Isaac (director of *Jason X*) described his film's setting as a virtual reality "Crystal Lake" set in a "future sort of campground," in Ferrends, *His Name Was Jason*. In a conversation I had with Kane Hodder (Atlanta, Georgia, September 7, 2009), who portrayed Jason in four of the *Friday* films (including *Friday the 13th Part VIII: Jason Takes Manhattan* and *Jason X*), he added that he merely tried to keep Jason consistent regardless of the setting.
84. Doug Bradley, personal conversation, Atlanta, Georgia, September 7, 2009.

85. Miller disavows the notion that the moralistic undertones of his film were intentional. Instead, he claims that those young people who were engaging in sexual acts and substance abuse were easy victims because they were "distracted." Instead of arguing that the adolescents in the film were learning a moral lesson, Miller seems to be saying they were learning a lesson in survival intimately related to their moral choices. To me, this seems a minor distinction at best. Miller, interview in Ferrends, *His Name Was Jason*.

INDEX

976-EVIL, 104, 108, 122–123, 186
976-EVIL 2, 122–123

Abbott and Costello Meet Dr. Jekyll and Mr. Hyde, 85–86
Abbott and Costello Meet Frankenstein, 35–37
adultery, 103, 149
After Midnight, 120–121
Alice, Sweet Alice, 91
aliens, 38, 57–58, 93–94
Altered States, 67
Amicus Films, 73, 167
animation, *see* cartoons
Antichrist, 121
anti-intellectualism, 19, 62
Anti-Intellectualism in American Life, 19, 62
anti-Modernism, 6, 137
Association for Improving the Condition of the Poor, 140
Audrey Rose, 91

Bad Seed, The, 90–91
Barrymore, John, 68–69
Bates, Ralph, 74–75
Black Christmas, 118, 124–126, 168
Blacula, 55–56, 84, 181–182
blaxploitation, 55, 83–86
Blob, The, 4–5
Bradley, Doug, 163
Bride of Frankenstein, 32–33, 170
Brides of Dracula, The, 49–50
Bronson, Charles, 13
Brood, The, 91

bullying, 3, 11, 98–105, 110–111, 160, 187, 189
Bundy, Ted, 117–118
Burning, The, 136, 151, 154, 157
Byron, Lord, 22, 24, 178

Cabinet of Dr. Caligari, The, 167
Cambridge Theological Seminary, 141
Camp Director's Association, 145
Campfire Girls, 144
Camp Harvard, 140
Campsite Massacre, 136
cannibalism, 90, 106, 139
Capra, Frank, 135–136
Carpenter, Edward, 159
Carpenter, John, 94, 105, 121, 125, 147, 158–159, 162–163, 168, 182
Carrie (1977), 2, 5, 99–101, 108, 110–112, 130, 160, 173, 186, 187, 189, 195
Carrie (2013), 190
cartoons, 78–80
Chaney, Jr., Lon, 30, 35–36, 181
Chaney, Sr., Lon, 167
Cheerleader Camp, 136, 151, 196
Chesterton, G. K., 15
Children of Men, 111
Children's Aid Society of New York, 140, 145
Children's Welfare Federation, 141
City Mission Society, 140
Civilization: Its Cause and Cure, 139

Clark, Bob, 168
Class of Nuke 'Em High, 123
Class of Nuke 'Em High 2: Subhumanoid Meltdown, 123
Clive, Colin, 31–32, 43, 61
Cohen, Barney, 151
Cold War, 144, 170
Columbine High School, 111–112, 118, 190
Cooper, Alice, 121
Coraline, 15
Craven, Wes, 13, 95, 109, 112, 168, 189
Crazies, The, 90
Cruze, James, 68
Cunningham, Sean, 150–151
Curse of Frankenstein, The, 39–40, 54, 168
Curtis, Dan, 55, 181
Curtis, Jamie Leigh, 103, 149, 158
Cushing, Peter, 40–62, 180, 181

Damien: Omen II, 91
Dark Shadows, 181
Darwinism, 84–85
Dawn of the Dead, 94, 130
Death Wish, 13
demons, 91, 130, 178
De Palma, Brian, 5, 99–100, 160
Dickens, Charles, 92
dime novels, 5
Don't Go in the Woods, 136
Dorm the Dripped Blood, The, 118, 123
Dracula (1931), 28–29
Dracula (1958), 47–49, 168
Dracula A.D. 1972, 50–52, 168
Dracula's Daughter, 29–30
Dracula Has Risen from the Grave, 50
Dracula: Prince of Darkness, 50
Dracula vs. Frankenstein, 55, 85, 181
Dr. Black, Mr. Hyde, 83–85
Dr. Faustus, 77

Dr. Hekyl and Mr. Hype, 84
Driller Killer, The, 96
Dr. Jekyll and Sister Hyde, 74–78

Ebert, Roger, 96, 150, 185, 194
Ebola, 8
Edison, Thomas, 20, 24
Empire Strikes Back, The, 150
Englund, Robert, 104
Enlightenment, 21–23
eugenics, 23, 72
Evil Dead, The, 96
Exorcist, The, 54, 91, 188–189
Exorcist II, The, 91

Faust, 5
Feldman, Corey, 155
feminism, 24, 97
Final Exam, 118–119, 129
folklore, 25, 51, 53, 146–148
Forest, The, 136
Frankenstein (1932), 31–32, 170
Frankenstein and the Monster from Hell, 45–47, 54
Frankenstein Created Woman, 42–43
Frankenstein Meets the Space Monster, 55, 56–58
Frankenstein Meets the Wolf Man, 35–37
Frankenstein Must Be Destroyed, 43–45
Frankenstein's Daughter, 55
Frankenstein: The True Story, 55
Freddy's Dead: The Final Nightmare, 95, 110
Freed, Herb, 111
Fresh Air Federation of New York, 141
Fresh Air Fund, 141
Freud, Sigmund, 70–71, 78, 80
Friday the 13th (1980), 106, 148, 150–153, 159–160, 184, 188, 190, 194–195
Friday the 13th (2009), 136

INDEX

Friday the 13th: Part II, 153–155
Friday the 13th: Part III, 194
Friday the 13th Part V: A New Beginning, 151
Friday the 13th Part VI: Jason Lives, 155–156
Friday the 13th Part VII: The New Blood, 151
Friday the 13th Part VIII: Jason Takes Manhattan, 157–158, 163, 196
Friday the 13th: The Final Chapter, 151

Gaiman, Neil, 15
Garrett, Leif, 196
Gein, Ed, 149, 194
German Expressionism, 20, 30, 167
Girls Nite Out, 130
Godwin, William, 24
Godzilla, 8–9
Goethe, Johann Wolfgang von, 5
Ghost of Frankenstein, The, 33–35
Golding, William, 90
Golem, The, 167
graduation, 1–3, 106–108, 132, 172
Graduation Day, 2, 106–108, 111, 186
Gulick, Luther, 144

Hall, G. Stanley, 138–139, 141, 144
Halloween, 94–96, 103, 105–106, 108, 111, 125, 147, 149–151, 158–159, 162–163, 168, 169, 182, 184, 185, 187, 190, 194
Hammer Films, 21, 38–41, 46, 50–57, 75–77, 168, 179, 180, 181, 182
Happy Birthday to Me, 106, 190
Hawthorne, Nathaniel, 135–136
hazing, 3, 11, 129, 131, 133, 173
Hell Night, 130
Hellraiser, 163
Hills Have Eyes, The, 90

Hiltzik, Robert, 159, 195–196
Hinkley, George, 143
Hitchcock, Alfred, 21, 76, 90, 93–94, 149, 167, 189, 194
Hodder, Kane, 196
Hofstadter, Richard, 19, 62
Home Alone, 13
homosexuality, 75, 160–161, 170, 182
Hooper, Tobe, 149, 168
House of Dracula, 30–31
House of Frankenstein, 35–37
House on Sorority Row, The, 118, 132–134, 190

I, Monster, 77–78
Incredible Hulk, The, 67
Industrial Revolution, 6, 21–22, 91, 143
Initiation of Sarah, The, 130
initiation (fraternities and sororities), 3, 126–131, 173
institutional review boards (IRBs), 82
Invisible Man, The, 27
Irving, Washington, 5
Isaac, Jason, 196
I Spit on Your Grave, 96
It's Alive, 91
It's Alive III, 91
It Lives Again, 91
I Was a Teenage Frankenstein, 55, 58–61

Jack the Ripper, 76–77
Jason Goes to Hell, 151
Jason X, 196
Jennifer, 100–101, 186, 189
Jesse James Meets Frankenstein's Daughter, 55

Karloff, Boris, 31, 44, 56, 167
Kent State University, 117
King Kong, 9, 84–85
King, Stephen, 99–100

Krueger, Freddy, 9, 14, 109–110, 173

Lady of the Shroud, The, 25
Lair of the White Worm, The, 25
Last House on the Left, The, 13
"The Legend of Sleepy Hollow," 5
Lee, Christopher, 43–44, 48–49, 77, 180, 182
Leigh, Janet, 149
Let the Right One In, 190
Little Darlings, 195
Lord of the Flies, The, 90
Lugosi, Bela, 27, 28, 30, 34, 36, 49, 167, 182

Madman, 136, 151, 154
Mad Monster Party, 79–80
Majaska, 147–148
Mamoulian, Rouben, 69–70, 81, 87
mandatory schooling laws, 4, 138, 172
Marcus, Adam, 151
Marlowe, Christopher, 77–78
Meatballs, 195
menstruation, 99, 108, 160, 173
MGM Studios, 27
mock ordeals, 147
Monkey Shines, 122
Monster on the Campus, 67
Motion Picture Production Code, 169
Mr. Smith Goes to Washington, 135
Mummy, The, 27
Murnau, F. W., 20
Muscular Christianity, 143–144
My Bloody Valentine, 106
Myers, Michael, 9, 105, 151, 158–159, 169

NASA, 57
Nietzsche, Frederick, 74
Night of the Creeps, 130–131
Night of the Living Dead, The, 54, 91, 94–96, 110, 149

Nightmare on Elm Street, The, 8, 89, 95, 109–111
Nightwish, 121
Nosferatu, 20, 167
nuclear war, 8, 23, 57, 59, 170
Nutty Professor, The, 67

Omen, The, 91
One Dark Night, 131
Other, The, 91

Palance, Jack, 55, 70, 81–83
Paramount Pictures, 27, 150–151, 181, 188
Parsons, William, 140
Peeping Tom, 184, 194
Picture of Dorian Grey, The, 77
Pinhead, 163
Poe, Edgar Allan, 5
Polanski, Roman, 91
Polidori, John, 22, 64
Powell, Michael, 184, 194
pregnancy, 89, 183
premarital sex, 136, 149
Prince of Darkness, 121–122
Prometheus, 45
Prom Night (1980), 2, 103–104, 186, 183, 188
Prom Night (2008), 111
Prom Night II, 104, 108–109, 186
Prom Night III, 104, 108–109, 186
Prom Night IV, 186, 188
Prowler, The, 1–3
Psycho, 21, 74, 90, 93–94, 149, 167, 189
puberty, 160
pulp fiction, 5

Quatermass Xperiment, 38

Rage: Carrie II, The, 190
recreation, 137–138, 142, 193
Red Book, 139–140
Redeemer, The, 100–102, 128, 186, 187, 194

Rennie, Michael, 80
Resident Evil, 111
Return to Horror High, 111, 186
Revenge of Frankenstein, The, 40–41
Romanticism, 6, 22–24, 77, 99–100
Romero, George, 90, 91, 94, 122, 130, 167–168, 184
Rosemary's Baby, 91, 94–95, 110, 149, 167

SARS, 8
Satanic Rites of Dracula, The, 50–53
Satan's School for Girls, 118, 130
Scars of Dracula, The, 50
Scream, 168
Scream, Blacula, Scream, 55–56, 181–182
Scuddamore, Simon, 188
school dance, 1–3, 89, 104, 106, 108, 183
school enrollment rates, 4, 7, 171
Shakespeare, William, 29, 89
Shelley, Mary, 5–6, 10, 20–24, 31, 45, 86, 180
Shelley, Percy Bysshe, 24, 26
Sherlock Holmes, 48, 52, 181
Significance of the Frontier in American History, The, 137
silent film, 15, 20, 24, 68–69, 167
Silent Hill, 111
Siskel, Gene, 96, 151–152, 185, 194
Sisters of Death, 118, 128
Slaughter High, 102–103, 112, 127–128, 186, 188
slavery, 55–56, 84–85, 180
Sleepaway Camp, 136, 152, 159–161, 195–196
Sleepaway Camp II: Unhappy Campers, 153–154, 161–162
Sleepaway Camp III: Teenage Wasteland, 162
Sloan, Edward von, 28, 47–49, 61–62
Son of Dracula, The, 30–31
Son of Frankenstein, The, 33–34

Sorority Babes in the Slimeball Bowl-O-Rama, 118, 129
Sorority House Massacre, 118, 125–127, 190
Spell, The, 5, 100, 187
Splatter University, 118, 190
Stevenson, Robert Louis, 5–6, 10, 67–71, 77–82, 84
St. Nicholas, 141
Stoker, Bram, 6–7, 10, 20, 22, 24–26, 53, 181
suburbs, 8, 93–95, 98–99, 110, 143, 184

Taste the Blood of Dracula, 50
Teen Wolf, 123, 131, 187, 189
Teen Wolf Too, 123
Terror Train, 2, 127
Texas Chainsaw Massacre, The, 54, 90, 149, 168
Thoreau, Henry David, 137
To the Devil a Daughter, 54
Tracy, Spencer, 71
transcendentalism, 137, 148, 164
transgender, 75–76, 160–161, 196
Troma Pictures, 123
Turner, Frederick Jackson, 137
Tuskegee syphilis experiments, 78, 84
Twain, Mark, 92
Two Faces of Dr. Jekyll, The, 73–74

Universal Pictures, 20, 26–39, 47, 50–51, 167–168, 182

Vamp, 131
Vampyre, The, 22
Vidal, Gore, 80
video nasties, 96
Vietnam War, 2, 8, 56, 117
Voorhees, Jason, 14, 151–159, 195
Voorhees, Pamela, 14, 153, 159, 195

Wack, Henry Wellington, 139
Walden, 137
Waxwork, 118

Wilde, Oscar, 77
Whale, James, 31, 170, 179, 180
white flight, 94
Whitman, Charles, 117–118
Wolf Man, The, 27
Wollstonecraft, Mary, 24
Wood, Walter, 143
word problems, 89

World War II, 1, 14, 38, 59, 71, 144–145

YMCA, 143–145, 193
"Young Goodman Brown," 135
YWCA, 144

Zombies, 8–9, 31, 91, 111, 121

www.ingramcontent.com/pod-product-compliance
Lightning Source LLC
LaVergne TN
LVHW011821060526
838200LV00053B/3854

GPSR Compliance

The European Union's (EU) General Product Safety Regulation (GPSR) is a set of rules that requires consumer products to be safe and our obligations to ensure this.

If you have any concerns about our products, you can contact us on ProductSafety@springernature.com

In case Publisher is established outside the EU, the EU authorized representative is:
Springer Nature Customer Service Center GmbH
Europaplatz 3
69115 Heidelberg, Germany